STUDIES IN THE HISTORY OF CHRISTIAN MISSIONS

R. E. Frykenberg
Brian Stanley
General Editors

STUDIES IN THE HISTORY OF CHRISTIAN MISSIONS

Susan Billington Harper

In the Shadow of the Mahatma: Bishop V. S. Azariah and the Travails of Christianity in British India

D. Dennis Hudson

Protestant Origins in India: Tamil Evangelical Christians, 1706-1835

Brian Stanley, *Editor*

Christian Missions and the Enlightenment

Kevin Ward and Brian Stanley, *Editors*

The Church Mission Society and World Christianity, 1799-1999

Judith M. Brown and Robert Eric Frykenberg, *Editors*

Christians, Cultural Interactions, and India's Religious Traditions

Christians, Cultural Interactions, and India's Religious Traditions

Edited by

Judith M. Brown

&

Robert Eric Frykenberg

Associate Editor

Alaine Low

William B. Eerdmans Publishing Company
Grand Rapids, Michigan / Cambridge, U.K.

RoutledgeCurzon
London

Published jointly 2002 by
Wm. B. Eerdmans Publishing Co.
255 Jefferson Ave. S.E., Grand Rapids, Michigan 49503 /
P.O. Box 163, Cambridge CB3 9PU U.K.
www.eerdmans.com
and by
RoutledgeCurzon
11 New Fetter Lane, London EC4P 4EE

RoutledgeCurzon is an imprint of the Taylor & Francis Group

Printed in the United States of America

07 06 05 04 03 02 7 6 5 4 3 2 1

Library of Congress Cataloging-in-Publication Data

Christians, cultural interactions, and India's religious traditions /
edited by Judith M. Brown and Robert Eric Frykenberg;
associate editor, Alaine Low.
p. cm. — (Studies in the history of Christian missions)
Includes bibliographical references and index.
Eerdmans ISBN 0-8028-3955-X (pbk.: alk. paper)
1. Missions — India — History. 2. India — Church history.
I. Brown, Judith M. (Judith Margaret), 1944- II. Frykenberg, Robert Eric.
III. Low, Alaine M. IV. Series.

BV3265.3.C48 2002
275.4 — dc21

2002023820

British Library Cataloguing-in-Publication Data

A catalogue for this book is available fron the British Library.
RoutledgeCurzon ISBN 0-7007-1601-7

Contents

Acknowledgments

The Editors would like to thank those who, apart from the contributors, have enabled the production of this collection of essays. The initial discussion of contributions to a volume on the theme of "Cultural Interactions" in India took place at a conference in Oxford in September 1999. This would have been impossible without the help of the staff at Balliol College. Stephanie Jenkins provided secretarial assistance throughout the conference and the publishing project, and Dr. David Washbrook, Reader in Indian History at the University of Oxford, helped with the planning and was an valuable colleague and chairman. The authors in this volume were joined at the conference by other invited scholars, whose comments and contributions were invaluable at the time and subsequently to the Editors. They included Dr. L. Caplan, Dr. P. Carson, Dr. G. Cederlof, Professor D. Hudson, Professor D. Jeyaraj, Dr. D. Mosse, Dr. G. Oddie, Professor A. Porter, and Professor T. Raychaudhuri. We should also like to thank The Pew Charitable Trusts for helping to fund the conference and the subsequent editorial costs.

Contributors

Peter B. Andersen is Associate Professor in the Sociology of Religions in the Department for the History of Religion, University of Copenhagen. He wrote his doctoral thesis on the Santals in India and has conducted statistical investigations on religious change and modern religious movements in Denmark.

Michael Bergunder is Lecturer in Ecumenics and Religious Studies in the Theological Faculty, University of Halle. His research has focused on the Pentecostal movement; modern esotericism; religion and society of modern South India, especially Tamilnadu; and the Tamil-speaking diaspora. He is working on the Theosophical Society and its impact on the religious history of India and the West.

Judith M. Brown is Beit Professor of Commonwealth History in the University of Oxford and a Professorial Fellow of Balliol College. Her research and writings have focused mainly on Indian politics in the twentieth century, and particularly on the career and thought of M. K. Gandhi. She is currently working on a political portrait of Jawaharlal Nehru.

Susan Billington Harper, formerly the Executive Director of the Templeton Prize for Progress in Religion, is now a writer and consultant. She lectured in history, literature, and expository writing at Harvard University, 1992-96, and was later a program officer at The Pew Charitable Trusts. She is the author of *In the Shadow of the Mahatama: Bishop V. S. Azariah and the Travails of Christianity in British India.*

Robert Eric Frykenberg is Emeritus Professor of History at the University of Wisconsin-Madison. His works include *Guntur District, 1788-1848: A History* *of Local Influence and Central Authority in India.* His edited works include *Christians and Missionaries in India: Cross-Cultural Communication and Consequences since 1500* (Curzon, forthcoming).

Bengt G. Karlsson is Visiting Professor at the South Asia Language and Area Center, University of Chicago. Previously he taught anthropology and coordinated a research seminar in development studies at Uppsala University, Sweden. His research focuses on indigenous peoples in India. He is author of *Contested Belonging: An Indigenous Person's Struggle for Forest and Identity in Sub-Himalayan Bengal.*

Indira Viswanathan Peterson is Professor and Chair of the Asian Studies Program, Mount Holyoke College, and specializes in Sanskrit and Tamil literature. She is author of *Poems to Siva: The Hymns of the Tamil Saints* and editor for Indian literature, *Norton Anthology of World Masterpieces.* Her most recent research is on literature and culture in eighteenth-century South India.

Avril A. Powell is Senior Lecturer in the History of South Asia at the School of Oriental and African Studies, University of London. Her recent publications include "History, Textbooks and the Transmission of the Pre-Colonial Past in North-Western India in the 1860s and 1870s," in *Invoking the Past: The Uses of History in South Asia,* edited by Daud Ali.

Gerald Studdert-Kennedy retired from the Department of Political Science and International Studies at the University of Birmingham in 1989, with an Honorary Chair in the School of Social Sciences. His publications include *British Christians, Indian Nationalists and the Raj,* and *Providence and the Raj: Imperial Mission and Missionary Imperialism.*

John C. B. Webster is a Diaconal Worker of the Worldwide Ministries Division, Presbyterian Church (USA). His recent publications include *The Dalit Christians: A History* and *Dalit Liberation: An Examination of Perspectives.* He is currently working on a history of Christianity in northwest India during the nineteenth and twentieth centuries for the Church History Association of India.

Richard Fox Young is the Elmer K. and Ethel R. Timby Associate Professor of History of Religions at Princeton Theological Seminary. His research interests focus on the history of encounter between Christianity and various religions of Asian origin, especially Hinduism and Buddhism; the place of Christianity in non-Western pluralism; and contemporary understandings of interreligious dialogue.

CHAPTER ONE

Introduction

JUDITH M. BROWN

The South Asian subcontinent has for centuries been a meeting place for diverse religious and cultural traditions. Here many of the world's major religious traditions have coexisted and interacted, influencing and being influenced by their neighbors. Not least among the processes of interaction was the way in which converts, for example to Christianity or Islam, often carried with them much from their former allegiances and beliefs. So marked a feature of India's history was this religious pluralism that when nationalist politicians began to articulate what they saw as central to national identity in the twentieth century, some of the most thoughtful identified a "composite" and multireligious culture as crucial to their inheritance.[1]

In the eighteenth and nineteenth centuries, however, the dynamics of cultural and religious interaction on the subcontinent were significantly changed by new Protestant and Catholic missionary movements from Europe and America.[2] Christianity had, of course, long been one of India's own religious traditions, in the form of the Syrian Christian communities in the south of the subcontinent, which claimed roots dating to apostolic times, and in the groups of Catholic Christians whose origins lay in the missions of the sixteenth century. There was now, however, a new drive to convert Indians of

1. See, for example, the discussions by Mahatma Gandhi in his 1909 pamphlet, *Hind Swaraj* [Indian Home Rule], or the attempt by Jawaharlal Nehru to capture the essence of India: A. J. Parel, ed., *Gandhi: Hind Swaraj and Other Writings* (Cambridge, 1997); J. Nehru, *The Discovery of India* (1st ed., 1946; London, 1947).

2. K. Ward and B. Stanley, eds., *The Church Mission Society and World Christianity, 1799-1999* (Grand Rapids, 2000); and D. Hudson, *Protestant Origins in India: Tamil Evangelical Christians, 1706-1835* (Richmond, Surrey, 2000).

other traditions, a drive which was rooted in new theological understandings of the significance and meaning of individual conversion. It was fired by a vision of personal and social godliness and responsibility that had already done much to alter the domestic world of Europe and America and had encouraged both men and women to engage in political and social work of compassion and reform.

In the particular context of South Asia in the nineteenth and early twentieth centuries the new piety and zeal for conversion had momentous implications because of the timing and broader context of the movements it generated. For the first time on the subcontinent Christianity was the religion of imperial rulers, as Islam had earlier been. From 1813 missionaries were allowed into the territories controlled by the East India Company. Increasingly through the century the missionary presence was able to thrive under the protective structures of British imperial rule. Christianity was also highly visible on the subcontinent as a defining mark of the ruling race and a central element in their domestic mores and as one of the boundary markers between rulers and the majority of their subjects. Moreover, at times and among particular groups of British officials in India as well as the British domestic public, the British empire itself was consciously thought to be part of a divine plan for India's "uplift" and "salvation."[3]

The Christian message was also tied, almost inextricably, with other aspects of Western intellectual influence that were brought to bear on India through modern forms of education and the presence of a Western imperial power. Few Indians educated in India's growing numbers of new schools, colleges, and universities could fail to encounter aspects of Christianity and to hear the criticisms of Hindu and Muslim tradition and social customs that were embedded in Western critiques of Indian "tradition." Some were powerfully attracted by the Christian Scriptures and by the teachings of Jesus. Yet even those who were hostile to Christianity, and the methods of some missionaries, became involved in their own reassessments of Indian religion and society and were profoundly concerned with the need to consider what was of value, what was essential, and what could be reformed or thrown out.[4] It was,

3. This was still evident in the early twentieth century. See C. Dewey, *Anglo-Indian Attitudes: The Mind of the Indian Civil Service* (London, 1993), particularly the section on Frank Brayne and his work in the Punjab; also G. Studdert-Kennedy, *British Christians, Indian Nationalists and the Raj* (Delhi, 1991), and his *Providence and The Raj: Imperial Mission and Missionary Imperialism* (New Delhi and London, 1998).

4. Gandhi was an example of this process: see his autobiography, first serialized in 1927: *An Autobiography: The Story of My Experiments with Truth* (London, 1966). A discussion of the self-analysis of Hindu tradition by educated Hindus in the nineteenth and

perhaps, the technology of communication that made the "new Christianity" such a powerful presence and cultural catalyst in India in this period. This was the time when modern printing presses began to turn out a voluminous literature in English and in India's vernacular languages on a wide range of social and religious issues, in book and pamphlet form as well as in the burgeoning popular press. The audience for this vast output of the printed word was the growing number of literate individuals who were becoming part of an educated and discerning Indian public.[5]

Given this context of imperial power, Western influence, and the development of an Indian public deeply concerned with issues of religious truth, morality, and social identity, it is hardly surprising that Christianity in India became a crucial element in many kinds of cultural debates and encounters. It is also clear why, for many Indians, Christianity had become far more problematic and challenging than it had been in previous centuries, and why the presence and role of foreign missionaries in particular became ambiguous and, at times, threatening to those Indians who were seeking to understand and reformulate their traditions and identities. As a result, the history of Christianity in modern India has often been written in starkly partisan terms. Such an approach masks the many and various ways in which Christianity interacted with South Asia's religious traditions. In these complex processes Christian practice and belief were themselves modified by South Asian religions, while simultaneously contributing to the processes of religious and cultural reevaluation and reform on the subcontinent.[6]

This collection of essays seeks to explore some of the ways Christianity has interacted with India's many religious traditions. Of course it must be underlined at the outset that "Christianity" was no single, homogeneous system of beliefs, practices, and authority structures. Western Christians exported to India their many denominational differences — differences that profoundly affected their understanding of their role in India, their relations with Indians, and their ecclesiastical structures. These essays focus on Protestant

---

early twentieth centuries can be found in ch. 2 of B. Parekh, *Colonialism, Tradition and Reform: An Analysis of Gandhi's Political Discourse,* rev. ed. (New Delhi and London, 1999). Aspects of Indians' "internal" responses to the West are explored in T. Raychaudhuri, *Perceptions, Emotions, Sensibilities: Essays on India's Colonial and Post-colonial Experiences* (New Delhi, 1999), pt. 1, "Perceptions, Sensibilities, Belief."

5. For a discussion of some of the implications of this process see the later part of C. A. Bayly, *Empire and Information: Intelligence Gathering and Social Communication in India, 1780-1870* (Cambridge, 1996).

6. A useful survey of the many reform movements at this time is K. W. Jones, *Socio-Religious Reform Movements in British India* (Cambridge, 1989).

Christianity, partly because of the connection between Anglicanism and the imperial rulers. Even among Protestants there were subtle differences in approach among different denominations and among different national groups of missionaries. Although Christian churches and missionaries figure prominently in this collection, this is not "Church history" or "mission history." It is, rather, a varied exploration of aspects of India's society and culture at a time of change and debate on many issues at many levels of sophistication, an exploration that focuses on the way aspects of Christian believing, belonging, and practice were a part of complex processes of cultural and religious interaction.

The first three chapters deal with the world of "High Culture" among Hindus and Muslims. Among educated, sophisticated Indians of high social standing there were few converts to Christianity. However, these sorts of Indians developed a deep awareness that they were living in a changing world, where their religious traditions were being challenged by secular and religious forces emanating from the Western world. In their milieu the debates about tradition, authority, the nature and relevance of Scripture, and the morality of a range of social customs with ostensibly religious sanction were real and extended.[7] Educated Hindus and Muslims did not merely "react" to Christian critiques, refuting Christian claims, or at times using insights from Christianity to reinvigorate elements within their own traditions, as Gandhi did in his reworking of the meaning of such themes as charity and sacrifice. They also noted the "techniques" of missionaries in teaching and social welfare, and their organizational and authority structures, and in some situations used them as examples for the reconstruction of their own traditions. This was clear, for example, in the work and beliefs of the Arya Samaj, one of the major reformist bodies within the spectrum of Hindu belief and practice.[8] When educated Indians did become Christians, they did not leave behind their cultural inheritance but often used the cultural and devotional resources of their earlier traditions in the expression of their new faith. Thus, in the longer run, they contributed to new Indian modes of Christian worship and theological emphasis and understanding.[9]

7. Among Hindus a deeply contested issue was that of caste and untouchability. Gandhi's life and work is an obvious example. See also the debates discussed in S. Bayly, *Caste, Society and Politics in India from the Eighteenth Century to the Modern Age* (Cambridge, 1999).

8. K. W. Jones, *Arya Dharm: Hindu Consciousness in Nineteenth Century Punjab* (Delhi and Berkeley, 1976).

9. An example of Indian Christian theological reflection on being Christian in the subcontinent was the large output of the first Indian Anglican bishop, V. S. Azariah (1874-

Indira Peterson, for example, examines the way a prominent Protestant poet in South India used Tamil forms of Hindu devotion embedded in local culture to tell a specifically Christian story, thus making existing cultural forms serve new religious and cultural purposes. Richard Fox Young's focus is on how Hindu participants in the new forms of cultural interaction felt and articulated their responses. He examines how educated Indians were drawn into an encounter with Christianity and how they viewed missionaries — an illuminating and ironic approach when set alongside the simultaneous and generally unflattering assessments by missionaries of Indian religions and their functionaries.

Avril Powell takes up the theme of cultural interaction within the world of Muslim high culture in the later nineteenth century. She examines the literary encounter between three serious scholars, two Muslim and one British, and their debates on Islam, Islamic history, and Islamic society. Of particular interest here is the way the British official, a committed Protestant Christian, examined issues relating to Islam in a genuinely scholarly way; and how both Muslim participants in the literary interaction engaged through a "modernist" mode of discourse. All three were heirs of earlier and cruder modes of encounter and had moved on to a new intellectual way of understanding religion in the context of history and society, in strong cultural contrast to the more popular "bazaar debates" between Muslims, missionaries, and Indian Christian converts.

The next group of chapters are devoted to Christians and Christianity within the diverse worlds of more popular culture. Again, the structuring theme is that of interaction, with an emphasis on the way Christian converts were deeply embedded in their local religious traditions, of linguistic region and locality: how Christian expression was molded by this context, and how Christian belonging and living were forged within it. Michael Bergunder's essay stands by itself in this group (though it echoes some of the themes raised by Peterson) in that he focuses on popular linguistic interaction. Historians of Asia and Africa have acknowledged the very significant cultural role of Protestant Christians, with their particular emphasis on literacy and the translation of Scripture into the vernaculars in mission fields. Missionary provision of education in India, often to the underprivileged, as an aspect of enabling Christian formation and growing spiritual maturity is well known. Far more work needs to be done on the rather more technical but important

1945). See Susan Billington Harper, *In the Shadow of the Mahatma: Bishop V. S. Azariah and the Travails of Christianity in British India* (Grand Rapids and Cambridge and Richmond, Surrey, 2000).

subject of how vernacular translations of the Bible have related to local languages, to their development, and often to their flowering. More research will reveal the extent to which Indian Christians themselves played a crucial part in the processes of co-opting local people into the work of Christian mission and education, initially as the language teachers and linguistic informants of foreign missionaries, and then as leaders of local Christian churches. Bergunder opens up the contemporary world of new translations of Scripture in a "postmission" period. He shows how Tamil Christianity appropriates certain types of vernacular for the key text of the Bible and is in turn influenced by the cultural trends in the linguistic region.

Three contributions in this group on cultural interaction at a more popular level (Peter Andersen, Beppe Karlsson and John Webster) take groups of Dalits and Tribals as their focus because it was from these groups that most of the converts to Christianity came. These were individuals and whole groups at the base of Hindu society or on its margins, geographically as well as culturally. Because they were often illiterate both before and often after their conversion to Christianity, it is difficult for historians to hear their "voices" except through the filter of missionary accounts. The latter were inevitably colored by their own Western prejudices and intentions, as well as the domestic audiences for which missionary literature was intended. (Both Andersen and Webster note this problem, directly or indirectly; and Andersen focuses on the nature of an apparently Indian Christian source and indicates some of the problems it poses for historians.)

The mass conversion movements of such marginal groups in the nineteenth and twentieth centuries were one of the most dramatic and unexpected aspects of the Christian missionary presence in India. They forced foreign missionaries to rethink the meaning of "mission" and the nature of the expanding Christian communities and churches. Here, in such movements and their results, was the site of some of the most profound interactions between Christianity and some of India's little religious traditions, as opposed to the high Brahmanical tradition of the more educated and higher caste. Much work remains to be done on these movements, on the reasons for conversion, and on the meaning of conversion in individual belief, in lifestyle, and in wider social relations. We also need to know more about the internal dynamics of the new Christian communities and their self-understanding, as well as the way they are perceived in contemporary India.

The papers here focus specifically on conversion, its meaning and dynamics. One way to understand the varied process of conversion is to see it as part of a broad spectrum of religious change in India in the nineteenth and twentieth centuries, where disadvantaged groups were using religious "resources" of many kinds to find meaning in their lives as individuals and as groups, particularly in a time of socioeconomic change. Andersen, in particular, stresses the context of change as vital in his study of Santal conversions. Some of these disadvantaged groups used resources within Hindu myth and tradition to claim new histories for themselves and new status and meaning for their lives. B. R. Ambedkar and his untouchable followers who abandoned Hinduism in the mid twentieth century used the religious and cultural resources of Buddhism. Yet others have turned to Christianity. "Resources" here must be widely understood to include the spiritual, social, and material — diverse aspects of a changing situation that enabled people to make new meaning of their inner lives and of their lives as a group, and to situate themselves in new locations in the wider society. Webster makes this plain in his exposition both of the role of the missionary in terms of a new "patron" for rural Christians and of the misunderstandings between convert and missionary that could result. What soon became clear was that conversions to Christianity among families and kin groups led to changes not just in self-esteem but in health, education, and the prospect of social and economic advancement. Such changes occurred after the bonds that tied converts to the lowliest place in village society had been loosened by their interaction with Christianity and its Indian and foreign representatives. As Webster points out, however, conversion must not just be seen as a change of belief or allegiance located at a specific point in time, though Protestant theology has often highlighted the critical nature of a "conversion experience." In the Indian context conversion should be recognized as a process that encompasses several generations, as new Indian Christians lay hold on the multiple opportunities offered to them through their new status that enable them to forge new identities, relationships, and roles in a changing world.

Issues relating to conversion in large numbers link this group of papers to those on the final theme, that of churches in India. Indian churches have been treated by historians in the past very narrowly, mainly in institutional terms. These chapters open up deeper issues relating to how new Christian communities are formed and disciplined and, in particular, how ill-educated converts are led to refashion their lives and to produce men and women who could in turn form a new Christian leadership. For Church leaders, who were of course in increasing numbers Indian rather than foreign in the twentieth century, a profound problem was to help to build a truly Indian church; yet also to extract converts from some aspects of their older cultural inheritance that were deemed incompatible with Christian profession while retaining those that were seen as conducive to Christian living and worship (see Susan Billington Harper). A further aspect of cultural interaction at a different level, and particularly acute within the Anglican Church, was the dilemma of how a "colonial" church, with all its webs of connection in Britain's own authority structures and ruling classes, could begin to become an Indian church in terms of theology and authority (see Gerald Studdert-Kennedy)

These essays discuss many of the ways in which Christianity (as belief, worship, way of life, and community) and Christians (from India and abroad) have interacted with India's other cultural traditions. It encourages readers to see Christianity, Christians, and the work of missionaries in India in the nineteenth and twentieth centuries as a vital part of a broad spectrum of cultural and religious change on the subcontinent. Here are fields for important historical research into the making of contemporary Indian culture and society, the product of a long period of interaction among the different regions and peoples of the subcontinent, as well as between the subcontinent and the world at large.

CHAPTER TWO

Bethlehem Kuravañci of Vedanayaka Sastri of Tanjore: The Cultural Discourses of an Early-Nineteenth-Century Tamil Christian Poem

INDIRA VISWANATHAN PETERSON

The Cultural Milieu of a Nineteenth-Century Tamil Protestant Poet

On a September day in 1809 the Tamil Protestant congregation of St. Mathias Church in Vepery, Madras, gathered before the church porch to felicitate a Tamil poet. Vedanayaka Sastri of Tanjore (Tanjavur) had been a guest at the home of a lay elder, Muttucamiya Pillai, for two months and had given readings and performances of his poetry to the congregation.[1] The premiere of the dramatic poem *Bethlehem kuravañci (The Fortune-Teller Drama of Bethlehem)* had been the highlight of the readings. At the church gathering, presided over by Reverend Paezold, the German missionary pastor, the Tamil congregation conferred upon the poet the title "King of Poets of the Light of Wisdom," along with a testimonial signed by forty members. Sastri was given rich ceremonial cloths, seated in a splendid palanquin that was a gift from Muttucamiya Pillai, and led in procession with pomp and music around Vepery, accompanied by the entire Tamil congregation.

Public readings of poetic works and the felicitation of learned poets with

1. The account of the felicitation of Sastri in Vepery on 19 September 1809 is based on descriptions in two biographies of the poet: D. V. Devanesan, *Tañcai Vedanayakam Sastiriyar* (Madras, 1947; 2nd ed., 1956), pp. 27-35, and Dayamani Manasseh, *Vētanāyaka Vētasastiri* (Madras, 1975), pp. 41-43.

processions, titles, and gifts are old traditions in Tamil literary culture. Such ceremonies formed part of the milieu of secular and sacred poetry in the eighteenth and nineteenth centuries.[2] That this particular ceremony took place in a Christian context was not unusual. From early on major Tamil literary works had been written by poets of diverse religious and sectarian backgrounds, including Buddhism, Jainism, Hinduism, and Islam.[3] In the seventeenth and eighteenth centuries Christian writers, including European missionaries, such as the renowned Jesuit Joseph Constantius Beschi (a.k.a. Viramamunivar, 1680-1747), had written original literary works in Tamil.[4]

Two aspects of the event, however, were unusual. First, the Tamil congregation of the Vepery church was led by German Pietist missionaries from Halle, who had established the first Protestant mission in India in the Danish territory of Tranquebar in 1706 and who were active in Tanjore, Madras, and other towns in the Tamil region.[5] These missionaries had focused on producing Tamil translations of the Bible and European hymns, and dictionaries and other linguistic works, rather than on creating original works, especially religious poems, in Tamil.[6] Vedanayaka Sastri was the first major poet to emerge from the Tamil Evangelical community in South India and to produce a substantial body of poetic works on Protestant themes in Tamil literary genres.[7]

2. For accounts of such ceremonies in the nineteenth century, see U. V. Swaminatha Iyer, *The Story of My Life: An Autobiography of Dr. U. V. Swaminatha Iyer,* translated by Kamil Zvelebil (Madras, 1990).

3. For instance, the first courtly epic poem in Tamil was written by the Jain ascetic, Iḷaṅkōvaṭikaḷ. See Kamil V. Zvelebil, *Tamil Literature,* Handbuch der Orientalistik, Zweite Abteilung, *Indien,* edited by Jan Gonda, Band 2: *Literatur und Bühne,* Abschnitt 1 (Leiden/Cologne, 1975).

4. See "Christianity and Tamil Literature," in *The Encyclopedia of Tamil Literature,* vol. 1 (Tiruvanmiyur, 1990), pp. 391-409.

5. The term "Evangelical" is used in the same sense as it was by the early Tamil Protestant community of South India and by the German missionaries. For the history of Protestantism in South India, see Stephen Neill, *A History of Christianity in India, 1707-1858,* vol. 2 (Cambridge, 1985). For the Danish Halle mission in Tranquebar, see Arno Lehmann, *Es begann in Tranquebar: Die Geschichte der ersten evangelischen Kirche in Indien* (Berlin, 1956).

6. On the writings of the Halle missionaries in South India, see Lehmann, *Es begann in Tranquebar,* and C. S. Mohanavelu, *German Tamilology: German Contributions to Tamil Language, Literature and Culture during the Period 1706-1945* (Madras, 1993).

7. On Tamil Protestant poets and authors and Tamil music in the Church in the period before Sastri, see Daniel Jeyaraj, *Inculturation in Tranquebar: Der Beitrag der früher dänisch-halleschen Mission zum Werden einer indisch-einheimischen Kirche (1706-1730),* Missionswissenschaftliche Forschungen, Neue Folge, Band 4 (Erlangen, 1996), pp. 235-36, 243-44.

Second, the *Bethlehem kuṟavañci* (henceforth *BK*) was the first Protestant work in the *kuṟavañci* genre. The *kuṟavañci* was one of several highly popular, musical-dramatic Tamil genres dating from the early eighteenth century.[8] The premiere of *BK*, which was to become Sastri's most celebrated poem, marked an important moment in the Tamil literature and the Tamil Evangelical Church. The literary, religious, and cultural discourses that shaped *BK* are the subject of this chapter.

Born in 1774 in Tirunelveli, the son of Devasahayam Pillai, a Catholic catechist who had converted from Śaivism, Vedanayaka Sastri received early schooling in the traditional Tamil manner.[9] In 1785, when Sastri's father and his family converted to the Evangelical Church, the German missionary Christian Friedrich Schwartz (1726-98) took the eleven-year-old boy to the city of Tanjore, the capital of the kingdom of Tanjore, which was ruled by a Maratha king under the authority of the British East India Company. Tanjore City in the eighteenth century was an important center of Tamil and South Indian literature and arts, as well as a meeting place of diverse languages and cultures.[10] In 1789, following a period of instruction with Schwartz, Sastri was sent to Tranquebar where he studied theology and the European systems of astronomy, anatomy, and mathematics with C. S. John and other German missionaries. In 1794, at age nineteen, he became headmaster of the Tamil school for catechists in Tanjore. From then until 1829, when he was removed from the school after disputes with the missionaries, he taught mathematics and astronomy and trained catechists. Sastri served as a court poet of King Serfoji II of Tanjore from 1829 until Serfoji's death in 1832, and he occasionally worked as an interpreter, Tamil teacher, and research assistant for British and German individuals. Throughout his life, however, he directed the major portion of his energies toward writing literary works in Tamil.

By 1809 Sastri had already written fifty-two Tamil poetic works on Protestant religious themes,[11] and by the time of his death in 1864, he had

8. On eighteenth- and nineteenth-century Tamil genres, see Zvelebil, *Tamil Literature.* For the *kuṟavañci* genre: Marina Muilwijk, *The Divine Kuṟa Tribe: Kuṟavañci and Tamil prabandhas* (Groningen, 1996); and Indira Viswanathan Peterson, "The Evolution of the *Kuṟavañci* Dance Drama in Tamil Nadu: Negotiating the 'Folk' and the 'Classical' in the Bharata Nāṭyam Canon," *South Asia Research* 18.1 (1998): 39-72.

9. For Vedanayaka Sastri, see Devanesan, *Tañcai;* Manasseh, *Vētanāyaka;* also Noah Jnanadikkam, *Tañcai cuvicēṭa kavirāyar Vedanāyaka Sāstriyār (Life of Vedanayagam Sastriyar, the Evangelical Poet of Tanjavur)* (Tanjavur, 1899; reprinted 1987).

10. On cultural diversity in Tanjore, see S. Seetha, *Tanjore as a Seat of Music During the Seventeenth, Eighteenth and Nineteenth Centuries* (Madras, 1981), and Peterson, "Evolution of the *Kuṟavañci*."

11. Vepery testimonial, 1809, cited in Devanesan, *Tañcai*, p. 31.

produced 120 Tamil works. He wrote several prose tracts on didactic and polemical topics and a Tamil textbook of arithmetic, but his most celebrated works are poetic.[12] The writings include nearly five hundred hymns and devotional songs.[13] Yet Sastri's enduring reputation as an eminent Tamil Christian poet rests above all on his longer poems.

For the greater part of his career, accompanied by his sons and daughter, Vedanayaka Sastri recited, sang, and discoursed on his longer works to Tamil Christian audiences in Tanjore and other towns. Several of these works were published in the late nineteenth and early twentieth centuries. Preeminent among these is *BK*, his masterpiece. The dramatic poem is Sastri's best-known work within the Tamil Protestant community, while historians of Tamil literature consider it to be a *tour de force* in the *kuṟavañci* genre. In 1979, long after the demise of nineteenth-century performance traditions, *BK* was performed as a dance-drama by students at the Women's Christian College, Madras.

Vedanayaka Sastri's choice of the *kuṟavañci* genre for a major work and the problems and challenges he faced in shaping the formal, thematic, and performance conventions of this popular genre to serve his ends as an Evangelical are the subject of this chapter. I argue that in *BK*, Sastri drew on a common pool of older and contemporary Tamil literary and performance genres to articulate a distinctively Tamil refraction of the Evangelical religion brought to South India. Sastri's poem shows that Tamil Protestants were fully engaged with the dynamics of social and cultural change in the Tamil region in the early nineteenth century.[14]

A Poetics for Tamil Evangelical Literature

In 1809, when Sastri came to Vepery, he had already been acclaimed by the Tamil Protestant communities of Tanjore and Tranquebar (1808) and awarded the titles "Evangelical poet" and "the Principal Evangelical jewel, the monarch of the divine poets." In 1815, during the forty-five days of Lent, the

12. Sastri's works are listed in Jnanadikkam, *Life*, pp. 111-13.

13. These hymns comprise the bulk of the Tamil hymns in the collection of the American missionary E. Webb and remain some of the most popular in the Tamil Protestant repertoire; see E. Webb, ed., *Christian Lyrics for Public and Social Worship* (Madras, 1853).

14. For studies of Sastri's contribution to Tamil literary and religious cultures, see P. A. Sattiyacāṭci, *Tañcai Vētanāyakar Tamiḻviruntu* (Madras, 1975), and T. Dayanandan Francis, *Christian Poets and Tamil Culture* (Madras, 1978).

poet presented two long poems, *Cāstirak kummi (Poem on Superstition)* and *Pēriṉpak kātal (Desire for Salvation),* before the Protestant congregations in Trichinopoly and received yet another testimonial, along with the title "Doctor of Biblical Theology."[15] In this way the Tamil Protestants celebrated the originality and range of Sastri's works and their importance to its religious and cultural life. The testimonials indicate that, although missionary priests presided over such events, the Tamil congregations were the real patrons and audience of Sastri's works. In 1815 the Tanjore congregation bestowed a "perpetual agreement" on the poet and his descendants, promising its uninterrupted support to them "till the day of the Last Judgment" for the fostering and performance of his works.[16]

The signatories of the testimonials included a number of interpreters, brokers *(dubash),* catechists, school teachers, clerks, doctors, and servants of Europeans (peons, butlers, personal servants) — men engaged in professions associated with European activity in colonial India. Like Sastri himself, Muttucamiya Pillai of Vepery and other elders and elite leaders of the Tamil Evangelical congregations belonged to the Tamil Vellāla community.[17] The dominant group in late-nineteenth-century Tamil society in Tamilnadu and Jaffna (Ceylon), Vellālas are mainly Śaiva in religious affiliation; they had been the principal custodians of Tamil literary traditions. The Tanjore testimonial states:

> He has besides well searched the Old and New Testaments and according to it has compiled 52 books containing the system of Christian doctrine sweetly and metrically. We therefore jointly and with exceeding gladness testify that he is a well-learned person and better versed than all whom we have known since the spreading of the saving Gospel in this part of India to this long period, that he ought to be esteemed as a more celebrated person than all worldly poets.[18]

15. For complete texts of the testimonials, see Devanesan, *Tañcai,* pp. 17-44, and Jnanadikkam, *Life,* pp. 96-109. I thank Dr. Daniel Jeyaraj for pointing out that the phrase *vēdacāstiram* (literally, "scholarly knowledge of Scripture"; Veda = the Bible) included in Sastri's title "Vedasastri" could refer more specifically to *Wedasastiram,* a Tamil compendium of Pietist theology by the Halle missionaries B. Ziegenbalg and J. E. Gründler, 1717. See Jeyaraj, *Inculturation,* pp. 136-38.

16. The agreement was reaffirmed in 1818. Devanesan, *Tañcai,* pp. 43-46.

17. On the Vellāla roots of the Tamil Protestant community, see D. Dennis Hudson, "The First Protestant Mission to India: Its Social and Religious Developments," *Sociological Bulletin* 42.1-2 (March-September 1993): 37-63; and Hudson, *Protestant Origins in India: Tamil Evangelical Christians, 1706-1835* (Richmond, 2000).

18. Devanesan, *Tañcai,* p. 18.

The Vepery congregation praised Sastri's competence as a learned Tamil poet:

> We perceived that the 52 books of songs . . . are all of them well revised according to the grammatical and poetical prosodical rules, and that even the most famous poets are not able to find any fault in them, and that such plain and elegant verses cannot be composed by any one unless he understands perfectly the contents of the Old and New Testament.[19]

In 1815, the Trichinopoly congregation similarly declared that "he excelled in knowledge all the Hindus who are well versed through all-India."[20] What cultural forces impelled Sastri to become an Evangelical poet and the Tamil congregations to discern these particular values in his works? Every religious community in India has produced a distinctive body of literature, and poetry plays an important role in most Indian religious communities. Hymns and songs of *bhakti* devotionalism have been ubiquitous in Hindu and other religious literary traditions from the seventh century, when *bhakti* movements arose in South India, led by Tamil saints who wrote hymns dedicated to the gods Śiva and Viṣṇu. In his Evangelical hymns Sastri used the forms and discourses of Śaiva and Vaiṣṇava hymn literature.[21]

Devotional lyricism, the singing of "divine songs," was important in German Pietist religion.[22] In the late eighteenth century, Sastri and his fellow Tamil Evangelicals had been brought up on Tamil translations of German Pietist hymns, and Sastri greatly admired the Tamil hymn translations of J. P. Fabricius.[23] Why did Sastri choose to write original Tamil hymns on indigenous models? It would seem that missionary translations did not fulfill the aesthetic needs of Sastri and his fellow Tamils. To be authentic, Tamil hymns had to be composed according to certain prosodic and stylistic requirements, including such elements as metaphors and tropes, specific metrical forms,

19. Devanesan, *Tañcai,* p. 31.

20. Devanesan, *Tañcai,* p. 38.

21. On the devotional hymns of the Tamil Śaiva and Vaiṣṇava poets, respectively, see Indira Viswanathan Peterson, *Poems to Śiva: The Hymns of the Tamil Saints* (Princeton, 1989), and A. K. Ramanujan, *Hymns for the Drowning: Poems for Viṣṇu by Nammāḻvār* (Princeton, 1981). On Sastri's use of Śaiva models, see Francis, *Christian Poets and Tamil Culture,* pp. 12-29.

22. Gudrun Busch and Wolfgang Miersemann, eds., *"Geist-reicher" Gesang: Halle und das pietistische Lied,* Hallesche Forschungen 39 (Tübingen, 1997).

23. Jeyaraj, *Inculturation,* pp. 236-43, discusses the use of translations from European hymns in the early Tranquebar Church. On Sastri's treatment of Fabricius's hymns, see the commentary in Vedanayaka Sastri, *Jepamālai by Vedanāyaka Sastiriyār,* edited with a commentary by S. W. Savarimuthu (Madras, 1987), pp. xvi, 80-81, passim.

and conventions of alliteration and rhyme. Thus Sastri was not satisfied with merely transforming Fabricius's Tamil translations of European hymns into metrical Tamil versions.[24]

Further, Tamil hymns had to be true songs, composed in the tradition of "musical Tamil," one of the three modes of poetic composition in Tamil. According to traditional accounts and performance practices, specific melodies and beat patterns were structural elements of the hymns of the Śaiva and Vaiṣṇava poet-saints.[25] In the manner of the Hindu *bhakti* saints, in his hymns and songs Vedanayaka Sastri identifies himself as God's poetdevotee, addressing a Lord who "comes in response to Tamil song."[26] In Sastri's time, South Indian composers of art music created both the music and the devotional lyrics for their compositions.[27] These cultural practices explain, in part, why Sastri viewed the Psalmist David as his model. According to oral tradition among his descendants, the foundations of Sastri's career as a poet were laid by Schwartz, who gave the young boy the Psalms of David.[28] There are many references to David and the Psalms in Sastri's works, and he viewed his vocation as that of an original poet-devotee-composer, a David who would sing and praise his God in his own words and music.

Sastri's father was also a poet, and as a child Sastri had been exposed to the rich *pulavar* (learned poet) culture of his native region (where the most famous poem in the *kuṟavañci* genre was written).[29] Learned poets composed in the *pirapantam* form, which consisted of numerous genres; the major Hindu devotional poets wrote long poems as well as shorter lyrics. Vedanayaka Sastri composed several works in older *pirapantam* genres that were concerned with courtly and sacred themes. In *Ñāṉa antāti (Poem on Wisdom),* composed in 1796, a poem partly based on the *Song of Solomon,* he uses an old poetic form in which each following verse begins with the last word of the previous verse. *Ñāṉa ulā (Procession Poem of Wisdom),* composed in 1835, is in the genre describing the procession of a king or a god.

24. Sastri, *Jepamālai.*

25. The melodic modes and rhythm patterns of these ancient hymns are forerunners of the later *rāgas* and *tālas.* See Peterson, *Poems to Śiva,* pp. 20-23, 59-66.

26. *BK,* pp. 202-3. All citations from *BK* in this chapter refer to Vedanayaka Sastri, *Bethlehem kuṟavañci with a Preface by E. Vedabothagam,* 3rd ed. (Tanjavur, 1938).

27. Indira V. Peterson, "The *kṛti* As an Integrative Cultural Form: Aesthetic Experience in the Religious Songs of Two South Indian Classical Composers," *Journal of South Asian Literature* 19.2 (Fall-Winter 1984): 165-79.

28. Jnanadikkam, *Life,* p. 20.

29. Puliyangudi, where Sastri received his early education in Tamil, was a center of learned Tamil poetry in the nineteenth century. Swaminatha Iyer, *My Life,* p. 68.

In the eighteenth and nineteenth centuries, not only hymns but many of the Tamil literary *pirapantams* belonged to the repertoire of traditions of performance. The hymns translated into Tamil from European languages were sung by the congregations to European tunes, but Sastri's hymns were sung by specialist singers at the Tanjore church to indigenous tunes, in a manner similar to the established tradition of the performance of Śaiva hymns at temples by professional singers.[30] Sastri's long poems and his hymns reflected the influence of contemporary performance practices, especially in the traditions of classical (Carnatic) music and *(catir)* dance. These practices had been developed in innovative ways from the seventeenth century in the Tanjore region. Sastri composed his Evangelical hymns in the *rāgas* (modal scale types) and rhythmic beat cycles of the music of the courts and temples of the Tamil region. The hymns were modeled on the newly developed *kīrttaṉai,* the major art song form of the Carnatic repertoire, and a form with a sophisticated and compact melodic and rhythmic structure.[31] In Sastri's time, music and dance were increasingly used in the longer literary *pirapantam* genres, and some dramatic and poetic genres, like the *kuṟavañci,* were comprised entirely of songs and were enacted in dance.

The missionary leaders of the Tamil Protestant congregation welcomed Sastri's hymns and his longer works, but by 1829 controversies had erupted between some groups among the high caste Vellāla Evangelicals and the German and English missionaries in Tanjore and Madras, mainly concerning the observance of caste practices among the congregation, but also regarding the "heathen" manner in which the Tamil hymns were performed in church.[32] Sastri's Tamil hymns were temporarily removed from church ceremonies but were later reinstated. By the 1850s, however, the Rev. G. U. Pope and other missionaries raised objections to certain elements in Sastri's hymns and poems, such as verses that included the poet's name. For a brief period, Sastri's hymns were proscribed from performance in church. At no time, however, did these hymns and poems decline in popularity with the Tamil congregation. In their view, Sastri had given them what the missionaries had not: a body of comprehensive, wide-ranging, original sacred poetry in Tamil idioms, which in their eyes surpassed the religious literature of the Hindus, especially the Śaiva and Vaiṣṇava Vellālas. In Sastri's poems the Tamil Evangeli-

30. Peterson, *Poems to Śiva,* pp. 51-67.

31. Peterson, "The *kṛti.*"

32. On the Vellāla Evangelicals' controversies with the missionaries, see Devanesan, *Tañcai,* pp. 110-20; Manasseh, *Vētanāyaka,* pp. 91-103; Hudson, "The First Protestant Mission"; and Hudson, *Protestant Origins,* pp. 140-88.

cals found a powerful instrument for expressing their sensibilities as a *Tamil* Christian community.

Bethlehem Kuṟavañci and Dramatic Poems in Nineteenth-Century South India

In addition to the pan-Indian epics *Rāmāyaṇa* and the *Mahābhārata*, which flourish in innumerable regional language retellings, self-identified communities in India, including religious sects, have created their own master narratives, epics, and *purāṇas* (stories, histories). These works are traditionally expounded to large publics in discourses and other types of performances. Cēkkiḻār's twelfth-century hagiography of the sixty-three Nāyaṉār saints serves as the *purāṇa* of the Tamil Śaiva sect.[33] Father Beschi had tried to fill the need for a Tamil Catholic epic by writing the *Tēmpāvaṇi*, a life of Joseph in ornate and erudite Tamil verse, modeled on the great Western epics yet using conventions from Tamil poetry, a genuine *tour de force*.[34] In the late nineteenth century the Tamil Protestant poet H. A. Krishna Pillai attempted a similar feat with his version of Bunyan's *Pilgrim's Progress*.[35] A study of *BK* suggests that Vedanayaka Sastri intended his poem to be an Evangelical master work, a *purāṇa* for the Tamil Protestant community. In the verse preface to *BK*, Sastri says that he worked on the plan of the poem for an entire year.[36] He completed a version of *BK* in 1800, premiered it in 1809, and revised it and formally presented it to the Evangelical church in 1820.[37]

Sastri intended his long poems to serve as Evangelical rivals and alternatives to the most famous Hindu (especially Śaiva) *pirapantam* works. "The Garland Poem in Praise of the Lord" was composed in 1794 as a counterpoem to the popular Śaiva works *Katirkāmamālai* and *Ampikaimālai*.[38] In the *Ñānak kummi* (*Song of Wisdom*, 1796) Sastri used the images and rhetoric of the Cittar poets' radical critique of Hindu practices in the *Cittar ñānak kummi*, at the same time displacing the path of wisdom advocated by the

33. Zvelebil, *Tamil Literature*, pp. 178-81.

34. "Christianity and Tamil Literature," pp. 391-93.

35. "Christianity and Tamil Literature," pp. 400-401; and Francis, *Christian Poets*, pp. 38-60. For a detailed study of this poem, see D. Dennis Hudson, "Protestant Faith as Tamil Bhakti: The Writings of Krishna Pillai," *Dharma deepika* 1.2 (December 1997): 55-74.

36. *BK*, p. 2, *Pāyiram* (prefatory verses), v. 4.

37. *BK*, Preface, p. xi.

38. Manasseh, *Vētanāyaka*, p. 33.

Cittar adept with Evangelical "wisdom," that is, the wisdom embodied in the gospel.[39] Sastri was working within a tradition of sectarian rivalry expressed through poetry.[40] Indeed, by writing counter-works to well-known Hindu poems, he was simultaneously imitating them, subverting their influence, and challenging their authority. In the verse preface of the *BK,* we read:

> The pack of poets who do not know the One God, but worship many gods, have written many *purāṇas* and *kāvyas* [ornate narrative poems] on the misdeeds of these false gods, and now have composed *kuṟavañci* poems that are performed in dance. Seeing these, I, who have written many faith-inspiring works on the Lord Jesus, thought: "I, too, should compose a *kuṟavañci.*"[41]

Sastri's statements in the prose and verse prefaces to *BK* show that writing a *kuṟavañci* was a different sort of enterprise from writing in traditional poetic and sacred genres such as the *kōvai* or *antāti.* For the Evangelical poet, an important motivation for writing a *kuṟavañci* was to make use of a contemporary performance genre that was enormously popular for the expression and affirmation of Evangelical Christian ideas. This was no easy task. Although *kuṟavañci* dramas were often written in praise of a god of a local temple, the *kuṟavañci, noṇḍi* (cripple's play), and other poetic genres of the eighteenth century focused equally on human affairs and contemporary social, political, and historical themes, and on Hindu gods, myths, and temples. The principal characters in these plays included courtesans, farm laborers, horse thieves, and, in the case of the *kuṟavañci,* an itinerant woman fortune-teller of a hill tribe and her bird-catcher husband. In the eighteenth-century *pirapantam* genres, local kings and noblemen were praised as often as the gods, and erotic themes dominated these works. The new genres incorporated combinations of older forms. They blended courtly and folk styles, and the most popular

39. On Sastri and the Cittar poets, see Francis, *Christian Poets,* pp. 17-18. Dennis Hudson discusses the controversies carried on through the *kummi* (a women's folksong genre) by Hindu and Christian intellectuals of Ceylon and Tamilnadu in the nineteenth century, in "Arumuga Navalar and the Hindu Renaissance among the Tamils," in *Religious Controversy in British India: Dialogues in South Asian Languages,* edited by Kenneth W. Jones (Albany, 1992), pp. 27-51, esp. pp. 30-31.

40. See Indira V. Peterson, "*Śramaṇas* against the Tamil Way: Jains as Others in Tamil Śaiva Literature," in *Open Boundaries: Jain Communities and Cultures in Indian History,* edited by John E. Cort (Albany, 1998), pp. 163-85, esp. p. 179.

41. *BK,* p. 1, *Pāyiram,* v. 3. The prose preface states that Sastri wrote *BK* to challenge the *Kuṟṟālakkuṟavañci,* a celebrated work by a Tirunelveli author.

among them were dramatic genres composed mainly or entirely in song forms and enacted in dance. *Kuṟavañci* plays were comprised of *kīrttaṉais* and narrative *daru* songs[42] and were performed at temples and courts by female dancers, and apparently also by folk performers, such as the male *kaṇiyār* in the countryside. The *kuṟavañci* was a favorite genre at the Maratha court in Tanjore. Between 1700 and 1830 more than ten fortune-teller plays in several languages were written and performed at the Tanjore court alone. King Serfoji II of Tanjore is himself the hero of one that was enacted at the great temple of Śiva in Tanjore until the middle of the twentieth century. Serfoji is also credited with the authorship of *Devendra kuravañji,* a fortune-teller play in Marathi.

The fortune-teller's play is named after its principal character, the wandering female fortune-teller of the *kuṟavar* hill tribe. It is an opera-like drama with a stereotyped plot and conventional subthemes. A lady of the courtly milieu is stricken with unrequited love for the local king or god of the local temple, whom she has seen in a procession. As she wastes away with lovesickness, a fortune-teller appears, performs rituals of divination, foretells the lady's happy union with her lover, and is richly rewarded. In the course of the episode, the fortune-teller describes her travels, her mountain home, her exploits as a fortune-teller, and the ways of life of her wandering tribe. She lavishly praises the noble lord and his realm, as well as the local god and his temple. The fortune-teller's husband, the bird catcher Ciṅkaṉ, appears in the rice fields, netting and snaring birds. Missing his wife, he sets out to find her. At the end of the play they are reunited in the town where she went to tell the noble lady's fortune.

The *kuṟavañci* genre arose as a literary expression of changing relations among populations of diverse linguistic and social affiliations in South India.[43] Ruled successively by the Telugu Nayakas and the Marathas, dynasties of non-Tamil linguistic and cultural origins, and under British authority in the eighteenth and nineteenth centuries, Tanjore was a major center of artistic responses to the transition from the premodern to the colonial modern in South India. Encompassing an eclectic array of themes — foretelling the future; mountain and agricultural landscapes; urban and temple scenes; dialogues between courtly and folk characters; narratives of travel and migration; and local history — the plot of the fortune-teller's play constituted a

42. Structurally similar to the *kīrttaṉai,* the *daru* songs were distinguished by their narrative, descriptive, and dramatic content.

43. Peterson, "Evolution of the *Kuṟavañci,*" and Peterson, "The Drama of the *Kuṟavañci* Fortune-Teller: Land, Landscape, and Social Relations in an Eighteenth-Century Genre," in *Tamil Geographies: Cultural Constructions of Space and Place in South India,* edited by Martha A. Selby and Indira Viswanathan Peterson (Albany, forthcoming).

commentary on new social formations, landscapes, and geographies. The details of the drama include elements that correspond closely to the actual practice of specific nomadic tribal communities in the Tamil region. A sense for the expanding geographical and cultural horizons is conveyed in the faraway places (China, Mecca, Delhi) to which the fortune-teller claims to have traveled. The genre owed its enormous popularity to its innovative treatment of heterogeneous themes, combined with its attractive plot and colorful characters — most importantly, the charismatic and exotic fortune-teller.

The drama's appeal also owed much to the genre's foundations in the seminal themes and discourses of older Tamil secular and sacred poetry, especially the complex homological relationships among kings and gods in Tamil civilization.[44] Its geographic and topographical focus, a characteristic feature of Tamil poetry from the early classical period (first-third centuries A.D.), is based on a sophisticated system of five idealized aesthetic "landscapes" that correlated both to actual Tamil ecotypes — hill, field, seashore, pasture, and wasteland — and to the inner states of human beings present in these landscapes.[45] Tamil religious poetry and myth are profoundly place oriented; every *kuṟavañci* poem is written about the god, king, and temple of a specific town or village, and, like the "Lord of Bethlehem," the god or king is the "lord of the place."[46]

The identity of the fortune-teller as a woman of the mountain *kuṟavar* tribe is based in part on the literary identity of the *kuṟavar* as a tribe of the hill landscape, one of the five conventional landscapes of the classical poems. In the oldest Tamil poems the *kuṟiñci* landscape is connected with dangerous and mysterious sacred powers. The hills are the abode of Murukaṉ (the god of the *kuṟavar*), and the landscape, of the clandestine sexual union of lovers, a situation that is itself a manifestation of the sacred.[47] These older associations of the *kuṟavar* tribe are carried forward in medieval religious literature and eventually in the *kuṟavañci* drama. Lastly, the fortune-teller's persona combines aspects of various diviner figures and divination techniques described in classical and later Tamil poetry.[48] It seems likely that Sastri, who was an intellectual rooted in Tamil traditions, the leader of a small religious commu-

44. For these relationships, see V. Narayana Rao, David Shulman, and Sanjay Subrahmanyam, *Symbols of Substance: Court and State in Nayaka Period Tamil Nadu* (Delhi, 1992).

45. For the landscape system of classical Tamil poetry, see A. K. Ramanujan, *The Interior Landscape: Love Poems from a Classical Tamil Anthology* (Bloomington, 1967).

46. On localization in Tamil religious and secular poetry, see Peterson, *Poems to Śiva*, pp. 33-41.

47. Ramanujan, *Interior Landscape*, pp. 105-9.

48. Peterson, "Drama of the *Kuṟavañci*."

nity, and an agent of new systems of learning, recognized in the *kuṟavañci* genre a flexible instrument. Writing an Evangelical *kuṟavañci* play entailed the transformation of many of its generic conventions.

Writing an Evangelical *Kuṟavañci:* The Past, Present, and Future of Christianity in *Bethlehem Kuṟavañci*

BK employs the conventional plot, situations, and characters of the *kuṟavañci* drama, but the poem is longer than the average drama. Sastri also uses the characteristic rhythms, meters, and song forms of the genre.[49] In fact, many of the songs in *BK* quite closely resemble the songs of the famed *Kuṟṟālak kuṟavañci,* but the Evangelical *kuṟavañci* also differs from other major examples of the genre.

First, Sastri frames the plot of his drama as a grand allegory. Tēvamōkiṉi, "She who is in love with the Lord," who is none other than the Daughter of Zion, humankind personified, falls hopelessly in love with Jesus Christ, the Lord of Bethlehem, whom she sees entering Jerusalem in procession, riding an ass. Faith comes to Tēvamōkiṉi in the form of the wandering fortune-teller Vicuvācak *kuṟavañci* (Cinki, or Vicuvācac cinki, "Faith, the fortune-teller") and predicts (prophesies) that Tēvamōkiṉi will become the Bride of Christ. Meanwhile, the catechist and his assistant, as the bird catcher Ñāṉacciṅkaṉ (Ciṅkan, "The Bird Catcher of Wisdom [of the Gospel]"), and his assistant Nūvaṉ, use the Gospels as nets and snares to trap birds in the form of the peoples of the world, thus thwarting the evil attempts of the False Bird Catcher, the Catholic Church, to corrupt them. The Thief, who is their adversary, is the pope of Rome. He tries to gather birds, not for Christ, but for himself. For Sastri and the Evangelical Church of Tanjore, the chief rival appears not to have been the Śaiva sect (this was dangerous only insofar as it continued to be the "cultural home" of the Vellāla adherents of the Protestant churches) but the Catholics, whose practices are shown in Sastri's poems as wicked stratagems destined to prevent men from becoming true Christians. Indeed, while Sastri offers no direct criticism of Hindu practices in his poem, he criticizes and abuses the Catholic Church at the end of many of *BK*'s songs, following the practice of the authors of the Tamil Śaiva hymns, whose hymns often ended with invective against the Jains and the Buddhists.[50] Sastri clearly

49. In several songs early in the poem, Sastri engages in various kinds of play with numbers, meters, words, riddles, etc.; see *BK*, pp. 4-15.

50. Peterson, "*Śramaṇas* against the Tamil Way."

had approval, and perhaps encouragement, from the missionary leaders, both for his poem and his critique of the Papists.

Sastri's *BK* is a *tour de force* based on the Tamil critics' definition of poems about fortune-telling as poetic representations of "the telling of the past, present, and future."[51] The drama contains "all the principal histories of the Holy Bible."[52] Further, through the allegory of the Church as the Bride of Christ, Sastri offers a poetic history of the spread of Christianity in the biblical tradition of messianic prophecy, ending with the prophecy of an entirely Christian (i.e., Protestant) world in the future. However, in *BK* these histories and narratives of epic and *purāṇic* scope are not related in a narrative discourse but through mythic and thematic allusion in a dramatic-poetic framework.

Encyclopedic in nature, Sanskrit *purāṇa* texts begin with cosmological sections narrating the cyclical creation and reabsorption of the universe. Tamil *kuṟavañci* dramas, as a rule, do not include these. In *BK*, however, Sastri turns the *kuṟavañci* convention of the lady playing with balls into a lesson in the heliocentric cosmology. In narrating her travels, Faith, the fortune-teller, gives an account of the topography of the Bible lands. Ñāṉaccinkaṉ and his assistant spread their nets over the seven churches of Asia, and then over all the countries of Asia and the world. In short, the allegorical mode allows Sastri to expand the scope of the fortune-teller drama to "epic," *purāṇic*, and encyclopedic proportions.

On the one hand, the *kuṟavañci* plot with its emphases on wandering, exotic tribes, and mountain, forest, and urban landscapes lent itself well to the domestication, through Tamil cultural discourses, of the myths and narratives of the Bible, of new systems of learning, and even of new cosmologies. On the other hand, the genre made it possible for Sastri to express enduring values in Tamil literature and culture, especially a deep love of landscapes and particular places and the celebration of love between man and woman, the central themes of the oldest Tamil secular and religious poetry.[53]

The Allegorical Mode in *Bethlehem Kuṟavañci*

In his poetry the Protestant Sastri used allegoresis to empty indigenous literary forms and themes of their erotic, idolatrous, or otherwise "unaccept-

51. *Paṉṉirupāṭṭiyal, cuttiram,* edited by M. Irākavaiyaṅkār (Madurai, 1904), 53.

52. *BK*, p. vii. Dayamani Manasseh, descendant and biographer of Sastri, sees *BK* as comparable to Cruden's *Concordance* to the Bible; Manasseh, *Vētanāyaka*, p. 38.

53. On landscape and love as major themes in classical and *bhakti* poetry in Tamil, see Ramanujan, *The Interior Landscape*, and Peterson, *Poems to Śiva*.

able" attributes. But metaphor, symbol, and allegory are also favored interpretive instruments in Protestant Christian traditions, most often used to construct theological and doctrinal interpretations of historical narratives in the Bible.[54] As an Evangelical theologian, Sastri often upheld the validity of the allegorical mode in interpreting biblical Scripture. This is evident in the record of his debate with the Catholic theologian Savarimuttu Mutaliyar in Jaffna in 1811.[55] Mutaliyar argued that the reference in Revelation 12:14 to a woman "clothed with the sun, with the moon under her feet, and on her head a crown of twelve stars," and the description of the woman as "pregnant . . . and crying out in birth pangs" were to be read as references to the Virgin Mary, the sun and moon her adornments, and to her labor pains. Sastri considered this an absurd interpretation. According to him, the woman symbolized the Church, the Daughter of Zion, and the sun and the moon were her symbolic adornments, while the pains were the sufferings of the Church.[56] Sastri ridiculed Mutaliyar for believing that the Virgin could actually be clothed in the sun or tread upon the moon. Both were great celestial bodies, located far from each other. In other words, a "literal" interpretation would yield only logical absurdity.

Allegory has also been a major literary mode in Western Christian traditions, and Tamil Protestant writers such as Sastri found it very congenial for the transposition of indigenous literary forms and motifs in Christian contexts.[57] Some indigenous genres appeared to lend themselves especially well to allegoresis: for example, the plot of the eighteenth-century cripple's play genre shows how a horse thief performs many wicked actions, becomes crippled, and then repents, until his leg is restored by the grace of the god of the temple at which he worships. In "The Cripple's Play of Wisdom," another cel-

54. The discussion follows: Alex Preminger, ed., "Allegory," in *Princeton Encyclopedia of Poetry and Poetics,* enlarged ed. (Princeton, 1974), pp. 12-15, and Philip Rollinson, *Classical Theories of Allegory and Christian Culture* (Pittsburgh, 1981), esp. pp. 42-64. For traditions of biblical exegesis, see Jonathan Z. Smith, ed., "Bible, Interpretation of the Christian," and "Christian Theological Systems," in *The HarperCollins Dictionary of Religion* (New York, 1995), pp. 113-14, 265-67. On August Hermann Francke and the Halle Pietists see F. Ernest Stoeffler, *German Pietism during the Eighteenth Century,* Supplements to *Numen* 24 (Leiden, 1973), pp. 9-11, 46-49.

55. Jnanadikkam, *Life,* pp. 47-53.

56. Sastri's interpretation corresponds to that in the note on this passage in Bruce M. Metzger and Roland E. Murphy, eds., *The Oxford Annotated Bible with the Apocrypha: A New Revised Standard Version* (New York, 1994).

57. Several Tamil translations of Bunyan's *The Pilgrim's Progress* appeared in the nineteenth century, including H. A. Krishna Pillai, *The Pilgrimage of Salvation* (Madras, 1894).

ebrated dramatic poem by Sastri, he adapted the metaphorical elements of the plot of the cripple's play to an allegorical treatment of the Christian themes of sin, repentance, grace, and redemption. In the eighteenth century, Tanjore saw the revival of an older genre of religious and philosophical allegorical drama, exemplified by the popular eleventh-century Sanskrit *Prabodhacandrodaya (Moonrise of Enlightenment)* of Krishnamishra, imitated in dance dramas composed at the Maratha courts.[58]

The *kuṟavañci* genre emerged from a culture in which kings were both devotees of gods and counterparts of the gods themselves. Under the seventeenth-century Nayaka rulers of Tanjore and other South Indian centers, the king-god and court-temple symbiosis had developed in complex and pervasive ways.[59] In the later *kuṟavañci* dramas, the Lord of the love-lorn lady could be a king or a god, and in many *kuṟavañci* plays the praise of a hero-king was juxtaposed with the praise of the local god whom the king worshipped, as in the play in which King Serfoji of Tanjore is the hero. Sastri's faith included love mysticism in the allegory of the Church as the Bride of Christ. By transforming the all-too-human courtly lady of the *kuṟavañci* into the Daughter of Zion, the personification of the Church, Sastri brought the central love plot of the genre into the framework of the enduring Christian allegory of bridal mysticism. The kingship of the Lord of Bethlehem plays a central role in *BK*'s discourse, but it excludes the possibility of conflating Christ with human kings.

Both erotic mysticism and allegorical interpretation were part of the early traditions of Tamil religious poetry. A very influential tradition of *bhakti* love mysticism, which drew on the erotic imagery of classical Tamil secular love poems of the *akam* (interior) type, provided Sastri with indigenous counterparts to biblical bridal mysticism. Uncomfortable with the male *bhakti* poets' frequent use of the female persona (the woman in love) and the first person voice in erotic-mystical poems of this sort, the later commentators tended to interpret these poems allegorically.[60] The Tamil *bhakti* tradition of erotic mysticism explains in part Sastri's particular fondness for the Song of Songs, which he rendered in Tamil in *Ñāṉa antāti,* and whose images and themes he used in a number of other poems.

58. E.g., a Telugu dance drama attributed to the Tanjore Maratha King Tulajaji I (1729-35); see S. Seetha, ed., *Sivakāmasundarīpariṇayanāṭakam* (Tanjavur, 1971).

59. Rao, Shulman, and Subrahmanyam, *Symbols of Substance.*

60. For the allegorical interpretation of erotic imagery and themes in Śaiva and Vaiṣṇava religious poems, see Norman Cutler, *Songs of Experience: The Poetics of Tamil Devotion* (Bloomington, 1987), pp. 92-109.

The Transformation of *Kuṟavañci* Characters, Motifs, and Conventions in *Bethlehem Kuṟavañci:* Christ as King

In Jesus Christ, the lordly hero of *BK*, Sastri combines in a single figure the divine and royal personae of the Tamil fortune-teller play — divested of worldly connotations — and the traditional imagery of the kingship of Jesus Christ, including his role as the bridegroom of the Church. In *BK*, the *kuṟavañci* topic of the king's procession is filled by the narrative of Christ's entry into Jerusalem, riding on an ass. The song that describes the hero's procession begins thus:

> The exalted Lord of Bethlehem, he who sustains the world
> as end and beginning, as Alpha and Omega,
> he who is borne by the celestial Cherubim,
> mounted an ass;
> accompanied by his twelve disciples,
> he rode in procession,
> so that the devoted people of Jerusalem city
> could adore him.
> Here comes the Lord of the celestial world,
> the Lord divinely bright,
> the Lord who is the Son of God.[61]

In the segment in which the fortune-teller describes the attributes of the king-god whom the lady wishes to marry, Sastri adds the ten (sacred) attributes of the king, a set topic found in Tamil epic poems, in poems on kings, and in some major devotional poems.[62] King Jesus has Sinai for his hill and the Jordan for his river. Canaan, Galilee, and Nazareth are his cities. The cross is the emblem on his flag, the rosary is his "garland," and the ass is his royal elephant. Christ rides on a cloud-horse, his seven heralds sound seven drums, and he wields his scepter over the entire universe.

The admiring reactions of the women lining the streets to watch the hero pass by are a major convention of the *kuṟavañci*. In *BK*'s "The plaints of the women" segment, the women of Jerusalem compare the Lord of Bethlehem to the men of the Old Testament, beginning with Adam, Cain, Abel, Noah, and Abraham. They compare Christ's perfect integrity of character with the less than noble deeds of each of the Old Testament figures: Adam ate the forbid-

61. *BK, Pavaṉiccintu* (procession song), p. 24.
62. *BK, Akaval*, pp. 61-70.

den fruit, Cain slew Abel, Joseph dominated his brothers, Samson fell because of his lust, and David caused Uriah's death. Jesus alone is sinless, and he alone performed the great deed (the Passion).[63] In reciting Jesus' genealogy, the women rehearse the convention of exalting a hero by narrating his lineage, but this account is also meant to help the audience recall the major personages and narratives of the Old Testament through brief, topical allusions. In this manner, throughout *BK* the narratives of the Old and New Testament are interwoven with the conventional plot elements of the *kuṟavañci.*

Tēvamōkiṉi's Dance with the Planets: Enlightenment Science and New Cosmologies in *Bethlehem Kuṟavañci*

In the *kuṟavañci'* drama the lord's procession is usually followed by the appearance of the noble heroine. The Daughter of Zion is introduced as a beautiful and pious young woman.[64] In the next song, Tēvamōkiṉi speaks, introducing herself as the eternal virgin, the chaste maiden who is the perfect bride for "the great fruit of the Virgin Mary."[65] The Daughter of Zion compares herself with the women of the Old Testament; her list begins with Eve and includes Rachel, Sarah, Dinah, Tamar, Deborah, Jael, Bathsheba, Susannah, and Judith. Each of the women is shown to have been guilty of a sin, but the virgin Daughter of Zion is beyond reproach. These allusions to sin are later balanced by several laudatory references, in the fortune-teller's song, about the same women.

With Tēvamōkiṉi's entrance, *BK* shifts briefly to new cosmologies, information drawn from the Enlightenment sciences that Sastri taught at the Tanjore school. The *kuṟavañci*'s lady in love addresses the moon in a conventional song, berating him for cruelly directing his "hot rays" at her and making her burn with longing for her lover. In *BK*'s version of this song, Tēvamōkiṉi tells the moon to stop being conceited, since it is only one of many moons — twenty-four, to be exact, twenty-four satellites created by God.

> Earth has one moon, Jupiter (Poṉ) has four.
> Saturn's moons number eight, Tiṅkaḷ's number six,
> Uranus has four, Neptune has one —
> God made all these twenty-four satellites.[66]

63. *BK,* pp. 33-35, vv. 4 and 5.
64. *BK, Nāṭṭiyat taru,* pp. 39-41.
65. *BK, Tēvamōkiṉi pirastāpam,* pp. 44-51.
66. *BK, Veṇṇilāt taru* ("Song Addressed to the Moon"), pp. 51-53.

In the remaining verses, the lady refers to episodes in the Bible in which the moon is shown in a subservient position — bowing to Joseph (Gen. 37:9) and being compelled to stand still by Joshua (Josh. 10:12-13). At the allegorical level, the moon represents worldliness and vanity, but the purpose of the first verse is to teach the new discoveries about the satellite moons of planets other than Earth.[67]

Next, Tēvamōkiṉi begins to play ball. The lady of the fortune-teller plays enters tossing balls in the air — one of the conventional scenes of the genre but the "balls" that *BK*'s heroine is tossing up in the air are no ordinary balls but the planets of the solar system:

> The Daughter of Zion, destined to become the bride
> of the One who placed the sun, moon, and stars in space,
> marveled at the vast courses of the planets,
> and played ball with them — I shall sing of her skillful play![68]

In this song, the narrator provides, in sing-song verse, with poetic epithets for the planets, facts and figures relating to the celestial bodies. The topics include the distance of the planets from the sun (in Indian units *yojana*, and in English, miles); the rotational period of each of the planets, the orbital speed per hour of each planet in English units, and the orbital period of the planets around the sun, in Earth-time units (days, hours, minutes, seconds).

Like the catalogs of epic poetry, mnemonic verses are common in didactic poems and in poems that are designed to teach facts and figures. The songs about astronomy in *BK* are clearly intended to help the readers (or listeners) memorize facts about the solar system. Indian treatises and textbooks in the sciences have always used oral techniques and mnemonic verses as a means for teaching facts and principles. In Sastri's song, poetic elements, including a lilting meter, alliteration and figures of speech, and the use of a number of traditional epithets and names for the planets, enliven the verses. In *BK*, Sastri uses traditional means to teach new ideas, for example, to replace the Hindu geocentric universe with the heliocentric one, in relation to the tropical in-

67. I suggest that in the revised version of *BK* Sastri incorporated the latest European astronomical discoveries available to him through his German missionary friends; see my "Science in the Tranquebar Mission Curriculum: Natural Theology and Indian Responses," in *Missionsberichte aus Indien im 18. Jahrhundert: Ihre Bedeutung für europäische Geistesgeschichte und ihr wissenschaftlicher Quellenwert für die Indienkunde,* edited by Michael Bergunder (Halle, 1999), pp. 175-219, esp. 200-201.

68. *BK, Pantaṭikkum taru* ("The Song of the Girl Playing Ball"), pp. 57-60, introductory verse.

stead of the Hindu sidereal zodiac. Tēvamōkiṉi's dance with the balls is intended to teach the Copernican world system as opposed to the cosmology of the Hindu *purāṇas,* in which the sun and moon rise and set on either side of the golden mountain Meru, which is located at the center of the island continent of Jambu-dvīpa and upholds the celestial abodes of the gods.[69]

The revolutionary nature of Sastri's assertion of the Copernican system must be understood in the light of the history of the Hindu view of the relationship among planetary astronomy, the cosmos, and human life, which is dramatically different from the European eighteenth-century perspective. Sastri presents the Copernican system as the basis of an alternative cosmology to the Hindu theories of infinite space, interminable cycles of time, impersonal forces of creation, and the ideas of *karma* and rebirth. The poet offers, instead, a theory of knowledge based on the empirical observation and study of nature. For him it is important that the figures and the calculations he cites are the results of actual observations of the European astronomers, and that those figures should alter one's understanding of the universe.

Sastri's enthusiastic presentation of Enlightenment scientific knowledge, in his work, was based on the philosophy of physical or natural theology, which was central to seventeenth- and eighteenth-century Pietist thought.[70] According to natural theology, the continuing scientific discoveries of humankind constituted the continuing expansion of human knowledge of God's universe, an expansion that was a celebration of the continuing revelation of the Creator's glory. This natural theological perspective was the reason that astronomy, natural history, mathematics, and other sciences played such an important part in the Halle curriculum taught by the German missionaries at Tranquebar and Tanjore. Sastri's independent, innovative, and culturally Tamil agency in transmitting these ideas is seen in the typically Tamil combination of poetry, performance, and theology in which he embedded his teaching of science.

69. In a widely accepted version of the *purāṇic* geography, the Earth consists of seven concentric island continents, each surrounded by an ocean. For the cosmology of the *purāṇas,* see Cornelia Dimmitt and J. A. B. van Buitenen, *Classical Hindu Mythology: A Reader in the Sanskrit Puranas* (Philadelphia, 1978), pp. 15-58.

70. In Peterson, "Science in the Tranquebar Mission," pp. 191-209, I discuss natural theology in "The Drama of the Architect of Wisdom," another of Sastri's poems on biblical themes, with European scientific information on the Copernican system, geography, human anatomy, and the taxonomy of animals and plants.

Faith, the Fortune-Teller: Prophecy and the Praise of Hills

Sastri's transposition of *kuṟavañci* themes is strikingly apparent in his treatment of fortune-telling, the central theme of the genre. First, Sastri identifies the Herald, who traditionally announces the characters as they appear on stage at the very beginning of the play, as John the Baptist. Second, Sastri's fortune-teller is no mere member of the *kuṟavar* hill tribe, but Faith, the personification of the wisdom of the gospel (faith in salvation through the Savior), embodied in the biblical tradition of prophecy. Sastri simultaneously appropriates the generic trope of foretelling the future and rejects its worldly and non-Christian implications.

Faith sings a number of songs about her qualifications and heritage in biblical traditions of prophecy. Interestingly, she begins her account with narratives about the miraculous feats achieved by nonprophetic figures in the Bible, and she exalts the women of the Bible in this song, entitled "Miracles."[71] Faith speaks of "Rachel's husband" (Jacob), who bred a speckled and spotted flock, Deborah the Judge, who sent Jael to kill Sisera, Esther, whose exemplary courage effected a miracle, Susannah's victory over the elders, and Elizabeth's miraculous conception. In the song entitled "The Glory of Prophecy" she recounts the prophecies and miracles achieved by her illustrious ancestors, the great prophets and eminent figures of biblical history.[72] She speaks of Joseph's interpretation of Pharaoh's dream, Daniel's interpretation of the dream of Nebuchadnezzar, Jonah's prediction regarding Nineveh, and the miracle of the cakes with which the widow of Zarephath fed the prophet Elijah. Her list of prophets includes Isaiah, Jeremiah, Hosea, and Malachi. In this manner, Faith establishes her credentials as the personification of the prophetic tradition of the Bible.

Before she performs her rites of divination, the fortune-teller of the *kuṟavañci* dramas praises the play's lordly hero and his lineage and sings of the glories of his city and land. The genre requires that a large part of the nomadic *kuṟatti*'s description be devoted to hills, hill landscapes, and the naming of faraway lands. The fortune-teller describes the mountains and hills of the hero's land, as well as her own native hills. She names the many lands she has visited during her travels. In the conventional manner, Faith praises the twelve tribes of Israel, Christ's lineage, the temple in Jerusalem, and the town of Bethlehem, of which he is Lord.[73] However, in keeping with generic con-

71. *BK*, pp. 102-3.
71. *BK*, pp. 104-5.
73. *BK*, pp. 81-99.

ventions, her songs are dominated by descriptions and narratives of the hills of the biblical lands.

The identity of the fortune-teller as a woman of the hill *kuṟavar* tribe is based in part on the literary identity of the *kuṟavar* tribe of the hill landscape, one of the five landscapes of the classical poems. In the oldest Tamil literature, "hill *kuravar*" are a tribe who live in the hill landscape as hunters and managers of the produce of hill and forest. The classical hill landscape is connected with dangerous and mysterious sacred powers. The hills are the abode of Murukaṉ (the god of the *kuṟavar*) and the landscape of the clandestine sexual union of lovers, a situation that is itself a manifestation of the sacred.[74]

The fortune-teller's entrance song and the one describing her native hills, the most popular songs in the *kuṟavañci* dramas, have a stereotyped folksong form and describe real scenery in the Tamil countryside. The hill song of the famed *Kuṟṟālak kuṟavañci,* for example, celebrates the hill and temple of Kuṟṟālam near Tirunelveli, situated at the foot of the Western Ghats mountains. *BK*'s Vicuvācack ciṅki, however, paints imagined (for Tamil Indians) landscapes, of Bethlehem and of hills in faraway lands. Imagining the landscapes of the Bible is not a difficult task for Tamil audiences already accustomed to the elaborate mythic landscapes of Hindu, Buddhist, and other texts. Nevertheless, the rhythms of the hill song and the generic idioms of the description of hills in the fortune-teller's song help to bring the far near, to make the imagined "real." Faith's "Praise of the Hills" begins with the following lines, which strikingly echo the first verse of the *Kuṟṟālak kuṟavañci.*

> The celestials gather there to sing prayers and praises,
> there great adepts practice difficult penances,
> wise shepherds come there to worship.[75]

Beginning with the second verse of the song, Faith lists the hills and mountains of the biblical narratives and speaks of her connection with each of these hills:

> The hill of Eden is our native hill,[76] lady,
> it is the hill where God created us, lady,
> it is the hill where he gave us the gift of his Law, lady,

74. Ramanujan, *Interior Landscape,* pp. 105-9.
75. *BK,* p. 77.
76. Literally, "hill of origin," "original hill." *BK,* p. 78.

it is the hill where we had immortality, lady,
it is the hill where Satan corrupted us, lady,
it is the hill where the Lord cursed us, lady,
and after we had left that hill in disgrace, lady,
Bethlehem hill became our great hill, lady.

Continuing in this vein, in the remaining verses of this song the fortune-teller describes Ararat, Noah's mountain; "lofty, cloud-covered Pisgah, from whose summit Moses saw Canaan"; Moabian Nebo, where he died; "Mount Olive, hill of the Lord's time of prayer"; Golgotha, "the hill of Jesus' passion"; Lebanon, the "high mountain in Canaan"; Gilead; Adullam; "Meribah, which became a flood of water when Moses struck it with his staff"; Zion; Abarim; Moreh; Sinai; and so on. But in the refrain of the song, the hill of Bethlehem, Christ's place of birth, receives her highest praise as the best of the hills of her tribe. In *BK*, Jesus is called, after the Tamil custom, "Lord of Bethlehem" since Bethlehem is his "native place." Running through *BK*'s fortune-teller segment, the motif of hills reappears in the benedictory song at the end of the play:

Resurrected on one hill,
he took the form of Prayer
on another holy hill,
he gave up his life on the hill of Grace —
I praise that Lord![77]

In addition to the emphasis on hills, what is striking about Sastri's treatment of biblical landscapes is the absence of the desert and wilderness landscapes. The few detailed landscape descriptions refer to the flora of the Kaveri delta, the location of Tanjore and the Tamraparni valley, and the location of Tirunelveli, famed as the rice-bowls of South India. The groves of *BK* harbor mainly plants and trees typical of the Tamil region. Thus, according to Faith, in Bethlehem pomegranates grow side by side with areca, mango, plantain, *champak*, coconut, and sandalwood trees, and the groves are lush with bamboo, turmeric, ginger, and sugarcane![78] We may surmise that the desert or wasteland landscape was inappropriate for Sastri's allegory of the prophecy of the joyous union of bride and bridegroom, since *pālai*, the wasteland landscape of Tamil poetry, is associated with the separation of lovers.

77. *BK, Vālttu*, p. 202, verse 8.
78. *BK*, p. 72, vv. 122-28.

Sastri shifts the descriptions of travel and foreign lands, normally a part of the fortune-teller segment, to the bird-catcher segment. Faith says that she knows the four continents of the Earth (Europe, Asia, Africa, and America),[79] but she does not describe these lands. Following her narrative songs, and the songs of her prophetic heritage, she performs several rituals of divination, including palm-reading, and foretells the Daughter of Zion's union with Christ.[80] Where the *kuṟatti* of other plays would invoke a number of Hindu, tribal, and village gods and become possessed by them, Faith invokes the Bible and the Eucharist; in her rite, in place of the materials of Hindu and tribal worship, wheat bread serves for the body of Christ and cashew wine for his blood. The motif of fortune-telling is enfolded into the symbolism of Evangelical religion.

Expanding Landscapes: The Bird Catcher of Wisdom and the Making of a Christian World

In *BK*, the bird catcher segment functions as an extension of the prophetic aspect of the *kuṟavañci* play. Using the net of the gospel, Ñaṉaccinkaṉ, the catechist, catches the birds, who are the peoples of every continent in the world, landing in the paddy fields that are the Bible lands and, eventually, the whole world. In a sequence of songs, beginning with the "Song of Sighting the Birds" and ending with the "Song of the Birds Arriving," Ñāṉaccinkaṉ describes the peoples of the world outside India, then the communities and tribes of India and South India, "flocking to the path of the sweet Tamil gospel, in the age of the religion of the New Testament."[81] He names ethnic groups by both the traditional and the modern nomenclature. The list of "tribes" in the first song includes, in one verse: Ethiopians, Chaldeans, Jews, the English, Arabians, Roarians, Pharisees, Magogians and Gogians, Prussians, and Russians. In another verse of the same song, he lists "the cunning French, Mesopotamians, Elamites, Hindustanis, Allemands, Corinthians, Spaniards," followed by "Sidonians, Moabites, Latins, Danes, Palestinians, and Abimalecians, all joyfully entering the path of the gospel of the Son of God." The order of names in these lists seems to be dictated as much by the requirements of meter and Tamil alliterative conventions as by "geographical" logic.

79. *BK*, p. 99, v. 22.
80. *BK*, pp. 107-20.
81. *BK*, p. 136, v. 1. See also *BK*, pp. 136-46.

In the verses that follow (5 and 6), Sastri gives the traditional Indian list of fifty-six countries and tribes: "In the fine subcontinent of India there are fifty-six territories, in which live peoples beginning with the people of Aṅga, Kirāta, Drāviḍa." However, in verses 7 and 8, the poet names the ethnic and occupational groups and castes that were found in the Tanjore region in the eighteenth century: Saurashtran silk weavers, Marathis, toddy-tappers, nomadic hill tribes, Jains, Paravar fishermen, Telugu settlers, untouchable Paraiyas, and "Pathans" (Muslim soldiers), to list but a few.[82]

In the songs that follow, the bird catcher describes the birds gathering "like the birds that went into Noah's Ark, two by two."[83] The next song abounds with similes for the birds seeking the fields: they are like Jacob, who fled to Laban at Paddan-Aram, for fear of Esau, or like the tribes of Israel fleeing from Egypt and finally arriving in Canaan.[84] The birds land in all of the Bible lands and spread out into the "fields" of the seven churches of Asia.[85] Finally, in the "Song of Setting the Snares" the bird catcher says to his assistant; "O Nūvaṉ, to gather the Lord's followers from every community all over the world in the Kingdom of Bethlehem's Lord, go to the vast continents of Europe, Asia, Africa, and America, and quickly set your snares."

The geographical movement in the poem is from historical sacred geography to the ethnographies of the immediate present and the glorious future geography of the globe encompassed by Christianity. At the same time, the geographical vision presented is an essential component of the Evangelical cosmology and its basis in natural theology. Well into the eighteenth and early nineteenth centuries both the Halle institutions and the Tranquebar missionaries continued to use the concept of the pair of globes, the celestial and the terrestrial, to represent the complementarity of the disciplines of astronomy and geography as components of a complete cosmography.[86] In *Noah's Boat Song*, a poetic version of the narrative of Noah's ark, composed in 1829 for King Serfoji, Sastri directly correlates cosmogony and a scientific, empirically verifiable (terrestrial) geography.[87] In this poem, as Noah's ark

82. For a list of castes and communities in nineteenth-century Tanjore, see T. Venkaswamy Row, *A Manual of the District of Tanjore in the Madras Presidency* (Madras, 1883).

83. *BK*, p. 140, v. 5.

84. *BK*, pp. 141-42, vv. 2, 4.

85. *BK*, pp. 144-45.

86. Peterson, "Science in the Tranquebar Mission," pp. 210-11.

87. *Nōvāviṉ kappaṟṟamiḻ* was later incorporated into Sastri's longer poem, *Drama of the Architect of Wisdom*. The *Devendra kuravañji*, a fortune-teller play attributed to King Serfoji, is a modern terrestrial geography. Like Sastri, Serfoji was educated by Schwartz. See

drifts around all the five continents of the globe (by this time Sastri is aware of Australia), the narrator names the major countries and territories on these continents, along with their capitals, such as London in England, and Philadelphia in Pennsylvania. In Sastri's *Noah's Boat Song* the voyage of the ark is transformed into a circumnavigation of the terrestrial globe of the nineteenth century. The connection between the various sciences and the world as an object of study (as God's Creation) comes across explicitly in the Creation context of *Noah's Boat Song.* Yet in *BK* Sastri also highlights the importance of the historical and ideal landscapes of the Bible lands in the "circumnavigable" world.

In his Evangelical *kuṟavañci* Vedanayaka Sastri ingeniously and effectively deploys the genre's tension between intensely localized and widening spheres of topographical description and experience. The *kuṟavañci* is a dramatic poem of expanding landscapes made palpable and accessible. The genre domesticates the "foreign" and the exotic without diminishing their mystery. In *BK,* Tamil geographies expand into world geographies, while the Evangelical worldview and ideal of the spread of the gospel are encompassed in Tamil cultural discourses. The universalism of Protestant Christianity is thus rendered into a particularly Tamil universalism.

A Christian *Kuṟavañci* and Tamil Traditions of Performance

The *BK* still has a role in contemporary Tamil Protestant discourses of identity. *Kuṟavañci* dance dramas were enacted in the dance style *catir* well into the nineteenth and early twentieth centuries. The female dancers were ritual specialists, employed by kings and temples, as well as entertainers.[88] Dedicated to the temple, they did not marry but had short- or long-term liaisons with appropriate men. The sexual mores of the *devadāsīs,* the erotic content of the Hindu mythological and secular texts to which they danced, and the style of their dance were condemned as "lewd" by most European observers, especially by the missionaries in South India.[89] Sastri had to solve the problem of the association of the dance-drama genres with *devadāsī* dancers and with texts con-

---

Indira Viswanathan Peterson, "The Cabinet of King Serfoji of Tanjore: A European Collection in Early Nineteenth-Century India," *Journal of the History of Collections* 11.1 (1999): 71-93, and Peterson, "Science in the Tranquebar Mission."

88. On the *devadāsīs,* see Saskia C. Kersenboom-Story, *Nityasumaṅgalī: Devadāsī Tradition in South India* (Delhi, 1987).

89. See, e.g., Abbe J. A. Dubois, *Hindu Manners, Customs and Ceremonies,* edited and translated by Henry K. Beauchamp, 3rd ed. (Oxford, 1959), pp. 584-88.

sidered lewd by the Tamil Christians. His solution was to treat this genre as a *sung* (musical) *pirapantam,* perhaps on the model of Cirkali Arunachala Kavirayar's *Irāmanāṭakak kīrttan̲ai,* an innovative late-eighteenth-century dramatic version of the *Rāmāyan̲a* epic composed in Tamil *kīrttan̲ais.* In Tranquebar and Tanjore, the *Irāmanāṭakak kīrttan̲ai* was arguably the most popular literary-musical narrative work of the nineteenth century.[90]

Sastri was a major innovator in the genre of the sung *pirapantam.* From 1814 until his death in 1864, he regularly expounded his *pirapantams* in Tanjore, in a format of discourse interspersed with music. His singers included his three sons and a daughter, as well as professional singers. The sons played the violin or accompanied themselves with hand cymbals. The performers executed *abhinaya* (dance gestures and facial expressions), and perhaps dance movements as well, in accompaniment to the songs. Sastri called these events *catur* or *catir,* combining *piracaṅkam* (expository discourse), the word used for the public verbal exposition of religious narratives such as the *Rāmāyan̲am* and *purāṇas,* and *catur* or *catir* (assembly, public arena), a word that in nineteenth-century Tanjore and Madras was applied to *devadāsī* dance and dramatic performance.[91] With Sastri's *catur piracaṅkam,* Tamil evangelism sounded in a new key, especially at church festivals. Sastri's format also anticipated the *kathākālaṭcepam,* a major expository form that developed in Tanjore in the mid to late nineteenth century, in which a male singer-performer expounded *purāṇic* narratives interspersed with song, accompanied by dance.[92] After Sastri's death, the performance of *catur pracaṅkam* was limited, surviving mainly in Tanjore, where Sastri's descendants carried on the tradition.

In 1979, 170 years after the premiere of *BK* in Vepery, Dr. Anjala Richard, a descendant of Vedanayaka Sastri and Professor of Tamil at the Women's Christian College in Madras, in collaboration with the Institute for Development Education, put on a performance of *BK* as a dance drama. It was in the classical Bharata Natyam dance style, the modern outgrowth of the *devadāsī* dance of Tanjore. The hereditary and specialist system of *devadāsī* dance had declined because of public criticism and legislation, and the efforts of Rukmini Devi and others in the 1940s had made Bharata Natyam a popular dance form in South India for those who were not from the traditional

90. This was followed and nearly replaced in the mid nineteenth century by Gopalakrishna Bharati's *Nantan̲ār Carittiram,* the retelling of the narrative of the untouchable Śaiva saint, Nantan̲ār, in *kīrttan̲ais.* Iyer, *My Life,* pp. 82-83.

91. On the *catur* formats devised by Sastri, see Devanesan, *Tañcai,* pp. 88-109.

92. On *kathākālaṭcēpam* see Premeela Gurumurthy, *Kathakalaksepa: A Study* (Madras, 1994).

devadāsī communities. Students of the Women's Christian College — mainly Hindus who had studied Bharata Natyam — danced in the 1979 performance.[93] For the Christian sponsors of the event, this first dance performance of Sastri's *kuṟavañci* by non-Christian performers, for an audience of Christians and others, signified the potential of art to transcend religious divisions. It also reaffirmed the Protestant community's sense of its artistic productions as an expression of their cultural identity as Tamils. According to Chandran D. S. Devanesan, son of Sastri's biographer and Director of the Institute for Development Education: "He [Sastri] teaches us how the Church can be redeemed from the charge of being an alien, Westernized transplant by sending its roots deep down into the soil of our Indian culture. Vedanayagam is an inspiring example of the complete identification that we need as Christians with our own people and culture."[94] Although it was not until the twentieth century that *BK* could be performed as a full-fledged dance drama, its Tamil aesthetic was never in question. And while Sastri's hymns tend to be encountered in sectarian contexts, his *magnum opus,* which had earned an enduring place in the Tamil literary canon as a different yet excellent exemplar of the *kuṟavañci* genre, continues to affirm for Tamil Protestants the Tamil cultural roots and character of their religion.

93. Both Hindu and Christian women performed in later productions (Dr. Anjala Richard, personal communication, 1994).

94. Chandran D. S. Devanesan, "Why Bethalem Kuravanji?" in *Bethalem kuravanji: Dance drama of Tanjai Vedanayagam Sastriar,* edited by Anjala Richard, a joint production of Women's Christian College and Institute for Development Education (Madras, 11, 12, 13 October 1979), p. 1.

CHAPTER THREE

Some Hindu Perspectives on Christian Missionaries in the Indic World of the Mid Nineteenth Century

RICHARD FOX YOUNG

> He claims to have knowledge of God,
> and calls himself a son of the Lord.
> Before us he stands, a reproof to our way of thinking,
> the very sight of him weighs our spirits down;
> his way of life is not like other men's,
> the paths he treads are unfamiliar.
>
> The Book of Wisdom 2:13-16 (New Jerusalem Bible)

Considered from an "insider" (by which I mean European) perspective, Christian missionaries, far from being cut from the same cloth, ecclesiastical or otherwise, are nowadays regarded as comprising an internally complex, self-differentiated cohort of individuals with little in common except an uncompromising faith in Jesus Christ as the one Lord and a collateral conviction that the gospel's salvific implications are universalistic. Apart from these absolutistic and therefore provocative orientations, always guaranteed to elicit astonishment, conflict, and resistance in newly evangelized communities, other commonalities appear to be few. Of personalities, little can be said that cannot be contradicted: for each who was forbearing and tolerant, another was overbearing and intolerant. The common denominators denominate a faith, not an ideology, and to trivialize theologies, ecclesiologies, and methodologies of mission would be to underestimate significant variables. Despite the ever-popular caricatures and stereotypes, every thesis generates its antithesis where missionaries are concerned. Scholars in mission studies take these variabilities with the utmost seriousness, recognizing that missionaries are shaped by a specific ethos, milieu, and tradition. It accordingly makes a world of difference about whom one is talking: Italian Jesuits, German Pietists, or British Baptists, to mention but a few possibilities. In addition, the more mission studies advance, the more keenly one realizes that concepts once taken for granted are more highly nuanced than previously supposed. The category "evangelical" is an example: one of the biggest surprises is that Alexander Duff, a tiger of a missionary whose roar made the Vedas tremble, has been recast in the role of a Calvinist with rationalist stripes, painted with a brush from the Scottish Enlightenment.[1]

Thus, although certain contrarieties appear less contrary than ever before, a dominant interest in the field of mission studies remains the missionary exemplification of distinctively Western mentalities, while "outsider" (here I mean Indian) perspectives on missionaries receive correspondingly less attention, except insofar as outsiders became Christians by virtue of an act or process of conversion. Without dismissing the historical significance of these advances in mission studies (indeed, my indebtedness to them will become evident), I attempt in this chapter to articulate three contrasting and clearly asymptotic perspectives on missionaries — what they were good (and bad) for — that circulated throughout the unchristianized Indic world of the mid nineteenth century, an era that proved to be as crucial for the Hindu discovery of Christianity as the seventeenth and eighteenth centuries had been for the Christian discovery of Hinduism.

The Missionary Way

> Missionaries stir and awaken, exasperate and vex,
> affect and make a difference to the lives of many:
> sometimes rudely, other times more gently, often indefinably.
>
> Kenelm Burridge[2]

My first submission in this connection is that the absence of commonalities between missionaries, the very stuff and substance of many a mission study,

1. See Ian D. Maxwell, "Alexander Duff and the Theological and Philosophical Background to the General Assembly's Mission in Calcutta to 1840," Ph.D. thesis, University of Edinburgh, 1995.

2. *In the Way: A Study of Christian Missionary Endeavours* (Vancouver, 1991), p. 10.

was hardly of concern to the unconverted, and to think otherwise is to suppose a certain degree of integration into the Western mentality. For the vast majority, it mattered little that missionaries came from different regions of the European world or that their social origin, education, and understanding of non-Western religions differed enormously. What mattered more was that, with very few exceptions, missionaries envisioned for India, always outlandishly and often outrageously, *the possibility of a new identity grounded in a different reality,* an identity ostensibly more satisfying than any provided by the *sanātana dharma,* which in having structured society for so long seemed to transcend time itself. In this view, missionaries were simply more alike than unalike, and their Christianity was of one piece despite clearly observable differences between Protestant and Catholic practice. If this perception of commonality was false, it was nonetheless prevalent; even metropolitan Indians, long familiar with different missions, glossed over the differences. As false as these (mis)perceptions were, I contend, with Robert Wilken, that their relevance for understanding the missionary encounter with India should be recognized, as they are in studies of early Christianity in the Mediterranean world, which accord a place to Celsus, Porphyry, and Julian alongside those of Origen, Tertullian, and Augustine: "How something is perceived," after all, "is an aspect of what it is."[3]

To expand upon the first submission, it helps to note that every missionary — Baldeus, Carey, Duff, Fabricius, Marshman, de Nobili, Plütschau, Schwartz, Ward, Xavier, or Ziegenbalg — was invariably neither a Baptist, a Jesuit, a Presbyterian, nor anything else, but only a *pādri* or (increasingly as memory of the Portuguese faded in the British era) a *mishanrī,* there being no terms of indigenous origin for such alien concepts.[4] Under this foreign, one might say *feringhi,* rubric missionaries were scripted into a role at variance with that in which they saw themselves. Consider, for example, Bartolomaeus Ziegenbalg (1682-1719) of the Danish Halle mission at Tranquebar on the

3. Robert Wilken, *The Christians As the Romans Saw Them* (New Haven, 1984), p. xiii.

4. *Mishanrī* is the standard pronunciation in Hindi; cognates in a host of other regional languages exist. Nowadays, *mishanrī* is a tag applied to anyone, foreign or Indian, involved in evangelism or social work. The term *pādri* for Protestant missionaries is less common now but survives in its original meaning as a designation for Catholic ecclesiastics. *Dharmpracārak* or *dharmadūt* have become functional equivalents for *mishanrī* in current Hindi but refer to individuals engaged in the modern phenomenon of Hindu missions. Interestingly, Christian missionaries seem to have been unconcerned with coining terms to describe their own endeavor. V. S. Apte's *Student's English-Sanskrit Dictionary* (Delhi, 1960) (s.v. mission) is one of few attempts at producing an etymological equivalent: *dharmārtham preritah* (lit., "one who is sent for the sake of dharma").

eastern coast of South India and his response in 1708 to some inquisitive "Malabarians" who raised the big question often asked of missionaries with the same disarming naiveté: "Pray, Sir, who, and what are you?" "I am, said I, a Minister or Servant of the Living God, who created Heaven and Earth, sent to you to warn you to leave the Idols of your own making, and to turn to the Worship of the true God."[5]

While this standard-issue rationale was only one among others that Ziegenbalg could have adduced to explain his presence in the Indic world, it or any other in the theological repertoire naturally derives its plausibility from the overall framework of Christian belief; it would, therefore, hardly suffice, as the record of Ziegenbalg's *Thirty Four Conferences* with the "Malabarians" abundantly illustrates.[6] The citation allows me to introduce my second submission, which emphasizes the obvious ramification of the first: envisioning the possibility of a new identity grounded in a different reality *necessarily places the Christian dharma in a relationship of tension with the Hindu dharma.* In deploying the characteristically Christian idiom of *metanoia,* leave and turn, a missionary signifies that the paths he treads are unfamiliar. As the faithful Jew of antiquity, so the Christian missionary — the inscription from The Book of Wisdom at the head of this chapter could equally apply to both. In merely existing, missionaries disturb a culture's equilibrium: "Before us he stands, a reproof to 'our way of thinking.'"[7] For our way of thinking substitute the *nomos* of Greek or the dharma of Sanskrit, and the spirit of the passage remains the same.

To add substance to the foregoing abstract on the missionary as potentially an unwelcome presence within a culture such as India's, anchored as it is (or was) in the dharma (a classic instance of a transempirical, or metacultural, integrating principle), I cite from anthropologist Kenelm Burridge's study with a wonderfully ambiguous title, *In the Way: A Study of Christian Missionary Endeavours,* which has influenced this discussion considerably.[8]

Burridge would have us understand that missionaries evoke mixed responses because *they give themselves over to the critique and transformation of other people's business* by envisioning the possibility of a new identity

5. Bartolomaeus Ziegenbalg, *Thirty Four Conferences between the Danish Missionaries and the Malabarian Bramans (or Heathen Priests) in the East Indies, Concerning the Truth of the Christian Religion: Together with Some Letters Written by the Heathens to the Said Missionaries. Translated out of High Dutch by Mr. Philipps* (London, 1719), p. 94.

6. See n. 5 above.

7. Book of Wisdom 2:14.

8. Burridge, *In the Way,* pp. 3-34.

grounded in another reality. Being a constant reminder that life can be different, they find themselves at odds with those whom they encounter: "in the way." Whether rudely or gently, more often than not what they say, or do, may also *impugn revered custom and usages and so provoke opposition, insult, and injury.* In transgressing the role prescribed by others in the communities with which they interact, missionaries arouse the oppositions they figure reflexively. By urging *metanoia,* they insinuate that traditional moralities are neither sacrosanct nor immutable. And what of those who come into contact with them? They begin to become aware that it is possible to change one's mind about life's fundamentals. Most of all, missionaries communicate choice, and in so doing "stir and awaken, exasperate and vex, affect and make a difference . . . often indefinably."

Although Burridge speaks mainly of missionaries working in Polynesian societies where transempirical realities are transmitted orally, his remarks apply equally to the literate echelons of the Indic social hierarchy to which I now turn. It should be clear at this juncture that I look to anthropology for a universal typology of the category "missionary" that subsumes the particularities of mission studies and integrates the three perspectives outlined below into an interpretative whole to help explain what missionaries were good (and bad) for.

From here on I borrow from Burridge not only his insights but also his idiom. Since, as he says so well, missionaries exasperate and vex, I refer to one perspective as "getting in the way"; to another as "getting back on the way" (because missionaries also stir and awaken); and, since missionaries make a difference (often indefinably), to yet a third as "getting out of the way." Obviously, three perspectives hardly exhaust the ways in which missionaries were perceived. For case material I draw from what I elsewhere refer to as "resistant Hinduism," and in that milieu the spectrum of likely responses to Christianity is marked on one side by exclusivism, the view that missionaries were only good for "getting in the way," and by inclusivism on the other, the view that missionaries were good for "getting back on the way." The third perspective, "getting out of the way," transcends the parameters established by the others and therefore receives special attention at the end of the discussion. As a final preliminary lest anyone wonder whether pluralism lies within the spectrum as I conceive it, a genuine pluralism that does not rank or subordinate religions within a hierarchy is found only in a more modern neo-Hinduism, not the Hinduism dealt with here. As a complex religion, Hinduism is, of course, a multicultural, polyglot, semi-fictional entity. To clarify, therefore, individuals who exemplify the three perspectives outlined below comprise a literate subgroup within the larger entity, notable for recognizing one corpus of texts or another within the Veda, loosely defined, as self-authenticating authority sources of salvific truth.[9]

Getting in the Way

> I cannot approve of anyone who is so puffed up with insolence and impious, sham enlightenment as to attempt to abolish this religion which is so ancient, so useful, and so beneficial.
>
> Caecilius, pagan, to Marcus, Christian (*Octavius* 8.1)[10]

"Their business," fumed a Maratha pandit, speaking of missionaries in Bombay, "is to revile other religions!"[11] The much vexed and exasperated pandit was Krishna Shāstrī Sāthe, about whom little is known except that he studied at the Poona Sanskrit College and that his engagements with missionaries date to the mid 1840s when he came to the defense of his namesake, the god Krishna, a favorite target for aspersion. For his meteoric rise to prominence, however, followed by an equally quick return to obscurity, Krishna Shāstrī had to wait until the 1850s when he delivered a series of controversial lectures on Christianity under the auspices of a *dharmasabhā* (a society promoting Hinduism) operating out of Thākurdvār. This was a temple complex located in Girgaum, behind John Wilson's Scottish Mission College on Chowpatty Beach, in a volatile area with a mixed population of Christians, Parsees, and immigrant Hindus from Konkan, Gujarat, Kathiawar, and other parts of Western India.

Thākurdvār had been constructed in 1838 by Brahmins of the coastal area, Gaud Sarasvats, and Pathare Prabhus, and it was under their patronage that Krishna Shāstrī appeared on stage in September 1852, lecturing until the monsoon of the following year. Weather, as always, was a critical factor in limiting the popularity of events like this, and the public's ardor was evidently dampened when the cool, dry season came to an end. Although Krishna Shāstrī was a consummate orator, witty, and adept at repartee with Christian hecklers, his contribution to anti-Christian apologetics has not yet received the attention it should.[12] The lack of a press under the ownership of the

9. Paul J. Griffiths, *An Apology for Apologetics: A Study in the Logic of Interreligious Dialogue* (Maryknoll, 1991), p. 4.

10. Rudolph Arbesmann et al., eds. and trans., *Tertullian, Apologetical Works, and Minucius Felix, Octavius* (Washington, D.C., 1950).

11. *Jñānodaya* 11 (January 1835): 24.

12. But see Richard F. Young, *Resistant Hinduism: Sanskrit Sources on Anti-Christian*

Thākurdvār *dharmasabhā* may be the chief reason. Unlike Bālgangadhār Jāmbhekār, a leader of the Hindu reform party, who brought out the *Bombay Darpan* and *Prabhākar,* or Morabhatta Dāndekara, a leader of the conservatives who published the *Upadesha candrikā,* Krishna Shāstrī had no other means for disseminating his tirades than to see them printed up and put into circulation by *Jñānodaya* (Dnyanodaya), the Anglo-Marathi organ of his adversaries, the American mission.[13]

When Krishna Shāstrī stepped into the limelight, Western India was experiencing rapid social change, precipitated, in part, by the egalitarian educational activities of the missionaries. At mid century Bombay was a simmering cauldron of countervailing forces: missionary work did not move forward unimpeded. There were traditionalists such as Morabhatta, who insisted that the fundamentals of the dharma were immutable; there were modernists like Jāmbhekār (who died shortly before Krishna Shāstrī's heyday), who saw scope for gradual change from within the dharma; and, of course, there were a host of other movements that cannot be fitted into a simplistic traditionalist-modernist dichotomy. Most of these movements kept abreast of what the missionaries were doing in schools and chapels, on the streets, and in bazaars, where, as Burridge would say, they gave themselves over to the critique and transformation of other people's business.

Although Protestants had been active for a number of years, it was the 1830s that saw tensions mount to crisis proportions with the arrival of John Wilson (1804-75) of the Scottish Missionary Society, a renowned educator, eminent linguist, and indefatigable controversialist who engaged in debates with every major religious community in the city except the Jains. The first of these had been with the aforementioned Morabhatta in 1830, mere months after coming to India, when his grasp of Marathi was still infirm and his reliance on converts a handicap. One of these was a Pandit Rāmchandra, described as a *paurānik,* a specialist in the *Bhāgavata purāna.* Himself a Christian for only a

Apologetics in Early Nineteenth-Century India (Vienna, 1981); Frank F. Conlon, "The Polemic Process in Nineteenth-Century Maharashtra: Vishnubawa Brahmachari and Hindu Revival," in *Religious Controversy in British India: Dialogues in South Asian Languages,* edited by Kenneth W. Jones (Albany, 1992), pp. 5-26; and Rosalind O'Hanlon, *Caste, Conflict, and Ideology: Mahatma Jotirao Phule and Low Caste Protest in Nineteenth-Century Western India* (Cambridge, 1985).

13. Krishna Shāstrī's discourses were serialized in *Jñānodaya* from October 1852 to July 1853, under the title "Thakurdwar Lectures." While the anonymous "eyewitness" who contributed monthly summaries softened some of the Shāstrī's more acerbic criticisms and portrayed him as a buffoon, his reports reflect the same tone and substance found in the printed materials by other Hindu apologists independently of the various mission presses and periodicals.

short time, Rāmchandra was a poor match for the debates that occurred after Morabhatta bowed out; in the opposition were pandits more learned than he, including several attached to the courts of the Nizāmat Adaulat.[14] It was, however, difficult to resist a force like Wilson, whose access to the press promoted the impression of being unbeatable. Despite occasional setbacks, including a brouhaha involving his most prominent convert, Narāyan Seshādri, in 1843, public controversies continued unabated. It is small wonder, then, when the outcome of the seemingly free-wheeling debates of the past were perceived as rigged, that "apostates and mlecchas" (converts and missionaries) were excluded from Thākurdvār when Krishna Shāstrī joined the fray. What better evidence that missionaries were "getting in the way"?

Jñānodaya's coverage of the Thākurdvār lectures indicates that Krishna Shāstrī was both a garrulous speaker and a populist who could entertain his audience with missionary jibes and exploit its discontent with colonial rule. On virtually every occasion, the trope of progress occurs, with blistering commentary on its ill affects. Take, for instance, the following, which reflects Krishna Shāstrī's internalization of the most invidious aspects of colonial rhetoric:

> The British are very industrious and energetic. Not so the Hindus. On account of the enervating influence of the climate we possess very little physical strength. We cannot well get through breakfast before 12 o'clock, and then we must sleep till 3 o'clock at least before we are capable of any mental exertion. For the next two or three hours of the day our minds are in working order. But the English can easily endure ten or twelve hours of daily toil.[15]

The excess energy that Krishna Shāstrī observed was both a marvel — "While we are adjusting our turbans, an Englishman will make himself master of a new language"[16] — and a fright because it bordered on frenzy and issued from bad religion:

14. In a diary entry for May 1830, Rev. A. Graves of the American Board of Commissioners for Foreign Mission said this of Wilson and Rāmchandra in connection with the first debate: "I think the sooner the discussion is closed the better. . . . Ram Chundur's knowledge of Christianity is not sufficient to enable him to answer the cavils of those who are so well acquainted with the doctrines of the Gospel as some of his antagonists, and Mr. Wilson is not sufficiently versed in Murathu to enable him to express clearly the ideas he wishes to communicate" (Cambridge, Mass., Harvard University, ABCFM Archives, vol. 4, Bombay Mission, Journals, Letters, and Documents, 1824-30).

15. *Jñānodaya* 12 (March 1853): 69-70.

16. *Jñānodaya* 12 (March 1853): 70.

> They accuse us of being lazy, and of doing nothing but studying the Vedas. But this is not true. We believe the soul to be an emanation from the deity; and to establish and confirm this belief we study the Vedas. The English require nothing of this kind. Such an amount of righteousness has been accumulated by the death of Christ that they can get along without any of their own.[17]

It may by now be obvious that what the colonizers considered progress was for Krishna Shāstrī regress into the Kali Yuga, the age of degeneration. The English had in Christianity a religion that matched their avarice and mendacity. Citing the *Bhavishya purāna,* which tells of things to come (but was a *purāna* coeval with Krishna Shāstrī himself), he saw the future in the present and that the English, descendants of the *daityas* (demons), would rule from Calcutta until "the whole earth is subject to them." The *pādris* who propagated Christianity were likewise "demon-born," as was Jesus himself, and all who followed him were "carried away by the spirit of Kali."[18] *Artha* waxed, dharma waned: the missionaries' chief pursuit was wealth, each had a wardrobe of "seven jackets" and enjoyed a large income.[19] When their attention turned to religion, "their mouths move faster than chariot wheels,"[20] and one could hardly get a word in edgeways.

Bleak as the dharma's prospects seemed, Krishna Shāstrī was not deterred from defending Hinduism and engaging Christianity wherever he saw chinks in its armor. In religious controversy, as in contact sports, a strong offense is the best defense, and Krishna Shāstrī thus claimed to have forty reasons for disbelieving Christianity, whereas the missionaries only had eighteen against Hinduism. The most formidable argument in his repertoire, one that made eminent sense to a society anchored in the dharma, had been urged against Christianity since the second century in the Mediterranean world: "The Hindu religion, being without beginning, must be true." Wilken illuminates the assumption behind the argument in connection with the pagan Celsus: "what was handed down by the ancients was true because it was old."[21] In fact, the Thākurdvār lectures could be fruitfully read with *Jñānodaya* in one hand and a work of anti-Christian apologetics from the Greco-Roman period in the other; only the idiom differs. The idea that Jesus was neither a savior nor a sage but only a magician ("aided by demons and fairies"),[22] and not a very good

17. *Jñānodaya* 12 (March 1853): 70.
18. *Jñānodaya* 12 (February 1853): 56.
19. *Jñānodaya* 12 (June 1853): 162.
20. *Jñānodaya* 12 (January 1853): 12.
21. Wilken, *Christians As the Romans Saw Them,* p. 121.

one at that ("our Konkani gaudis are better"),[23] was there, as well as wonderment at the Christians' fascination with Jesus ("Ram saved Ayodhya but Jesus was pinioned by men"),[24] and, of course, the defense of divine unity against the charge of polytheism ("There's more than one way to fold a turban").[25]

As Caecilius, the pagan of Minucius Felix's *Octavius* cited at the head of this section, was vexed and exasperated by the Christians of his day, so was Krishna Shāstrī by the missionaries of his: they seemed puffed up, insolent, impious. Unlike Caecilius, he rounded off his lectures with a dogmatic claim, exceeding those of the critics of Western antiquity who "debunked" Christian absolutism without asserting an exclusivism of their own: "The Hindu religion is utterly opposed to the idea that anybody can be saved outside its pale."[26] There is, of course, no obvious reason why Krishna Shāstrī had to react in this particular way, and there were others who looked upon missionaries more benignly. Let me explain why he intrigues me. I find him more amenable to criticism than my brief summary would suggest. His concern was belief maintenance at a time when the dharma seemed vulnerable, and this in itself is enough to quash the idea that Hinduism is a spongy mass of unlimited tolerance. His lectures also reveal an interest in belief (re)formation; he was especially sensitive to missionary criticism of the way the Holi festival was celebrated. If one sees here a Protestant Hinduism on the horizon, it can be found even more clearly in his successor at Thākurdvār, Vishnubava Brahmachāri, like him a controversialist but more in the mold of Dayānanda Sarasvati.[27] Krishna Shāstrī's fulminations seem to confirm the negative effects of missionary polemics, which Arun Shourie calls "the wages of calumny."[28] In reading *Jñānodaya*, with its triumphant note of indefeasibility, one can appreciate Shourie's point of view: the gnashing teeth, the wagging forefinger, and the dagger looks relieved by flashes of biting humor are almost palpable. Be that as it may, Krishna Shāstrī had a keen sense of epistemic duty, Christian truth claims had to be countered, and of ethical duty, someone had to spring to the defense of communities anchored in the dharma.[29] Missionaries were getting "in the way" and had to be chased out.

22. *Jñānodaya* 12 (June 1853): 162.
23. *Jñānodaya* 12 (February 1853): 69.
24. *Jñānodaya* 12 (June 1853): 162.
25. *Jñānodaya* 12 (December 1852): 349.
26. *Jñānodaya* 11 (November 1852): 339.
27. Conlon, "Polemic Process," p. 23.
28. Arun Shourie, *Missionaries in India: Continuities, Changes, Dilemmas* (New Delhi, 1994), pp. 41-53.
29. My understanding of interreligious apologetics as an epistemic and ethical duty is derived from Griffiths, *Apology for Apologetics*, pp. 14-17.

Getting Back on the Way

> Who is wrong? Moses or Jesus? Or when the Father sent Jesus had he forgotten what commands he gave to Moses? Or did he condemn his own laws and change his mind, and send his messenger for quite the opposite purpose?
>
> Celsus (*Contra Celsum* 7.18)[30]

"Let the eternal and holy God . . . be praised" began a letter of 1843 in the *Morning Star,* the Anglo-Tamil organ of the missionaries of the American Board in Jaffna, Ceylon.[31] At first glance the effusive beginning must have seemed an encouraging affirmation of their activities, encouraging because the letter went on to say: "for his having condescended to the people of this land, and having sent the missionaries from a far country, from America, where civilization and Christianity prevail, and for employing means to chastise the people."[32] Strangely enough, the author was not a Christian but a Hindu. This was Ārumuka Pillai (1822-79), a Vellāla pandit who had been profoundly stirred by the missionary presence in this quiet corner of the Indic world where a great revival of Shaivism was about to occur. This revival would be initiated by the letter writer, but its precipitators were the missionaries who never envisioned the possibility that a new identity could be grounded in Hinduism or that the "eternal and holy God" who had sent them was the god Shiva. Still young at the time his letter appeared, Ārumuka was the product of one of the finest systems of education of which missionaries in the Indic world could boast. Not only were the Jaffnese exceptionally literate, they were also biblically aware. It was by British Wesleyans at St. Paul's, a school on the Jaffna esplanade, that Ārumuka had been educated, even though his letter had been sent to the Americans (who controlled the local press). For nine years he sat in their classrooms, listened to their admonitions in chapel, and read their tracts. As thoroughly as anyone, he had been exposed to their faith, was familiar with their civilizational ideals, and knew their mentality. After leaving St. Paul's, these connections continued. For the next half decade he assisted Peter Percival (d. 1873), a Wesleyan who was revising the Rhenius version of the Tamil Bible. In the intimacy of relationships like these, where little could be concealed, missionaries began to arouse *the oppositions they figure reflexively.*

30. Henry Chadwick, trans., *Origen: Contra Celsum* (Cambridge, 1965).
31. *Morning Star,* 26 January 1843.
32. *Morning Star,* 26 January 1843.

The same letter disabused the missionaries of their hope that Ārumuka was on the verge of becoming a Christian: "For a length of time," he wrote, "I professed Sivaism, but now, partly because I have heard the sermons which the charitable and benevolent missionaries have preached to the people of this country . . . and having had a desire to examine the Bible . . . *some doubts have arisen in my mind*" (italics added).[33] As with Krishna Shāstrī, Ārumuka's doubts were familiar both to the Mediterranean world of antiquity and the Indic world of his own time; they were doubts that might occur to anyone who reads the Torah without Christian blinkers. They had been voiced in the fourth century by Julian, the pagan emperor who had likewise had a Christian education, in *Against the Galilaeans.* Julian there argued that Christianity was an apostasy from Judaism, that the pagan rites he wished to revive matched the cult of Yahweh better than anything the New Testament offered, and that both Greeks and Jews had "temples, sanctuaries, altars, purifications, and certain precepts."[34] Monotheism aside, other differences seemed trivial. When missionaries first arrived in the Indic world, Hindu cultic practices brought the Old Testament to mind: "What is the Veda," asked Fr. J. Bouchet, a Jesuit, "but Moses in the medium of Sanskrit?"[35] In Jaffna, where even those who avoided contact with the missionaries were often well informed about the Bible, critics realized that Christianity was especially vulnerable at its interface with Judaism, where so many claims about Jesus were founded. Even before Ārumuka, Muttukkumārak Kavirāyar (1780-1851), a Vellāla poet, had composed a caricature of the missionaries, castigating them for apostatizing from the dharma of Israel. Ārumuka merely honed the argument to a fine edge by adducing the Bible itself to sever the New Testament from the Old. In so doing, the missionaries were made to appear foolish: "Those Christians who deride and abhor the doings of the Tamil people who perform services similar to those which the (Jews) performed according to the command of God . . . must then admit that . . . God in the time of old gave all those commandments through ignorance and foolishness."[36]

Thus, as Julian's Greeks, so also Ārumuka's Tamilians — both were closer to the Jews in respect of cultic norms for worshipping God than the missionaries were. In short, the Israelites practiced a temple-based cult; so did the Shaivites, and what was wrong with that? Like Julian, Ārumuka argued that

33. *Morning Star,* 26 Jan. 1843.

34. Wilmer C. Wright, trans., *The Works of the Emperor Julian,* vol. 3 (London, 1953), p. 407.

35. Cited in Wilhelm Halbfass, *India and Europe: An Essay in Understanding* (Albany, 1988), p. 44.

36. *Morning Star,* 26 January 1843.

the law of Moses was meant to last forever; what is more, "the Israelites more punctually attended the ceremonies than the Sivas."[37] While the missionaries were hardly routed by this remarkable display of biblical erudition, they were certainly put on the defensive: Ārumuka's *Annihilation of Calumnies against Shaivism (Caivatūshanaparikāram)* of 1854, which amplified the argument in the *Morning Star*, clearly made the Bible tremble in Jaffna. Tract after tract had scolded the Hindus for localizing the godhead in temples. Again like Julian, who paid back the Christian mentors of his youth by attempting to reconstruct the Jewish temple in Jerusalem, Ārumuka spent a lifetime trying to effect a change in the ritual life of his contemporaries by making the Kantacuvāmi temple, Jaffna's cultic center, a place befitting the presence of God.

Throughout the Indic world, Hindus familiar with Judaism through the medium of Christianity found missionary rhetoric about Hinduism unconvincing for the same reasons that Ārumuka did.[38] Some took umbrage, incensed that missionaries impugned revered custom and needlessly provoked opposition, insult, and injury. In Madras Presidency, for instance, where Hindu-Christian tensions were mounting, one Umāpati Mutaliyār of the Sacred Ashes Society (Vipūticankam), circulated a tract called "The Pādris' Secrets Disclosed," a salacious work that claimed to reveal the true reason behind the "evils" being inflicted upon society by the missionaries. One finds in Umāpati's tract a theodicy based on the familiar theme in the Tamil *purānas* of heaven becoming overcrowded. Too many souls, he believed, were enjoying the presence of God in heaven, having been released from the cycle of death and rebirth, while only a few remained in the world for another attempt at attaining liberation. The god Yama, who punished the witless and hapless for their failings during the interval between death and rebirth, appealed to the gods for redress, having little to keep him occupied. At their behest, a chain of events was obligingly orchestrated, beginning with the birth of Jesus, conceived by one of Yama's minions, and ending with the disruption of dharma by "those base men who call themselves Church Mission, Wesleyans, London Mission, and American Mission."[39] A remarkable theodicy indeed, proving

37. *Morning Star,* 26 January 1843.

38. It was reported of one Mohun Chund by a contemporary of William Carey in Bengal that "he seems highly pleased with the ceremonial washings of the Mosaic Dispensation, and desires to know if in these ceremonies the Hindoos are nearer the Bible than we are" (Regents Park College, Oxford, Baptist Missionary Society archives, John Thomas, Mudnabatty, 25 September 1795).

39. "The Padri's Secrets Disclosed" (written in 1843 or 1844), published in *Madras Christian Institution and Missionary Record* 2 (1844): 131-34.

that myths from the past were still useful at mid century for interpreting the tumult of the present.

"The Pādris' Secrets Disclosed" thus explained the disturbing existence of Christianity in the Indic world by invoking the principle that both dharma and *adharma* are necessary for keeping the cosmos in balance; Umāpati merely recycled a familiar theodicy. In Ārumuka's view, however, the work was flawed in one respect. Missionaries were not standard-issue demons from the kingdom of Yama: they were more than merely good (or bad) for depopulating the heavenly realms; they also exemplified certain dharmic qualities, and these qualities were compensation for the ruckus they were raising. It was Shiva's bidding that brought them, and their presence was purposeful, if not actually providential. Ārumuka needed a way of saying in terms congenial to his own perspective that missionaries exist because God intervenes in affairs of the world. To illustrate how he expressed himself I turn to a parable in the *Morning Star* that describes the experience of being stirred and awakened to faith:

> When I heard the doctrines of the Christian missionaries, my heart was moved and having entertained a thought that Sivaism was false and probably Christianity is true, I examined the Bible — but alas! it is as if a goblin came from a well, and fearing the country of the tiger, went to the country of the jackal, and the country of the jackal became the country of the tiger.[40]

The imagery is polysemic, but if the goblin represents the author, the jackal Christianity, and the tiger Shaivism, the meaning may be that Ārumuka's spiritual quest, from Shaivism to Christianity and back to Shaivism again, climaxed in discovering that both religions were grounded in the same reality, a transempirical unity that the missionaries denied because they were ignorant of the Bible's true purport. In fleeing from this reality, presumably as a young man being educated in missionary institutions, Ārumuka had found Shiva where he least expected him, in "the land of the jackal." The imagery would seem more obscure than it really is unless we revert to the operative word in the first sentence of Ārumuka's letter. *Chastise!* — that was what the missionaries were there to do. Raking the Jaffnese over the coals, the missionaries had unknowingly envisioned for them the possibility of a new identity grounded in an old reality. By his own account, being in "the land of the jackal" was for Ārumuka a punishing experience of being shamed into

40. *Morning Star*, 26 January 1843.

opposition. The "evil" that the missionaries meant to inflict was nonetheless transformed by Shiva into something good for Shaivism. If only for this, missionaries were good for getting back on the way. His recovery of religious identity seems to have transformed Ārumuka so thoroughly that one is tempted to speak of him, oxymoronically, as a convert to Shaivism, as Julian was to paganism. The experience, however, was a classic instance of revitalization. He was imbued by it with a focused sense of commitment to the reawakening of Shaivism, as if he, too, had become a missionary like those whose chastisements made him a more self-aware Shaivite.

From the discussion thus far, one might surmise that Ārumuka's subsequent endeavors on behalf of Shaivism would provide worthwhile material for testing the Protestantization thesis. While this is certainly so, and Ārumuka has been called, tongue-in-cheek, the best Wesleyan ever produced by the Jaffna missionaries, there is another line of thought to pursue. Although every missionary employed a pandit, the little we know about them — their aggravations of conscience, the stirrings and awakenings of new and old identities, even their names — emphasizes the remarkable importance of Ārumuka Pillai. Take, for example, the numerous pandits assisting the Serampore missionaries in the Herculean project of translating the Bible into Indic languages. Even the pandit in the famous portrait of William Carey, pen in hand, manuscript of the Sanskrit Bible on the desk, has been misidentified so often — Gopāla Nyāyalankāra, not Mrityuñjaya Vidyālankāra — that it hardly seems surprising that the others are barely remembered. When all was said and done, what impressions did the pandits take home? *The State of Religion in Jaffna (Yālppānaccamayanilai),* written by Ārumuka in 1874,[41] offers suggestive cues in connection with a missionary who may have been Peter Percival, whom he helped revise the Tamil Bible. This individual, Ārumuka claimed, was in fact a Shaivite at heart, like Cākkiya Nāyanār, one of the great exemplars of devotion whose stories are told in Periyapurānam. The transformation of Cākkiya, who was actually a Buddhist, *not* a Hindu, into a Nāyanār began with a stone he tossed absentmindedly at a lingam and ended with a theophany of Shiva, pleased with the attention he received, irreverent though it was. Missionaries were for Ārumuka more ambivalent figures than Cākkiya Nāyanār, situated as they were "in the land of the jackal" between dharma and *adharma.* All things considered, however, they were not on that account without a *raison d'être* in the "land of the tiger."[42]

41. Published in Jaffna, Ceylon (Sri Lanka).

42. Documentation for this discussion may be found in R. F. Young and S. Jebanesan, *The Bible Trembled: The Hindu Christian Controversies of Nineteenth-Century*

Getting Out of the Way

> You must guide your mind by this intention, that you hold the scales of justice most impartially and do not tend by inclination toward either side, lest the verdict seem not the result of our argumentation, but rather, the product of your personal feelings.
>
> Caecilius, pagan, to Marcus, Christian (*Octavius* 5.1)[43]

"If my one hundred doubts on Christianity may be removed," asked a skeptical young Hindu of a missionary whose presence in Benares (Banāras) in the 1840s affected the lives of many, "why may not my five hundred on Hinduism?"[44] At a time when Christian literature was becoming more accessible in Sanskrit than ever before, some of it written in Banāras itself around this same time, it seems ironic that it was the routine street preaching in Hindustani of William Smith of the Church Missionary Society that caught the attention of this young Hindu, a Chitpāvan Brahmin named Nīlakanth Goreh (1825-85), who sat at the feet of pandits and was himself honored as a *shāstrī.* "Church Sanskrit," as I have termed the belletristic writing in that language by Christians, soon began to have an impact on Nīlakanth. First impressions count, however, and it was Smith's "getting in the way" with his no-other-way-than-faith-in-Christ-the-avatar-of-God bazaar evangelism, mimicked by Nīlakanth in chaste Sanskrit as *īshāvatāre khrishtākhye vishvāsān nānyathā gatih,* that irked him. Already a self-aware Hindu, unlike Ārumuka Pillai, Nīlakanth did not need a missionary to chastise him into becoming one. Prompted by a keen sense of epistemic and ethical responsibility, he went forth, like Krishna Shāstrī, to engage Smith in a quintessentially panditic contest of *mandan-khandan,* defending Hinduism *(mandan)* and refuting Christianity *(khandan).*

To Nīlakanth's dismay, and to his chagrin, as he later testified, Smith was

---

Ceylon (Vienna, 1995). For detailed studies of Ārumuka Pillai, see D. Dennis Hudson, "Arumuga Navalar and the Hindu Renaissance among the Tamils," in *Religious Controversy in British India: Dialogues in South Asian Languages,* edited by Kenneth W. Jones (Albany, 1992), pp. 27-51, and "A Hindu Response to the Written Torah," in *Between Jerusalem and Benares: Comparative Studies in Judaism and Hinduism,* edited by Hananya Goodman (Albany, 1994), pp. 55-84. Hudson's interpretation of Ārumuka's letter in the *Morning Star,* especially the Tamil meaning of the term "chastise, " has significantly influenced my own.

43. Arbesmann et al., *Tertullian, Apologetical Works, and Minucius Felix, Octavius.*

44. William Smith, *Dwij: The Conversion of a Brahmin to the Faith of Christ* (London, 1850), p. 92.

hardly the "illiterate bucolic yokel" he took him to be,[45] unlike the Christians whom Celsus, the anti-Christian critic of antiquity, encountered in the Mediterranean world. From their retrospective remarks on the ensuing relationship, one gathers that Smith was to Nīlakanth what Marcus the Christian was to Caecilius the pagan in *Octavius.* The change he effected was gradual — no browbeating; no appeals to the Bible as an inspired text; no exhortations of the don't-ask-questions-only-believe variety — leavened by a good measure of patient responsiveness to endless questions without the offensiveness he seemed to exhibit when preaching on the streets. What transpired between the two was less like *mandan-khandan* and more like the authentic dialogue that occurs when two individuals, equally committed to their respective religions, encounter each other; that is to say, their relationship was essentially agonistic,[46] replete with intellectual skirmishes, strategic withdrawals, and occasional one-upmanship. Smith seems to have been honestly shaken by the subtleties of his opponent's arguments, but it was Nīlakanth, as is well known, his conversion being a landmark event in the history of Indian Christianity, who began to become aware that it is possible to change one's mind about life's fundamentals. Most of all, as a mid-century missionary and therefore an indefeasible individual, Smith *communicated choice.* The ensuing spiritual crisis was of long duration. Its indefinable resolution makes me place Nīlakanth outside the parameters of likely responses to Christianity from subgroups within Hinduism that recognize one corpus of texts or another within the Veda as self-authenticating authority sources.

At the end of one such engagement with missionary Smith, Nīlakanth returned home with a work in Church Sanskrit, mulling it over for nearly a year before returning for another round of discussion. This was the *Mataparīkshā (The Examination of Religions),* by John Muir (1810-82),[47] a Company servant imbued with a keen sense of mission, who at the time was in Banāras as the acting principal of the Sanskrit College. Written in the same dialogue format as *Octavius,* and in all likelihood modeled upon it, with a Christian *satyārthī* (truth-seeker) to match Marcus and a Hindu *Vedavidvān* (Vedic scholar) to match Caecilius, the *Mataparīkshā* was both a masterwork in the genre and a piece of pure *kampfliteratur* that marched inexorably toward the triumph of Christianity, ostensibly on rational grounds and without appealing to the Bible as an inspired text. It was not only the audacity of orchestrat-

45. Henry Chadwick, trans., *Origen: Contra Celsus* (Cambridge, 1965), p. 165.

46. For an understanding of dialogue similar to my own, see Griffiths, *Apology for Apologetics.*

47. Calcutta, 1839.

ing such an outcome that Nīlakanth found unbearable, but also the trivialization of faith and the subordination of it to reason seemed irreligious, the sort of cant one heard from Buddhists, Materialists, and other historic adversaries of the Veda. The *Mataparīkshā* said a great deal about the intellect *(buddhi),* analytical reasoning *(vichāra),* and proof *(upapatti)* and was forever arguing that all scriptures, the Bible included, were to be examined, investigated, and searched *(vichāranīya).* About faith *(shraddhā),* that disposition of the heart *(hridasya vrittih),* as Shankara defined it, without which one could never grasp transempirical truth, the book said nothing. To Nīlakanth, truth was to be apprehended by faith, not reason, because truth is revealed (timelessly and impersonally, the Veda being authorless according to his view). The *Mataparīkshā* had it all wrong, and to set the author straight Nīlakanth composed a full-blown text of *mandan-khandan* in Sanskrit, the *Shāstratattvavinirnaya (A Verdict on the Truth of the Scriptures),*[48] denouncing Christianity as a crude Kali Yuga religion of delusion *(mohadharma)* at the same time that he articulated a well-reasoned defense of the priority of faith — in Scripture, not God as such — over reason.

Reason, however, prevailed, or the idea of it exemplified by his Christian mentors who themselves signify, like Alexander Duff, that the stuff of which Evangelicals were made was a complex mix of soft-hearted concern and hard-headed rationalism. Nīlakanth literally cogitated his way into Christianity. It was a rough transition, attended by familial and societal ruptures; for every step forward there was a half-step back, until in 1848 he was baptized and renamed Nehemiah. He was held back at the last moment by a nagging doubt about the capacity of Christians for comprehending that God's love might extend beyond the realm of the human to the animals they voraciously consumed.

I have discussed Nīlakanth's preconversion objections to Christianity elsewhere;[49] what I have not emphasized strongly enough is that his transition from Hinduism was affected by his perception of how Christians think as much as what they think. There was no "knock-out" argument that convinced him to cease being a Hindu, although the idea that the Veda cannot be eternal because its linguistic features demonstrate development over time shook Nīlakanth to the core.[50] His transition was more effected by an impression accumulated over several years that logic, rightly exercised by an intellect func-

48. Written in 1844, edited and published by S. L. Katre (Ujjain, 1853).

49. Young, *Resistant Hinduism.*

50. In the same way modern form criticism takes the wind out of many a Christian's sails.

tioning as an impartial judge, punched more holes in Hinduism than Christianity. One sees this in his first postconversion writing, *Vedāntmat kā vichār aur Khrishtīyamat kā sār (An Examination of Vedānta and the Essence of Christianity)*,[51] written shortly after his baptism (later revised and published as the *Shaddarshandarpan* [*Mirror of the Six Philosophical Systems*] in 1860).[52] This was a work of logical incisiveness, long on *khandan* but short on *mandan:* Vedānta was examined and found to be fatally flawed by logical inconsistencies. His concern was how Vedāntins think, not what they think, whereas what passed for the essence of Christianity was a discourse on the right use of the human faculty for analytical reasoning *(svābhāvik vivek)*. There was here no message from the gospel to warm the heart but only an appeal to reason. Especially notable for its absence was the word *shraddhā,* so important a part of his vocabulary before becoming a Christian. As he grew into Christianity over a life of service to the Church, first as a Low-Church, then a High-Church Anglican, and finally as an Anglo-Catholic, Nīlakanth absorbed another idiom for expressing the changes that occurred when becoming a Christian, and duly accorded a place to grace in his self-understanding; but the obsession with rationality remained. The closer one gets to his early mentality, the more one sees that Christianity was for him another *darshana,* a school of philosophical thought, more logically consistent than the classical *darshanas* of Hinduism but no less and no more than a *darshana.* It was a conceit that missionaries flattered, thinking that having a Banāras pandit on the team added credibility to the claims of Christianity on the attention of the serious-minded.

That missionaries could be good for getting out of the way without also being good for getting into the way seems a valid inference from the discussion above. As he was an introspective individual, the historian has little access to Nīlakanth's inner agon. His correspondence, however, informs us that his conversion left him with a nagging sense of incompleteness — of being, in his own words, a *kaccha* (immature), not *pakkha* (mature), Christian — and that he tried to overcome this disappointment by perpetually seeking that elusive "knock-out" reason for not being a Hindu. That he was relatively unconcerned with demonstrating why he became a Christian seems to me significant. The missionary appeal to reason effected in him was not a capacity for more efficient reasoning but rather for stepping back from Hinduism to a vantage point where its philosophical coherence could be assessed objectively. Why it eventually came about that he saw the *darshanas* as fatally flawed on

51. Allahabad, 1853.

52. Best known under the formidable English title "A Rational Refutation of the Hindu Philosophical Systems" (London and Calcutta, 1861).

rational grounds is beside the point, despite the intrinsic interest of his arguments. What matters is that in becoming aware that it is possible to change one's mind about life's fundamentals, there was too much denial of Hinduism and too little affirmation of Christianity, a change in philosophical orientation that left the dispositions of the heart very much the same. To make the point in Christian idiom, Nīlakanth's experience seems to have fallen short of a *metanoia* that transformed the heart as well as the mind, giving constancy to belief and making it become conviction.

For an individual such as Nīlakanth, *metanoia* was obviously a process, not an aoristic event, the outcome of years, not moments (indeed, the assurance of it came to him in later life), but in the early postconversion period his self-identity expressed itself more in terms of not being a Hindu than in being a Christian. This can be illustrated by reverting to the *Vedāntmat kā vichār aur Khrishtīyamat kā sār.* In this short treatise the logic of Vedānta was declared to be fallacious, so much so that no rational person could accept it. One cannot help but feel, however, that the same analysis applied to Christianity might show it to be equally incoherent. Technically speaking, this type of refutation was called *vitandā* and was best exemplified in late Vedānta by Shrī Harsha's *Khandanakhandakhādya,* a treatise of the twelfth century that excoriated the inconsistencies of all opposing schools. With other systems disqualified, the truth of *Advaita* was upheld as self-evident; no demonstration was required. "The business of philosophy," as B. K. Matilal observed, "is thus regarded by Shrī Harsha as consisting simply in the refutation of rival views."[53] Likewise for Nīlakanth, Christianity was true because Hinduism was false. Having moved out of the way, he was nonetheless plagued by continuous doubts about the way, as were the pandits of Banāras to whom he addressed his writings. For them he remained a pathetic figure, his refutation ignored. When hardly a word in demonstration of Christianity's self-evident truth was forthcoming, it seems unsurprising that Pandit Baldev Upādhyāy, writing from the Banāras of today, accounts for Nīlakanth's conversion by invoking inimical cosmic forces: the convert, he laments, "fell victim to the Kali Yugic *māyā* of the Christians."[54]

Much effected by the missionaries, their impact on Nīlakanth nonetheless seems somehow "indefinable," and the role that was scripted for him coincided congenially with his own dispositional and philosophical proclivities. A pandit of pandits, as he was often called, Nīlakanth might have become an In-

53. Cited in P. E. Granoff, *Philosophy and Argument in Late Vedānta: Shrī Harsha's Khandanakhandakhādya* (Dordrecht, 1978), p. xi.

54. Baldev Upādhyāy, *Kāshi kī pānditya paramparā* (Vārānasī, 1994), p. 1059.

dian Justin Martyr, an Origen, or even an Augustine, putting the *darshanas* to use as the matrix for a new *chrēsis* of Christianity in the Indic world, just as Greek and Roman philosophy had been pressed into service for the gospel. Because he seemed indifferent to the task, posterity has not dealt kindly with Nīlakanth; a sense of disappointment lingers, stemming perhaps from its own failure to understand the dynamics of his transition to Christianity. And, unfortunately, to see *chrēsis* happening at mid century, it would be better to turn to Europeans, John Muir himself or — better yet — James Ballantyne (d. 1862), who at this same time was creating in the Banāras Sanskrit College a complete *shāstra* of his own, modeled on the Nyāya principle of the *vidyāchakra,* an expanding "circle of knowledge" that embraced both empirical *(paurusheya)* and transempirical *(apaurusheya)* knowledge. Whereas Ballantyne's work culminated in *The Bible for Pandits,*[55] Nīlakanth's legacy was a void left unfilled. As Andrew Walls observed, "No conversion is complete without a conversion of the past";[56] the new Indic *chrēsis,* a symptomatically theological act that transforms *kaccha* insights into *pakkha* truths, therefore required an individual less prone to continuous reassessment of his beliefs than Nīlakanth/Nehemiah Goreh. Although he was promising, the changes effected in him were simply too indefinable.[57]

Pray, Sir, Who and What Are You?

> Between the hagiography, the ordinary working missionary, and the twisted image of the stereotype, there is no single truth about missionaries as people.
>
> Kenelm Burridge[58]

Returning to the question of the "Malabarians," asked of Bartolomaeus Ziegenbalg and so many others who followed him — "Pray, Sir, who and

55. London and Benares, 1860.

56. Andrew Walls, *The Missionary Movement in Christian History: Studies in the Transmission of Faith* (Maryknoll, 1996), p. 53.

57. For further analysis of the dynamics of Nīlakanth Goreh's conversion, with comparative observations on other Indian Christians of the same era, see Avril A. Powell, "Processes of Conversion to Christianity in Nineteenth Century North-Western India," in *Religious Conversion Movements in South Asia: Continuities and Change, 1800-1900,* edited by Geoffrey A. Oddie (Richmond, 1997), pp. 15-55.

58. Burridge, *In the Way,* p. 32.

what are you?" — all that one seems warranted in saying is that the impact of Christianity on the three individuals discussed above (Krishna Shāstrī Sāthe, Ārumuka Pillai, and Nīlakanth Goreh) engendered a variety of asymptotic perspectives on what missionaries were good for (and bad for) in the Indic world. There is simply no obvious way of squaring these perspectives; they diverge, like lines that never meet. Whether one tries to comprehend them as an insider or an outsider would, *there is no single truth about missionaries.* The material, furthermore, suggests that the particularities entailed in being a missionary were of less consequence than we imagine. By envisioning the possibility of a new identity grounded in a different reality, a reality that would mean nothing for Christians were it not named with the name of Jesus Christ, missionaries necessarily placed the Christian dharma in a relationship of tension with the Hindu dharma. One could respond to their faith in the gospel and their collateral convictions about its salvific universality by braying, as Krishna Shāstrī did, about Hinduism's uniqueness *(extra Vedos nulla salus);* one could berate them for obtuseness, as Ārumuka did, and still allot them a niche within the dharma; one's entire belief-system could even become a shambles without experiencing the same compensatory certainty they enjoyed, as was tragically true of Nīlakanth. In any event, for anyone who recognized the Veda as a self-authenticating authority source, missionaries could be dismissed but hardly ignored.

Of course, for every individual like these three, countless others lacked the same keen sense of epistemic and ethical responsibility, and on them the impact of Christianity was even more indefinable. Among these reticent figures, I think, for instance, of one Rāmachandra Vidyābhūshana, a Bengali pandit who came in 1828 to William Hodge Mill, a missionary of the Society for the Propagation of the Gospel, with a specimen in Sanskrit of a paean to Jesus Christ, adoringly extolled as the *shabdāvatāra,* the Incarnation of the Word. Rāmachandra faltered and retreated into the shadows of history, but the magnificent *Shrīkhrishtasangītā (Hymn to the Blessed Christ),* which Mill completed a few years later, was the fruition of his inspiration. One can only wonder what it was about this missionary's presentation of the gospel that warmed the heart of his pandit, only to grow cool again because of the greater ardor he professed for the *Bhagavadgītā* of Lord Krishna.[59] Rāmachandra had pagan counterparts in the Mediterranean world, like the fifth-century Nonnus of Panopolis who, without being a Christian, and indeed

59. Anand Amaladass and Richard Fox Young, *The Indian Christiad: A Concise Anthology of Didactic and Devotional Literature in Early Church Sanskrit* (Anand, Gujarat, 1995), pp. 57-62.

being famous for an epic about the god Dionysius, had written a paraphrasis on the Gospel of John in Greek hexameters. What this and the other parallels drawn from the Western world seem to suggest is that a comparable dynamic was evident in the Indic world. Although the *chrēsis* with Greek and Roman philosophy that domesticated Christianity in the world of antiquity has yet to occur in South Asia, a transformation that some, underestimating the resilience of the dharma, believe would entail its demise, familiarity with Christianity made the presence of missionaries seem less abnormal than was the case initially. Familiarity proverbially breeds contempt, as it did in the classical world, but the indifference that the Indic world's exposure to Christianity seems to have fostered was more apparent than real. For the full-bodied response to occur, however, missionaries had to transgress the roles scripted for them by the land of the dharma and coax it into an encounter *it had not asked for.*

The period treated here represents the high-water mark of awareness of Christianity on the part of learned communities that recognized the Veda as a self-authenticating authority source. When the ensuing turmoil abated, and the dharmic center was seen to hold, the interstitial "Other" (as Burridge calls the missionary) was increasingly unable to seem anything but an incidental "by-the-way" presence in the Indic world. It would, however, take us beyond the scope of this chapter to enter into the whole complex of reasons for designating the mid nineteenth century a crucial period for the Hindu discovery of Christianity. Suffice to say that these reasons have to do with an epistemological shift within Hinduism in the second half of the same century, when the Veda was less widely recognized as the sole authenticating source of authoritative knowledge. One hears in later years more of the rhetoric of neo-Hinduism, which prioritizes experience *(anubhava)* and marginalizes revelation *(shabda)*. Significant though this was, I conclude with a document from the period before the shift occurred. The following extract, from a letter in Hindi sent around 1860 by a pandit of Banāras to a missionary (who might have been William Smith), brings us back to where we started, to the bewilderment of hearing missionaries speak, as Ziegenbalg did, of being *sent by the Living God:*

> If Jesus Christ had wanted to get his religion going in every country of the world, he would surely have gone to each one in person. Why would he have sent someone else? . . . But he didn't go anywhere, and he wouldn't have commanded anyone else to go in his place, because he would have known clairvoyantly that Shankar Swami [the philosopher] had already descended to India from heaven. . . . Anyway, if he really had issued such

> an order, you should have honoured it by going out to the whole world immediately. How come you waited for eighteen-hundred years, idle and silent?[60]

Actually, the pandit was making a backhanded compliment to the figure at the very heart of the missionary movement; he absolved Jesus of responsibility for it! To the Indic world, this movement was as puzzling as it had been to the Mediterranean world where Celsus (*Contra Celsum* 4.7), at a time when Christianity was considerably younger, wondered: "Is it only now after such a long age that God has remembered to judge the human race? Did he not care before?" Understanding of the missionary endeavor, on its own terms and others, was still a good way off in both worlds.

60. The extract is from *Dharmādharmaparīkshāpatra*, or, as the English title puts it, *Letters Discussing Religion and Irreligion* (Calcutta, 1861), a collection of correspondence between an unidentified missionary and several pandits, published by the Religious Tract Society.

CHAPTER FOUR

Modernist Muslim Responses to Christian Critiques of Islamic Culture, Civilization, and History in Northern India

AVRIL A. POWELL

A New Phase of Cultural Interaction between Islam and Christianity

The outbreak of the Rebellion of 1857 brought to a temporary halt a period of intensive interaction between spokesmen for Christianity and Islam in northwestern India. Such encounters had almost always taken place in Urdu, using traditional modes of communication, such as public debates, the issuing of *fatawa,* and the writing of tracts in Urdu, which, printed mainly in lithographed form, preserved the format of premodern communication in this region. Spokesmen for Islam were almost always drawn from members of the traditional *'ulama* class of scholars learned in Islam. When such cultural interaction resumed some ten years after the failure of the Rebellion, it continued to be conducted in the vernacular languages of the region. Spokesmen for Christianity were now often drawn from the small circle of recently baptized and sometimes ordained Indian Christians, rather than from the increasing numbers of European and American missionaries now settled in the northwest who had previously presented Christian claims. Considerable at-

This study forms part of a research project being conducted on "Scottish Orientalism and the Roots of Indian Religions" during a period of research leave funded by a Leverhulme Fellowship.

tention has been paid in recent years to the study of such interaction in the "popular" arena of bazaar confrontation.[1]

In the following discussion attention will be paid to some examples of a much rarer form of communication that occurred in the late nineteenth century between some European "Islamicist" and some Muslim "modernist" scholars who addressed, as well as belonged to, circles of "high culture." The question will be approached from a historiographical perspective, in order to assess how a trio of scholars, two Indian and one British, all in government service and all amateur rather than professional historians, through publications mainly in English, articulated their contested views on the religious and cultural constituents of high civilization as exemplified through history.

In the late nineteenth century a number of north Indian Muslim scholars chose to write on themes concerning Islamic history in modes that provoked overt comparisons with some other civilizations, notably with "Christian" Europe. Such histories provide a basis for examining the cultural interactions responsible for first triggering such studies, and then influencing their contents and perspectives. The principal Muslim authors, in contrast to most of the *'ulama* who had responded to Christian challenges in earlier decades, were "modernist"[2] in their own understandings of Islam. They chose to publish in English and from presses in London rather than in India. Although such authors certainly drew on Muslim sources, both classical and modern, they put a very strong emphasis on the authority of recent writing by Western apologists for Islam. This was clearly a new phase in interaction between Christian and Muslim scholarship. Among these authors, the two to be considered here, Sir Saiyid Ahmad Khan (1817-98) and Saiyid Amir 'Ali (1849-1928), have already been the subjects of considerable attention concerning their roles in the spheres of politics, education, and theology. They have not, however, been considered previously as historians of Islamic and comparative civilizations.[3]

1. Kenneth W. Jones, *Arya Dharm: Hindu Consciousness in Nineteenth-Century Punjab* (Delhi, 1989; reprint); Barbara Daly Metcalf, *Islamic Revival in British India: Deoband, 1860-1900* (Princeton, 1982); A. A. Powell, "Contested Gods and Prophets: Discourse among Minorities in Late Nineteenth Century Punjab," *Renaissance and Modern Studies* 38 (December 1995): 38-59.

2. Fazlur Rahman (*Islam*, 2nd ed. [Chicago, 1979], pp. 212-14) distinguished between intellectual, political, and social expressions of modernism. Francis Robinson (Francis Robinson, ed., *The Cambridge Illustrated History of the Islamic World* [Cambridge, 1996], p. 243) has defined "modernism" as aiming "to reconstruct [Islamic] knowledge in the light of western knowledge and the new economic and political realities." In this study the emphasis is on explanation and usage of the past in such modernist modes.

3. These authors anglicized their own names as, respectively, "Syed Ahmed" and

Traditional forms of response to Christianity also resumed in the late 1860s, notably among some *'ulama* belonging to a newly established *madrassa* at Deoband. The entry into the arena for the first time of a new type of "modernist" spokesman, as represented by Saiyid Ahmad and Amir 'Ali, however, was responsible for some new approaches to the problems presented by Christian claims, as well as some new strategies. There was, of course, considerable continuity in some of the themes, notably in a renewed emphasis on the lives, characters, and claims to authority of the "founders" of the two religious traditions, Jesus and Muhammad, at least as starting points for entry into some new and more extensive cross-cultural domains. Thus, simultaneously with a new phase of modernist apologetic in English, there also occurred around 1870 a resurgence of publications in Urdu of a genre of "miracle literature" that had first surfaced in northwest India in the 1840s. Yet it was a new awareness of the unsatisfactory tone and claims of some of the earlier publications on both sides (the unscholarly tracts of some Bible Society presses as well as the "miracle" genre of Muslim *maulud* writing) that subsequently led to the decisions of these modernists to adopt both a new format and some new foci of comparison between Islamic and Christian societies.[4] Instead of the claims to prophethood and miracle, and the charges of "corruption" and "irrationality," that had dominated much pre-1857 interchange, they now placed stress on claims to religious and cultural superiority as tested through the history of comparative civilizations.

The catalyst in the new process of interaction was an attempt by an influential evangelical scholar in British service to offset what he perceived to be the shortcomings of the Muslim-authored "miracle" *mauluds*, and some re-

---

"Syed Ameer Ali." They will be referred to here as "Saiyid Ahmad" and "Amir 'Ali." Among many studies of their careers and other contributions see: Christian W. Troll, *Sayyid Ahmad Khan: A Reinterpretation of Muslim Theology* (New Delhi, 1978); J. M. S. Baljon, *The Reforms and Religious Ideas of Sir Saiyid Ahmad Khan*, 2nd ed. (Lahore, 1958); Hafeez Malik, *Sir Sayyid Ahmad Khan and Muslim Modernization in India and Pakistan* (New York, 1980); K. K. Aziz, *Ameer Ali: His Life and Work* (Lahore, 1968); Martin Forward, *The Failure of Islamic Modernism? Syed Ameer Ali's Interpretation of Islam* (Bern, 1999). Other prominent Muslim scholars writing on Islamic civilization, culture clashes, and comparative civilization in late-nineteenth-century India include Chiragh 'Ali (1844-95), Shibli Numani (1857-1914), and Altaf Husain Hali (1837-1914).

4. For a critique both of religious tract society publications on Islam and of Muslim publications on the miracles associated with Muhammad's birth and childhood as then popularized in the *maulud* genre see William Muir, "Biographies of Mohammed for India and the Mohammedan Controversy," *Calcutta Review* 17 (January 1852): 387-421; Ghulam Imam Shahid, *Maulud sharif* (Lucknow, 1843); and Shahid's many editions in the 1860s and 1870s, which are referred to by Muir as "The Ennobled Nativity."

cent unsubstantiated claims in Bible Society tracts. He did this by embarking on a new "authoritative" history of the origins and early history of Islam. The first major publication of William Muir[5] (then secretary to the provincial government of the North Western Provinces but later to be Lieutenant Governor), *The Life of Mahomet from Original Sources*, published in four volumes between 1858 and 1861, provoked the publications on history and civilization by Saiyid Ahmad and Amir 'Ali. That both Muslim scholars chose to publish in London rather than in India may have been fortuitous in the case of Amir 'Ali, but for Saiyid Ahmad it was the result of a deliberate decision to present his first response to Christian criticism of Islam to a Western rather than an Indian readership.

The Making of Historians of Civilization

William Muir, Saiyid Ahmad, and Amir 'Ali belonged to very different traditions of historical writing. Muir had been a student in Edinburgh and Glasgow in the immediate wake of the Scottish Enlightenment but was mainly self-educated in history and was seemingly scarcely touched by the philosophical tradition that had been established in the second half of the eighteenth century by the historical works of David Hume, William Robertson, and Edward Gibbon.[6] Saiyid Ahmad had been brought up in the Mughal tradition of Indo-Persian chronicle writing that continued to exert a strong influence upon him. He had also come under considerable European influence during thirty years of British service before the compilation of his essays on Islamic society. Amir 'Ali, in contrast, was more directly influenced by the thoroughgoing English medium and Western education that he had received in the English department of the Hooghly College of Calcutta University, and he seems to have received his initiation into Arabic and Islamic sciences and history rather spasmodically and mainly through private tuition arranged in his family.

In adhering to a providential view of history, which assumed the unfolding of a divine plan and ascribed "virtue" only to those cultural norms that

5. Sir William Muir (1819-1905) entered the Bengal Civil Service 1837 and was Secretary to Board of Revenue, 1848; Secretary to NWP government, 1852; Foreign Secretary, Government of India, 1865; Lieutenant-Governor, 1868-74; Viceroy's Council, 1874-76; Council of India, 1876-86; and Principal, Edinburgh University, 1886-1903.

6. On history writing during the Scottish Enlightenment see David Allan, *Virtue, Learning and the Scottish Enlightenment: Ideas of Scholarship in Early Modern History* (Edinburgh, 1993).

reflected Christian precepts, Muir belonged firmly in the mainstream of much popular historical writing in early-nineteenth-century Britain. The Scottish historian David Hume and his English contemporary, Edward Gibbon, had certainly been innovators, and exceptions, in Britain in agreeing with Voltaire and Montesquieu's "commitment to explanations within the reach of the human and the natural, rather than the divine."[7] "Popular" history did not, however, follow where they had led. The only surprising factor in Muir's otherwise quite unexceptionable stance, was the opportunity he had seemingly had during his own Scottish education to have seen things rather differently. Yet by the time he had enrolled in Greek classes at Edinburgh in the early 1830s, following in his three elder brothers' footsteps, and then in logic at Glasgow, the intellectual atmosphere had changed. Debate continues on whether the Enlightenment ended with a "bang" or a "whimper" following the demise of the acknowledged innovators.[8] It is doubtful, however, whether history teaching within Scottish university classrooms had ever been as greatly affected by the most innovative of eighteenth-century thinking as some have assumed.[9] The lectures given by Professor Alexander Fraser Tytler, chair of Universal Civil History in Edinburgh from 1780 to 1800, ran through numerous editions in Britain and America, and there was also an Urdu edition published in Calcutta. The last major revision, the *Universal History, from the Creation of the World to the Beginning of the Eighteenth Century*, coincided in 1834 with William Muir's own time at Edinburgh University. That this was a poor reflection of the "philosophical" approach is best judged by a comparison of Tytler's histories with those of his "friend" and colleague, the Reverend William Robertson, Principal of Edinburgh University, who, apart from earlier studies on Scottish, European, and American history, published at the end of his life a highly original work on India.[10] In spite of his grandiose claims to "universality," Tytler's own lectures for students remained firmly grounded in "ancient" — that is, in Egyptian, Roman, and Greek — history,

7. Roy Porter, *Gibbon Making History* (London, 1988), p. 78.

8. "With the coming of the French Revolution . . . the world of the Scottish Enlightenment disintegrated" (David Daiches et al., eds., *The Scottish Enlightenment 1730-1790: A Hotbed of Genius,* 2nd ed. [Edinburgh, 1986], p. 40). For discussions of whether Enlightenment influences actually did fade see Anand C. Chitnis, *The Scottish Enlightenment and Early Victorian English Society* (London, 1986), and Allan, *Virtue, Learning and the Scottish Enlightenment.*

9. Daiches (*Scottish Enlightenment,* p. 9) refers to eighteenth-century Scotland as being "obsessed by history."

10. William Robertson, *An Historical Disquisition concerning the Knowledge Which the Ancients Had of India* (Edinburgh, 1791).

with only the merest of gestures toward the extra-Mediterranean world. Although he commenced the "modern" period of his lectures with the rise of the Arabs under Muhammad, such an emphasis reflected his perception of the significance of Arab expansion on Europe rather than any intrinsic interest in Islamic history. The omission of any substantial reference to Mughal India until the reign of Aurangzeb and the subsequent imperial "decline" demonstrates the limitations of his concern to the consequences for Europe of events in Asia.[11]

By William Muir's time at Edinburgh in the early 1830s, teaching history survived only in the study of the Latin and Greek languages, which formed the core of the Arts curriculum. At Glasgow "civil," as opposed to "ecclesiastical," history was not taught at all until the late nineteenth century. There, as at Edinburgh, the Arts students of the 1820s and 1830s imbibed historical understanding only through the reading of Thucydides, Herodotus, and Virgil in the Latin and Greek classes, thus maintaining the Renaissance attitude to the significance of the "classics" as a sufficient key to the lessons of the past. Scottish students in the early nineteenth century thus had little formal access to the nonclassical and non-European worlds.

Like other members of the educated and professional middle classes Muir was largely self-educated in history, and, like most other amateur historians of his day, he would not have not considered himself as belonging to a particular "school of history." He had read Gibbon in his leisure time, and, although he would cite him on particular points and indeed chose to mimic the title of the *Decline and Fall* in his own *The Caliphate: Its Rise, Decline, and Fall,* he took strong issue, like many other critics, with Gibbon's materialistic explanations of Christianity's rise and expansion and its role in the undermining of the Roman Empire, which were at opposite poles to his own providential understandings of the expansion of Christianity. It seems that the only sense in which Muir may have been a legatee of Enlightenment historiographical influences was his adoption in his analysis of Islamic (but not biblical) history of what Roy Porter has described as the explanation characteristic of the Scots, such as David Hume and William Robertson, as the "conjec-

11. Alexander Tytler is a neglected figure. The various editions of his major work show some modifications after reading Robertson, but subsequent "interference" in the 1830s by one of his sons brought his stance on "Hindu" institutions close to that of James Mill. See Tytler's *Plan and Outline of a Course of Lectures on Universal History, Ancient and Modern: Delivered in the University of Edinburgh* (Edinburgh, 1782); and his *Elements of General History, Ancient and Modern,* 2 vols. (Edinburgh, 1801) and the "family edition" of 1834 in 6 vols. There were also American and Indian editions, including an Urdu translation, *Lubb al-tawarikh,* 3 vols. (Calcutta, 1829-30).

tural" mode; this Muir would use in essaying explanations of, for instance, Muhammad's state of mind at the moment of the "first revelation."[12] His "conjecture" was not embedded, however, as was theirs, in an articulated philosophy of history; and it later led, unsurprisingly, to accusations from his critics, both Muslim and British, of reliance on "arguments from convenience," of "bias," or even of "bigotry."

Muir had begun his prolific output on Islamic history soon after his arrival in northwestern India in the late 1830s. His first researches were published, while he was still in his twenties, in journals such as the *Calcutta Review.* These articles were subsequently embodied in his *Life of Mahomet from Original Sources* (1858-61), to which the modernists responded in the early 1870s. After retirement from India in 1876 Muir resumed the charting of early Islamic civilization with his *Annals of the Early Caliphate* (London, 1883); *The Caliphate: Its Rise, Decline and Fall* (London, 1891); and *The Mameluke or Slave Dynasty of Egypt, 1260-1517 A.D.* (London, 1896). Apart from these academic though purposefully "popular" works, Muir later produced abridged editions of his biography of the Prophet, and various distillations of his views on Islamic society that were specifically intended for the edification of readers of religious tract society publications.[13] Some of his published lectures also provide insights on particular aspects of his understanding of the relations between Islamic and Christian civilizations.[14]

The two Muslim apologists for the claims of Islamic civilization against the criticism of Muir and other European Islamists belonged to *sharif* families, with a tradition of government service under former Muslim ruling powers, Saiyid Ahmad's in Delhi, and Amir 'Ali's in Awadh. At the time of writing his historical essays, Saiyid Ahmad was a district judge of some thirty years' standing. He traveled to London in 1869, ostensibly to accompany his son to the University of Cambridge, but also to consult both Western and Arabic sources on the early history of Islam. Amir 'Ali was a young law student who after his birth and education in the Calcutta region arrived in London in the same year, 1869, in order to read for the bar at Lincoln's Inn. Both scholars had been enabled to travel by the award of Indian government scholarships, in the former case to Saiyid Ahmad's son, and, in the latter, to Amir 'Ali in his own right.

The scholars both benefited from the help of a circle of British well wish-

12. Porter, *Gibbon,* p. 23.

13. For example, William Muir, *The Rise and Decline of Islam,* "Present Day Tracts," no. 14 (London, 1883).

14. For example, William Muir, *The Early Caliphate and Rise of Islam . . . Rede Lecture for 1881* (London, 1881); *The Crusades: A Brief Historical Sketch* (Edinburgh, 1894).

ers in India who gave them introductions to influential families in London. They researched, compiled, and published their studies before leaving England and then continued to write and to add to their original statements on themes of comparative civilization and history following their return to service in India and until their deaths. Although they met each other in London where they discussed political matters affecting Indian Muslims, no record survives of any discussions on their mutual interest in the history of Islamic societies.[15] Yet both worked in the India Office Library and the Library of the British Museum on the sources that would enable them, aided also by discussion with European scholars, to publish their responses to Muir within three years.[16] Amir 'Ali continued to write on aspects of comparative civilization until his death in 1928, but the focus here will be on his historical output prior to his permanent move to England on his retirement in 1904, thus setting his historical works within the same approximate time frame as that of Saiyid Ahmad, who died in 1898, and of Sir William Muir, who died in 1905.

The intellectual formation of the two modernist Muslim historians was considerably more complex than Muir's. Saiyid Ahmad had been educated entirely in the Islamic tradition of his *ashraf* and Sunni forebears, reading in his youth with relatives and then privately with scholars renowned in particular fields of Islamic learning. He never attended a *madrassa.* His biographer, Hali, mentioned a boyhood reluctance for study and proclivities to "unbridled excesses." He nevertheless developed an interest in mathematics and medicine in his early manhood, although there were at that time no signs of his later scholarly qualities beyond the apparent development of an "interest in reading."[17] He must have imbibed much general knowledge of Islamic history and was no doubt familiar with the innovative principles underlying Ibn Khaldun's late-fourteenth-century *Muqaddimah* or "introduction" to history and civilization, which bears a striking resemblance to the eighteenth-century European "Enlightenment" attention to factors such as climatic conditioning and the identification of materially conditioned "stages" of civilization. Saiyid Ahmad's early historical works, however, were firmly within the Indo-Persian *annales* tradi-

15. Amir 'Ali's "Memoirs" refer to "frequent opportunities" for discussing political matters with Saiyid Ahmad, but not to religious and cultural questions. See "Memoirs of the Late Rt. Hon'ble Syed Ameer Ali," *Islamic Culture* [hereafter *IC*] 5.4 (October 1931): 540.

16. Among other Orientalists, both met the renowned French scholar Joseph Garcin de Tassy in Paris and a German Talmud scholar Emmanuel Deutsch, who worked in the British Museum's oriental collection.

17. Altaf Husain Hali, *Hayat-i-Javed,* translated by David J. Mathews (New Delhi, 1994), pp. 33-42.

tion. They consisted mainly of dynastic tables or topographical *aides-memoires* and new editions of Persian chronicles.[18] Government service in the Delhi/Agra region in the 1840s brought him into close contact with some European amateur historians, including William Muir and Aloys Sprenger, Principal of the Delhi College, and also occasioned some commissions to compile local histories for government purposes. The most well known of these was his survey of the buildings and people of the city of Delhi, the *Asar al-Sanadid (Traces of the Past)*. The two editions of this, separated by some five years, testify, as Christian Troll has shown, to the growing influence of Western principles of historical inquiry upon him.[19] The establishment of a Scientific Society was but one facet of a more comprehensive scheme to take advantage of some lessons from European success and to prepare Indian Muslims for future emulation of some "progressive" aspects of European civilization. One function of the Society would be the translation into Urdu of European historical works, some on India, but mainly on the "ancient world, " as perceived in the so-called "universal histories" of the European Enlightenment era.

Preoccupied as he was from the late 1860s with both the present and the future of Indian Muslims, and with theological and educational concerns, Saiyid Ahmad did not write extensive original works on the Islamic past. His stance will be drawn mainly from two of the essays that he wrote in London in direct reply to Muir entitled, "On the Manners and Customs of the Pre-Islamic Arabians," and "On the Question Whether Islam Has Been Beneficial or Injurious to Human Society in General and to the Mosaic and Christian Dispensations."[20] Additional relevant material can also be found in a number of his articles in an Urdu journal that he established on his return to India

18. *Jam-i jam (The Cup of Jamshed)*, Persian (1840), a list of Muslim rulers from Timur to Bahahdur Shah; *Silsilat al-muluk* (1852), a list of "rulers" from the Pandavas to Victoria.

19. Christian W. Troll, "A Note on an Early Topographical Work of Sayyid Ahmad Khan: *Asar al-Sanadid*," *Journal of the Royal Asiatic Society* 2 (1972): 135-46. Troll finds that by the early 1850s Saiyid Ahmad was considerably influenced not only in "his working methods as a historian but also [in] his thought and attitude more generally" by a new intellectual and cultural milieu in Delhi, and more particularly by the "kind of historical and archaeological writing published by the Asiatic Society of Bengal and the Archaeological Society of Delhi."

20. Cited here from a reprint of the first English edition, *A Series of Essays on the Life of Muhammad and Subjects Subsidiary Thereto* (Lahore, 1968). On his return to India, Saiyid Ahmad did not complete the sequel to this volume that he had intended. The original Urdu text was not published in India until 1887: "Al-khutubat al-Ahmadiyah fi al-'Arab wa al-sirah al-Muhammadiyah," in *Tusanif-i Ahmadiyah*, vol. 1, part 2 (Aligarh, 1887).

from London, the *Tahzib al-akhlaq* (subtitled *The Mohammadan Social Reformer*). Some of the articles were republished after his death in an edited series of his works, under the title *Maqalat-i Sir Saiyid.*[21] More generally, his works on a wide range of theological and social issues were suffused with his perceptions of the Islamic past, indications of which sometimes surfaced more explicitly, for example, in a lecture to the Muhammadan Literary Society in Calcutta in 1863, and a month before his death in 1898, in an unfinished article, to which the title "Islami sultanat ka zawal" ("Decline of the Islamic Sultanate") was later given by his editor.[22]

Amir 'Ali, in contrast to Saiyid Ahmad, had followed a Western school and university curriculum — based on then current British ideas about higher education — and thereby satisfied the growing ambitions of some Bengali *ashraf* families to prepare their sons for British service. The Calcutta University history syllabus initially reflected the same emphasis on the Egyptians, Greeks, and Romans as has been noted in the Scottish universities at the beginning of the century.[23] In contrast to the Arts courses in Britain, however, which by this time (the 1860s) were beginning to teach the "civil" history of Britain, Indian students followed a parallel course in Indian history using set texts that included J. C. Marshman's *Brief Survey of History* and Mountstuart Elphinstone's *History of India.*[24] Although a course on "the principles of historic evidence" at the B.A. level suggests a more critical approach to the past than was current in British universities, the examination papers indicate that attention was concentrated on military and political issues, on the roles of individual rulers, and on the rise and fall of dynasties and empires.[25] Amir 'Ali

21. Maulana Muhammad Isma'il Panipati, ed., *Maqalat-i Sir Saiyid,* 16 vols. (Lahore, 1962-65).

22. Lecture read in Persian at the house of 'Abd al-Latif Khan, 6 October 1863, republished in *Mukammal majmu'ah lectures wa speeches* (Lahore, 1900), pp. 8-14; "Islami sultanat ka zawal," in *Tarikhi muzamin,* vol. 6 of *Maqalat* (Lahore, 1963), pp. 159-65.

23. The syllabus he followed, the set texts he read, the names of his teachers and examiners from 1862, when he took the entrance exam as a thirteen-year-old until his B.A. in 1867, his success in honors in 1868, and his M.A. and law qualifications prior to his winning a scholarship to study in London in 1869 can be traced from the Calcutta University calendars.

24. J. C. Marshman's *History of India from Remote Antiquity to the Accession of the Mogul Dynasty,* 3rd ed. (Serampore, 1842) was described as "for the use of schools." Marshman drew eclectically on William Jones, William Robertson, Edward Gibbon, and James Mill. See also Mountstuart Elphinstone, *History of India,* 5th ed. with notes and additions by E. B. Cowell (London, 1866). The first edition was published in 1839.

25. *The Calcutta University Calendar* (Calcutta, 1862-68); Amir 'Ali, "Memoirs," pp. 523-29.

graduated with "honors" in history from Calcutta University with much stronger credentials to be considered a trained historian than had Muir from his Scottish university thirty years earlier. Like Muir, he was a voracious reader from his early boyhood, recording in his memoirs that he had read most of Gibbon's *Decline and Fall* by the time he was twelve.[26]

The depth of Amir 'Ali's immersion in traditional Islamic scholarship is less easy to assess. A recent biographer has questioned his skills in the Arabic and Islamic sciences, pointing to the "largely superficial veneer of learning in his writings."[27] Yet his own memoirs stress the private teaching he had received from some prominent Bengali scholars, notably from Maulana Karamat 'Ali Jaunpuri. He was considered proficient enough to be asked to collaborate, at age nineteen, in the translation into English of Jaunpuri's scientific work, the *Makhaz-i ulum (Origins of the Sciences),* which included chapters on the transmission of knowledge from the Greeks to the Arabs, and from the Arabs to the Europeans.[28] The demands of his subsequent career, however, concentrated his attention on the legal aspects of the Islamic corpus, and it seems fair to suggest that he lacked the wide-ranging Islamic erudition of many scholars of the previous generation, including his modernist colleague, Saiyid Ahmad.

The evolution of Amir 'Ali's subsequent views on Islamic culture, civilization, and society can be drawn much more directly than can Saiyid Ahmad's from a series of overtly historical works, notably from *A Critical Examination of the Life and Character of Mohammad,* published in 1873, and his *A Short History of the Saracens,* first published in 1899.[29] Although his views on Islamic culture in the Indian context were less systematically expounded than his ideas on the Islamic heartlands, two hitherto neglected articles on the Ghaznavid, Sultanate, and Mughal eras of Indian history, written at the turn of the twentieth century but only published shortly before his death, allow some reconstruction of his views on the *longue durée* of Indo-Islamic civilization that is more instructive than anything written on Islamic culture in India by either Muir or Saiyid Ahmad.[30]

26. Amir 'Ali ("Memoirs," p. 520) commented on his boyhood reading of Gibbon: "The sixth volume in which the historian describes the rise of the Saracenic power I found especially fascinating."

27. Forward, *Failure of Islamic Modernism?* p. 69.

28. Amir 'Ali, "Memoirs," p. 528.

29. Amir 'Ali, *A Short History of the Saracens, Being a Concise Account of the Rise and Decline of the Saracenic Power and of the Economic, Social and Intellectual Development of the Arab Nation* (London, 1899).

30. See "Islamic Culture in India," *IC* 1.1 (January 1927): 450-56; "Islamic Culture

Religion in the Formation of Culture, Society, and Civilization

The interaction that resulted from the responses of these Muslim scholars to William Muir's provocative publications on Islamic history brought to the surface some hitherto unarticulated views on the role of religious traditions first in creating cultural norms and then in shaping the criteria for adjudging "civilization" during the historical periods preceding and following the first preaching of Christianity and Islam. Most Western critics of Islam, as well as most Indian Muslims who responded to them, were at one in agreeing that revealed religious precepts (the religious and moral injunctions instilled in a society by the original transmitters, and the subsequent written texts) are the main determinants of the "social virtues" and corresponding "vices" of any society.

William Muir, a particularly virulent critic of Roman Catholicism, held that Protestant Christianity was the single determinant of desirable cultural and "social virtues." He directed strong criticism against those social norms that he thought Muhammad's religious teaching had produced. His critique hinged on the notion that adherence to *taqlid,* the doctrines early established in the Muslim schools of law, rendered change impossible in all societies that had subsequently adopted Islam. His historical writings are suffused with references to the "static" and "stationary" character of Muslim societies that he deemed incapable of self-generated change. In his view, and that of many contemporary Christian commentators, "Islamic modernism," as later advocated by Saiyid Ahmad and Amir ʿAli, was a contradiction in terms.

Muir's critique, which included all aspects of Islamic society, centered on two main social consequences. The first, and frequently repeated, was the status of women and slaves in Muslim societies: "Polygamy, Divorce, and Slavery, are maintained and perpetuated; — striking as they do at the root of public morals, poisoning domestic life, and disorganizing society." Second, "freedom of judgment in religion is crushed and annihilated. The sword is the inevitable penalty for the denial of Islam. Toleration is unknown."[31] This reformulation, in dogmatic terms, of a critique that had been explicit in much Western writing on Islam for centuries has since exercised tremendous influence on the perpetuation of stereotypes about Islam. In spite of the subsequent efforts of Thomas Arnold and others to stress other modes of conversion to Islam, this view has remained the "popular" British one throughout

---

under the Moguls," *IC* 1.3 (July 1927): 457-84. References to Shibli and Hali in these texts prove he wrote these articles before 1914, the year both scholars died.

31. William Muir, *Life of Mahomet* (London, 1861), 4:321.

the twentieth century. It was stated most openly and simplistically in the homiletic works Muir wrote for a committed Christian readership during his retirement,[32] but it also underpinned all his more scholarly histories. He was unrivaled among British scholars of his generation in his Arabic learning, and he had long personal experience with Indian Muslim *ashraf* circles and a perhaps surprising degree of empathy with selective aspects of Islamic culture, particularly with the Arabic language and poetry. Yet his scholarly concern with the "heartlands of Islam" rather than their peripheries, and within them with ruling dynasties and elites rather than with the masses, with Sunni "orthodoxy" rather than with Shi'ism and Sufism, and, above all, with textual authority rather than with custom resulted in a neglect of nontextual influences in the formation of cultures. Some personal idiosyncrasies, notably insensitivity to the visual arts and to science, seem to have reinforced his narrowness of vision. For Muir "culture" was religiously determined, and true "civilization" was the monopoly of post-Reformation Christian Europe. The Enlightenment's identification of socially conditioned "stages" of civilization meant little to him: historical eras were mainly the sum of dynastic politics and military endeavors.

In reply, Saiyid Ahmad and Amir 'Ali, both advocates of just such "Islamic Modernism" as Muir deemed impossible, proceeded to set Islamic society (at various historical junctures that they considered to have been turning points) against pre-Islamic society and also against Vedic, Judaic, and particularly "Christian" society in order to emphasize some positive and morally estimable aspects of Islamic culture. These aspects were not only improvements on all earlier cultures but were themselves capable of further progress, thus heralding, in particular, the very "modernization" of Indian Muslim society that Muir and other British observers of mid-nineteenth-century Islamic societies deemed to be "impossible."[33] Some general characteristics of their handling of their subject should be stressed. First, the terms *tahzib* and *tamaddun* were frequently used interchangeably in Urdu for both "culture" and "civilization." Saiyid Ahmad, for example, used *tahzib* and "civilization" synonymously, whereas the poet Hali's use of *tamaddun* has been translated as "civilization."[34] Without suggesting that European writers were necessarily consistent in their use of any of these terms, the interchangeability of the Urdu terms

32. Notably, *The Rise and Decline of Islam* (London, 1884).

33. For example, Amir 'Ali, "The Modernity of Islam," *IC* 1.1 (January 1927): 1-5.

34. See, e.g., Saiyid Ahmad's article, "Tahzib aur us ki tarikh," in which he used the English term "civilization" synonymously with *tahzib*. For Hali's use of *tamaddun*, see Christopher Shackle and Javed Majeed, trans., *Hali's Musaddas: The Flow and Ebb of Islam* (Delhi, 1997), pp. 120-21, 227.

sometimes exacerbates problems in trying to capture both intention and meaning in the English texts of Indian Muslim historians.

Second, although the context of their responses was specifically Indian, several scholars have noted that late-nineteenth-century Indian Muslim writers tended to eulogize the Arabian roots of Islam and to minimize the Indian elements in the cultural history of the Muslim community in order, as A. B. M. Habibullah has commented, to "emphasize and concentrate on those which brought that community nearer to Islam, the world power, and the dominant world civilization."[35] Peter Hardy has also expressed the interests of the pre-1920s Western-influenced Indian Muslim intelligentsia as being "more Islamic than Indian and more religious than historical."[36] This trait, noted previously mainly in respect to the eulogies of Hali and Shibli on Arab cultural achievements, was certainly also characteristic of the historical perspectives of Saiyid Ahmad and Amir ʻAli. Efforts will be made in what follows to elicit their less well publicized perceptions on, in Amir ʻAli's phrase, the more neglected "Islamic culture in India." Apart from the obvious sense in which the roots of Indian Islam did lie in Arab soil, these writers were also influenced in their own preoccupations by Muir's emphasis on Arabia and neglect of India, and by the opportunity presented by the "high civilization" of ʻAbbasid Baghdad and Umayyad Spain to reject Muir's verdict on the inherently static character of Islamic culture.

Third, their responses are remarkable for the extent and nature of their dependence on a genre of Western writing that was sympathetic to, and sometimes supportive of, Islam's theological and cultural claims. While more conservative *ʻulama* tended to draw on European biblical criticism merely to refute missionary claims for the Bible, the modernists also trawled from a wide range of not always consistent Western publications on Islamic history and biography to support both their defense of Islamic norms and their counterclaims of shortcomings in medieval and contemporary Christian Europe. Apart from the influence of Gibbon, from whom both Saiyid Ahmad and Amir ʻAli quoted extensively, recourse was had to sources as varied as Charles Forster's historical geography of pre-Islamic Arabia, especially his support for Muhammad's Ismaelite legacy, to Thomas Carlyle's eulogistic typology of Muhammad as "hero," and, more incongruously, to the little-known but wide-ranging defense of both Muhammad's

35. A. B. M. Habibullah, "Historical Writing in Urdu: A Survey of Tendencies," in *Historians of India, Pakistan and Ceylon*, edited by C. H. Philips (London, 1961), p. 485.

36. Peter Hardy, "Modern Muslim Historical Writing on Medieval Muslim India," in *Historians of India, Pakistan and Ceylon*, edited by C. H. Philips (London, 1961), p. 296.

character and the "virtues" of Islamic as compared to "Christian" society by John Davenport.[37]

Stages of Islamic Society

In order to draw out the comparative aspects of their interaction, four "stages" of history that attracted particularly contested claims concerning comparative levels of culture and civilization will be considered here. These are pre-Islamic Arabia (the *jahiliyya,* or "age of ignorance," of many Muslim writers); the city-state established by Muhammad at Medina after the *hijrat;* the Arab caliphates under the Umayyads and the 'Abbasids; and, last, their hitherto neglected views on the cultural impact of Muslim rule on northern India under the Delhi sultans and the Mughals.

Pre-Islamic Arabia

The state of culture and society immediately prior to the preaching of Islam was the starting point for both the critics and the apologists. Both showed considerable ambivalence, although for different reasons. Muir evinced evangelical horror of idolatrous practices but indulged in romantic eulogy of desert "simplicity." He was also affected by the ambivalence within Western scholarship on the role and failure of Christian influence in the Arabian peninsula. While some modernists were at pains to reject earlier simplistic condemnations of an alleged *jahiliyya,* or "age of ignorance," in order to show a progress that would admit some "virtues," even in the pre-Islamic era, they too faced some difficulties in evaluating specific customs and practices. They shared with their critic a reliance on some recent contributions to the "histor-

37. "The gentlemen . . . for whose talents I shall ever cherish high esteem and respect, are Edward Gibbon, the celebrated historian, Godfrey Higgins, Thomas Carlyle and John Davenport" (preface to Syed Ahmed Khan Bahador, C.S.I, *A Series of Essays on the Life of Muhammad,* [Lahore, 1968 (reprint)], p. xiii). The works he cited frequently were: Rev. Charles Forster, *Historical Geography of Arabia or, the Patriarchal Evidences of Revealed Religion* (London, 1844); Rev. Charles Forster, *Mahometanism Unveiled: An Inquiry in Which That Arch-Heresy, Its Diffusion and Continuance, Are Examined on a New Principle, Tending to Confirm the Evidence, and Aid the Propagation of the Christian Faith* (London, 1829); Godfrey Higgins, *Apology for Muhammad* (London, 1829); and Thomas Carlyle, *On Heroes, Hero Worship and the Heroic in History* (London, 1841). John Davenport's study of the Prophet had been translated into Urdu by 1870: *Mu 'aiyid al-Islam: An Apology for Muhammad and the Koran* (Delhi, 1870).

ical geography" of the peninsula. Both Muir and Sayyid Ahmad chose to preface their works with tribal genealogies reconstructed from scriptural and Western classical evidence, as well as from indigenous sources. The most influential contribution to this genre was the Reverend Charles Forster's recently published *Historical Geography of Arabia,* a work suspect to Muir but attractive to Muslims because of its acceptance of the descent of Muhammad from Ishmael, yet drawn on by both because of Forster's unprecedented attention to genealogical detail. While both Muir and Saiyid Ahmad brought their own Arabic scholarship to bear, taking issue with Forster and others on specific points, it seems that Amir 'Ali, who was less initiated into original sources, was content to rely on European Orientalist conclusions on this period, including those of Muir and the Austrian Arabist Aloys Sprenger, with whose conclusions on later eras he would take strong issue.

Muir's ambivalence can be seen in the contrast between the dispassionate tone of his discussion of the Ka'ba practices in the introduction to the first volume of his *Life of Mahomet* and his open condemnation in subsequent publications, particularly those directed at readers of religious tracts, of the "spiritual torpor," and hence general passivity, that he felt was inculcated by idolatry. Yet it seems that from the beginning his admiration for the Arabic language, and in particular for Arabic poetry, qualified the repugnance he undoubtedly felt for other symptoms of "barbarity" and "rudeness."[38] The paradox implicit in his attitudes he resolved, to his own seeming satisfaction, with a distinction common to other Western Arabists of this period: the "free atmosphere of the desert" and its bedouin nomads he romanticized and idealized, in contrast to the "trammels and conventionalities of settled society."[39] Although he showed little sign of being drawn to the English and French romantic poets of his own youth, Muir essentialized the early Arab poet as "the child of nature" whose "poetical remains" provided "stepping-stones for the historian along the quicksands of oral evidence." The British should, he felt, be particularly interested, as rulers themselves, in the Arabic poetry that had formed "so powerful an element in moulding the character of the Moslem conquerors and rulers of the East."[40] While tribes rose and fell and commerce was energetically pursued at particular junctures, nomad life remained static and unchanging, "untainted by the most distant approach of the busy world," a virtue rather than a vice at this stage of history.[41] There are obvious contra-

38. See William Muir, "Ancient Arabic Poetry: Its Genuineness and Authenticity," *Journal of the Royal Asiatic Society* n.s. 11 (1879): 72-92.

39. Muir, "Ancient Arabic Poetry," p. 72.

40. Muir, "Ancient Arabic Poetry," pp. 79-91.

41. Muir, "Ancient Arabic Poetry," p. 74.

dictions in such a polarized representation of the city and the desert. Muir would later modify his positive admiration of a static and unchanging pastoral section of society into a general condemnation of a religion that would become, in itself, the cause of stagnation in all Islamic societies, whether urban or rural.

Saiyid Ahmad's initial response to Muir was contained in three of the twelve essays he published in London in 1870.[42] The first, a long essay on the "Historical Geography of Arabia," is very scholarly and, in spite of owing much to Charles Forster's work of a similar title, demonstrates Saiyid Ahmad's own command of the varied sources he drew on in building up the tribal genealogies of the peninsula. The second, on the "Manners and Customs of the Pre-Islamic Arabians," a choice of title redolent of much European writing on non-European societies during the Enlightenment, he modestly referred to as a "cursory sketch."[43] It is indeed little more than a superficial balance sheet of social "virtues" and "vices" loosely strung together by lavish quotations from pre-Islamic Arab poetry. The third, on the "Various Religions of the pre-Islamic Arabs," falls between the first two in that it consists of a brief survey, but with little reference to sources, of the main forms of religious practice in the peninsula, ranging through "idolatry," "atheism," and "deism" to the "revealed religions," in which he included Sabeanism, "the religion of Abraham," Judaism, and Christianity.

His depiction of "manners and customs," in the second essay, shared much ground with Muir's typology, particularly in the representation of the "plain and artless" life of the desert as being "almost entirely in accordance with the dictates of nature."[44] Significantly, however, he differed from Muir in attributing similar "national characters" to "settled or mercantile" and to "nomadic" tribes, a point that has a bearing on the later divergence of their perceptions of urban culture in Medina and other Muslim cities. If the "virtues" of "patriarchal simplicity," plainness of diet, early rising, and cleanliness probably owed their precise phrasing to the British "friend" who revised and corrected the manuscript, Sayyid Ahmad's emphasis on eloquence and poetic inspiration moved beyond Muir's evocations of uncorrupted "nature" in its derivation from essentially Islamic understandings concerning the particular readiness of the Arabs to be the transmitters of God's final revelation. Among the "vices" prevalent in pre-Islamic Arabia, which would subsequently be

42. Saiyid Ahmad, *Series of Essays on the Life of Muhammad: Essays 1-3* (London, 1870).

43. Saiyid Ahmad, "Manners and Customs of the Pre-Islamic Arabians," in *Series of Essays on the Life of Muhammad: Essays 1-3* (London, 1870), p. 123.

44. Ahmad, "Manners and Customs of the Pre-Islamic Arabians," p. 106.

condemned in Islam, he listed adultery, fornication, incest, drinking, gambling, usury, and robbery. Emphasis will be limited here, however, to his responses to those characteristics of Arab society that had been singled out by Muir for particular criticism.

Evangelicals, Muir included, equated idolatrous practices with a "barbarity" from which only Christianity could bring relief. In contrast, Saiyid Ahmad explained idolatry naturalistically and without any attempt at either "accusation" or "apology" as an early stage in the emergence in the peninsula of a number of different religious ideologies. Concerned as he was to show Islam as having then relieved Arabia of "her insufferable load" and the "heavy incubus" of discordant religious forces by drawing together in a "perfect combination" the partial truths of Sabeanism, Abrahamism, and Judaism, he saw no need to berate "half-savage and ignorant" people for following their natural instincts to worship idols, which then became "a general practice among the Arabs."[45]

Saiyid Ahmad did not linger long on the question of women's status, a constant theme of all Muir's publications on Islam. His own reticence is not surprising considering his conservative stance on the position of women in the context of much of his otherwise reformist writings on issues significant to Indian Muslims under British rule. In his historical writings he merely drew a firm line between strong approbation of *parda* and qualified support, which fell far short of Amir 'Ali's, for some progressive modifications in the customary position of women. Thus while conceding that "the fair sex was in a very wretched and degraded condition" in pre-Islamic Arabia because of the prevalence of customs of polygamy, divorce, and female infanticide, he expressed horror at the freedom of early Arab women to mix "publicly unveiled," for, he fulminated, they considered it "neither indecent nor immoral to expose any part whatsoever of their person to the public gaze."[46] Yet earlier in the same essay he had depicted women as assisting their menfolk on the battlefield in times of crisis, a selective but virtuous activism that he did not find in any way anomalous. Overall, his final balance sheet of virtues and vices represented the "domestic, social, and public life of the semi-savage but high-minded and open-hearted inhabitants of the great Arabian Peninsula" almost as ambivalently as had William Muir's.[47]

Amir 'Ali shared none of the reasons attributed to Muir and Saiyid

45. Saiyid Ahmad, "Various Religions of the Pre-Islamic Arabs," in *Series of Essays on the Life of Muhammad: Essays 1-3* (London, 1870), pp. 124-40; Ahmad, "Manners and Customs," p. 116.

46. Ahmad, "Manners and Customs," pp. 120-22.

47. Ahmad, "Manners and Customs," p. 123.

Ahmad for treating pre-Islamic Arab society ambivalently. Prepared, as he certainly was, to emphasize social shortcomings even in fully fledged Islamic society, he was forthright where he felt criticism of the early Arabs was called for, but he stressed at the same time the moral and social shortcomings of other, and particularly European, societies. Significantly, he deigned to quote Muir, with whom he would disagree strongly on other matters, to the effect that the "tide of indigenous idolatry and of Ishmaelite superstition . . . gave ample evidence that the faith and worship of Mecca held the Arab mind in a thraldom, rigorous and undisputed."[48] The populist rather than scholarly tone of his critique was shown in an offhand representation of idolatrous Mecca as "a sort of Rome or Benares" and of pre-Islamic Arabia as sharing with Vedic India in the "gross materialism" of an age of degradation, in short, of "a nation steeped in barbarism."[49] More provocative, at least in its implications for Muslim readers, was his seeming agreement with, and adoption of, Aloys Sprenger's controversial view, upsetting to many Muslim scholars and rejected also by Muir, that Islam was "in the air" before Muhammad actually began to preach.[50] In his case unequivocal condemnation of Arab idolatry was merely a prologue to an exposition of the dramatic social progress of society and civilization under Islam that would raise the Arabs and others "from the depth of social and moral degradation into which they had fallen," and that would carry with it the potential for further modernization and progress both in late-nineteenth-century India and elsewhere in the future.[51]

City of God: Medina as the Model of Civilization

In the late nineteenth century many Indian Muslim writers evoked the city of Medina as the model of a religiously rooted, "rightly guided" society to which all subsequent Islamic states should look for inspiration and emulation. Significant to the conflation of urbanity and virtuosity is the derivation of the Urdu word *tamaddun,* "civilization," from the Arabic *medina,* a city.[52] Yet William Muir, who had acknowledged the Meccan phase of Muhammad's mission as a genuine religious quest, castigated the "gross and earthly spirit"

48. Amir 'Ali, *Critical Examination,* pp. 19-20; cited in Muir, *Life of Mahomet,* 1:ccxxxix.

49. 'Ali, *A Short History of the Saracens,* p. 4; *Critical Examination,* pp. 3, 18, 147.

50. "Islam existed before Mohammed; just in the way, I should say, as Christianity existed before Jesus" ('Ali, *Critical Examination,* p. 18, n. 1).

51. 'Ali, *Critical Examination,* p. 25.

52. See n. 34 above for discussion of *tamaddun.*

that he considered had emerged during Muhammad's successful years in the city of Medina. In his view, the successful establishment of the city-state represented the loss of those desert virtues he associated with pre-Islamic Arabia. In response the modernists tried to show the ways in which the Prophet's city-state had marked epoch-making progression not only over pre-Islamic Arabia but also over Judaic and Christian societies, particularly over Christendom during the "dark ages."

Muir did not deny that the Medinan state marked an improvement in some significant respects over pre-Islamic Arabia. His balance sheet of "social virtues" and vices listed a new degree of "brotherly love," the protection of orphans, the prohibition of alcohol, and the treatment of slaves "with consideration."[53] In spite of such concessions, however, his repeated condemnations of other cultural, religious, and social "evils" meant he came down very firmly on the other side, justifying the charge that change is impossible from within Islamic society. The two main foci of condemnation were the status of women and coercion in both physical and intellectual contexts, a new accusation that appeared in place of the emphasis on idolatry in pre-Islamic Arabia. Muir blamed first Muhammad's "worldly" ambition once he had established himself in Medina, which led him to use force to extend his power beyond the city, and, second, a weakness for women, which resulted in the moral degradation he felt was implicit in the Qur'anic stipulations concerning marriage and divorce. He thus reinforced, with little change of tone, charges that had reflected European fears of Islam since medieval times.[54] In his view a married woman in Islam could be no more than "a dependent inferior creature," who, "restrained, secluded, degraded," became "the mere minister of enjoyment" for her husband.[55] The seclusion of women reinforced the emphasis on *taqlid* in matters of belief to produce a society that contained no mechanisms for allowing change from within. From this followed Muir's characterization of Islamic society under the Arabs as inescapably static, and hence semi-barbaric, throughout all subsequent history.

Saiyid Ahmad's counterview of Medinan and early Islamic society was set out in his essay, "Whether Islam Has Been Beneficial or Injurious to Human Society in General and to the Mosaic and Christian Dispensations." After quoting with approbation Muir's acknowledgment of some religious and social virtues in Islam, he countered that, far from slaves being merely "treated

53. Muir, *Life of Mahomet,* 4:320.

54. R. W. Southern, *Western Views of Islam in the Middle Ages,* 2nd ed. (Cambridge, Mass.: Harvard, 1978); Norman Daniel, *The Arabs and Medieval Europe* (London and New York, 1975).

55. Muir, *Life of Mahomet,* 3:304-5.

with consideration" as Muir had conceded, "Mohammad did almost entirely abolish slavery," for "in no case is it allowed, except in that of war captives, and that also with the benevolent intention of saving their lives."[56] Both protagonists were somewhat disingenuous on this contentious issue: clearly slavery in successive Muslim societies extended beyond the category of war captives. For his part, Muir made slavery one of the main burdens of his critique of Islamic society, yet he belonged to a merchant family in Glasgow whose business interests had benefited from the late trans-Atlantic slave trade.

Other additions by Saiyid Ahmad to Muir's list of the "social virtues" inculcated in Medina included Muhammad's prohibition of gambling and the use of "indecent words and expressions," the encouragement of loving family relationships, kind treatment of animals, and a system of almsgiving. In demonstrating these "virtues" he quoted at length from a number of Western apologists for Islam, notably Thomas Carlyle and John Davenport, and also from Edward Gibbon whose ambivalence toward some aspects of both religions was transmuted here into a eulogy of Islam at Christianity's expense.[57] Citation of Carlyle's view of the rise of Islam "as a birth from darkness into light for the Arab nation" thus reversed entirely the thrust of Muir's frequently employed "darkness and light" analogy to represent the early years of Islam not as the "dark age" of Arab civilization but as its awakening.[58] For Saiyid Ahmad, as for Shibli and Hali, Medina thus provided the turning point and the model for future emulation, although he would also draw lessons for the Indian present from other non-Islamic civilizations.

Amir 'Ali held a progressive view of social change, according to which institutions in all societies undergo modification to suit changing circumstances. Thus his representation of the state of Medina, during what he called the "republican" phase of caliphal rule under Muhammad's four successors, avoided the eulogies of many of his Muslim contemporaries. The consolidation of Medina and the spread of Islam "under the influence of one great Idea" was, nevertheless, in his view "one of the most wonderful achievements recorded in history."[59] He showed no reluctance, however, to acknowledge that, like the Nile floods that fertilize the soil but bring devastation in the

56. Saiyid Ahmad, "Whether Islam Has Been Beneficial or Injurious to Human Society in General and to the Mosaic and Christian Dispensations," in *Series of Essays*, pp. 158-62. For a later discussion by Saiyid Ahmad on slavery see *Ibtal-i ghulami* (Agra, 1893).

57. Saiyid Ahmad concluded the preface to his *Series of Essays on the Life of Muhammad* with long quotations from all three British authors' arguments against the popular European perception of Muhammad as a "mere imposter" (pp. xiii-xv).

58. Ahmad, "Whether Islam Has Been Beneficial," p. 146.

59. 'Ali, *A Short History of the Saracens*, p. 55.

short term, many people had suffered during the early struggles to assert the claims of Islam. He supported the generally "progressive" nature of Muhammad's legislation, compared, in particular, with both early Christian and with contemporary attitudes to practices such as slavery. He praised the "free" and public circulation of women in a society that had not yet adopted seclusion, and arts such as singing and flute playing at a time when "music had not been yet placed under the ban."[60] He also made distinctions between the early "republican" caliphs, praising 'Umar but criticizing 'Uthman, and praising the austerity and piety of the Medinites in comparison with the alleged frivolity of the Meccans, whose levities he considered to be "reproduced in a worse form at Damascus under the Ommeyades."[61] In spite of such apparent independence of judgment, some of his comments on political ideology and on domestic protocol seem to be those of an apologist who was eager to achieve a receptive hearing among a late-nineteenth-century English readership rather than make the discoveries of a serious Arabist.

Imperial Zenith: Umayyads and 'Abbasids in the Balance of Civilization

After completing his *Life of Mahomet,* Muir spent much of his leisure time in the next thirty years researching and writing the history of the Arab caliphates up to the Mongol victory of 1258. Through these histories, in which his concern was limited to political, military, and administrative issues, his convictions on the religious determinants of culture and civilization were tested, and all Islamic societies deemed to be "stationary." For most Muslim historians, in contrast, the cultural achievements of Damascus, Moorish Spain, and particularly 'Abbasid Baghdad were held up as exemplars of high civilization at a time when, it was frequently pointed out, European culture was at its lowest ebb.

Insofar as Muir admitted a preference for the Umayyad caliphate over the 'Abbasid, the judgment reflected his admiration for qualities such as simplicity, manliness, frugality, and hardiness, which he associated with the desert Arabs and which had underpinned his sympathetic portrayal of pre-Islamic Arabia, and of the Prophet himself before his alleged seduction by worldly ambition at Medina. In contrast, he associated the rise of the 'Abbasids with the dilution of Arab qualities by some negative characteristics he associated with Turkish and Persian adventurism, which led inexorably to enervation

60. "Social Life" at Medina, in 'Ali, *A Short History of the Saracens,* pp. 65-69.
61. 'Ali, *A Short History of the Saracens,* p. 67.

and demoralization. The cursoriness of his own treatment of the cultural achievements of Baghdad partly reflected the narrowly political bent of all his historical writings, and particularly of his *Caliphate,* but also showed a preconceived certainty that Europe held the monopoly on cultural achievement, conditioned, as he believed it to be, solely by Christian religious values.

Saiyid Ahmad, who valued the transmission of cultural influences and ideas between societies, was not inclined to make categorical judgments, whether in praise or criticism, on entire regimes and cultures. Like Ibn Khaldun he compared the rise and fall of civilizations to a human life cycle: from childhood, through youth to maturity, and subsequently to inevitable death. An organic, naturalistic explanation of this kind had little place for condemnation of the shortcomings of individual rulers.[62] In keeping with his characteristic wish to find meeting points rather than to emphasize religious and cultural differences, he traced a diffusionist line from Greece, 'Abbasid Baghdad, and caliphal Spain to the Europe of the Renaissance era in an effort to show the transmission of philosophical and scientific knowledge from pagan, through Islamic, to Christian cultures.[63] Significantly, although Saiyid Ahmad wrote little himself on the histories of early civilizations, he was the moving force behind the commissioning of translations of European histories of Greece, Egypt, and early China into Urdu, using his privately owned press for their publication.[64]

Amir 'Ali, like Saiyid Ahmad, did not uphold the strong contrast urged by Muir between the two main caliphal dynasties and preferred instead to trace evolution and adaptation to changing circumstances throughout the whole period of "Saracenic" rule. Nevertheless there is no doubting his personal preference for the 'Abbasid period over the Umayyad. Since he was a Shi'a of Persian ancestry, his preference was partly conditioned by an opposite bias to Muir's distaste for the detrimental influence of alleged "Persian" and urban enervation. A more significant reason for his eulogy of an 'Abbasid "golden

62. Ahmad's organic theory of the rise and fall of empires is indicated in "Islami sultanat ka zawal"; for the influence on his thinking of Henry Thomas Buckle's *History of Civilization,* 2 vols. (London, 1857-61), see his own preface to an Urdu translation of part of Buckle's work, in "Tahzib aur us ki tarikh," in *Tarikhi mazamin,* vol. 6 of *Maqalat-i Sir Saiyid,* pp. 1-8.

63. Hafiz Malik briefly discusses Saiyid Ahmad's ideas of historical cultural diffusion in *Sir Sayyid Ahmad Khan,* p. 23.

64. Listed for sale with works on farming, mechanics, electricity, and political economy in the *Aligarh Institute Gazette,* February 14, 1867, were histories such as: *Misr ki qadim tarikh* (1864), translated from Charles Rollin's *Ancient History of the Egyptians: Yunan ka kadim zamana ki tarikh* (1865), translated in two parts from Charles Rollin's *Ancient History of Greece: Tarikh-i Chin,* translated from *History of China* (Calcutta, 1864).

age," however, seems to have been his recognition that the achievements of the Baghdad court in the late eighth and early ninth centuries under Caliph Harun al-Rashid, and particularly al-Ma'mun, provided a convincing retort to those Western authors who denigrated all aspects of Islamic culture in comparison with the cultural and scientific achievements of Christendom and Europe. Thus, while Muir made only brief and grudging references to al-Ma'mun's cultural innovations, preferring the "more substantial grandeur" of the Damascus court under the Umayyads to the more "lustrous" atmosphere of Baghdad, Amir 'Ali not only made 'Abbasid cultural and scientific achievements the high point of his *A Short History of the Saracens* but used both Baghdad and Saracenic Spain as exemplars of the flowering of Islamic culture in countless references in articles and lectures on other subjects. Inspired by the Prophet's own emphasis on intellectual liberty, the 'Abbasids gave "the Islamic world her period of glory," making the Muslims "the repositories of the knowledge of the world."[65] In stressing "the latitude of private judgment" in Islam at this time, Amir 'Ali was at the farthest remove possible from Muir's position on the caliphal era. In a wider sense Baghdad became the answer of late-nineteenth-century Indian Muslims to the cultural critique of the West, as the poetry of Hali and Azad also suggests. The coupling of Moorish Spain with Baghdad could be said to bring the retort closer still to the consciousness of European critics of Islamic society, providing the opportunity to project within medieval Europe itself a picture of harmonious religious relationships as well as of architectural splendor, intellectual inquiry, and cultural achievement. In the final chapter of his *Critical Examination* he reached a crescendo of acclaim for the 'Abbasids, portraying medieval Europe as "groping in the darkness of absolute ignorance and brutality" while Islam "introduced into the modern world civilisation, philosophy, the arts and the sciences."[66]

Indo-Muslim Culture and Civilization

India during its seven centuries of "Muslim" rule was of much less overt concern to all these scholars than were the Arab heartlands during the formative centuries of Islam. Preoccupied with 'Abbasid Baghdad and Moorish Spain, they passed over Arab influence in Sind and other coastal regions of India almost without comment. As noted above, such neglect was conscious, for Hali,

65. 'Ali, *Critical Examination*, pp. 295-98.
66. 'Ali, *Critical Examination*, pp. 338-45.

Zaka-Allah, and Shibli, who "exhorted Muslims to pride in their past, viewed that past as more Islamic than Indian — they were interested in Muslim civilization under the 'Abbasids or under the Ummayads in Spain rather than in the civilization of medieval Muslim India."[67]

Muir did not undertake a history of Muslim rule in India. He ended his epic histories of the caliphates with the fall of Baghdad to the Mongols in 1258, and apart from a history of Mameluke Egypt, which he acknowledged to be largely dependent on German scholarship,[68] and a short lecture on the crusades, he published nothing of substance on any other period of Islamic history. His views on Sultanate and Mughal India are, therefore, drawn here mainly from remarks made in his administrative correspondence and, indirectly, from his support or criticism of the views of other historians of India, both British and Indian.[69]

At no point did Muir provide a full analysis of the ways in which the Indian environment and earlier cultural influences had influenced the impact of Islam. He held instead to the categories of forceful conversion, slavery, and the seclusion of women that had predetermined cultural consequences for him whatever the nature of the society on which they operated. There were differences only of degree. He thus adjudged the seclusion of women to be more complete in India, where it was adopted also by the conquered but unconverted "pagans," and he found the "evils" deriving from such a widespread practice of *parda* to be more extreme in India than in Arabia.[70]

Unappreciative of the flowering of civilization in Baghdad, Muir almost entirely passed over Akbar's era of cultural splendor even though he spent much of his early service career in Agra, surrounded by evidence of the "golden age" of Mughal cultural achievement. The Muir Central College, which marked his personal support for Muslim educational interests during his Lieutenant Governorship, he chose to construct in Indo-Saracenic style, but as much to encourage Muslim enrollment as to reflect any personal aesthetic enthusiasm for the Islamic cultural past. His anxiety to identify and preserve Persian chronicles and Arabic manuscripts of the traditions of the

67. Hardy, "Modern Muslim Historical Writing," pp. 295-96.

68. William Muir, *The Mameluke* (London, 1896), pp. ix-xii.

69. Muir was a professed admirer of H. G. Keene — author of *The Fall of the Moghul Empire: An Historical Essay* (London, 1876); *The Turks in India* (London, 1879); "Islam in India," *Calcutta Review* 71(142) (1880): 239-56; and numerous articles on Indo-Muslim civilization, including "Are Islam and Civilisation Irreconcilable?" *Calcutta Review* 84 (168) (1887): 243-56 — though Keene did not return the compliment.

70. Saiyid Ahmad, "The Veil; or Seclusion of Women in India," *The Indian Female Evangelist* 5.34 (April 1880): 74-75.

Prophet reflected a very real attachment to these languages, particularly Arabic, but also an awareness of their usefulness as evidence for his own and others' historical studies.

Saiyid Ahmad, as seen above, did make some very important contributions to the transmission of knowledge concerning the Indo-Muslim past by editing, under British patronage, some new Persian editions of important medieval chronicles (notably the fourteenth-century *Tarikh-i Firuz Shahi* and Abu'l Fazl's late-sixteenth-century *A'in-i Akbari*). He was also commissioned to research the history of the district of Bijnor in which he was serving at the time. The historical work that bears his own mark much more strongly is the *Asar al-sanadid*, a guide to the buildings and *literati* of Delhi. None of these European-influenced publications, however, concerned as they were mainly with buildings, dynasts, and the historical basis of land claims, allows a full appreciation of Saiyid Ahmad's understanding of the relative cultural value of the various Indo-Muslim regimes, their elites, and the results of cultural patronage. Nor is much to be drawn from his various articles in Urdu and Persian on historical themes, few of which focus on Indian, rather than on Arab, culture and civilization.[71] In spite of his intervention in some controversies over the writing of history textbooks for schools, Saiyid Ahmad, like William Muir, left no integrated and comprehensive account of his own understanding of the Indo-Muslim past.[72]

Of these three scholars, Amir 'Ali provided the most direct and detailed comments on Indo-Muslim culture even though his best-known historical works also neglected India.[73] The French Orientalist Garcin de Tassy suggested that as early as 1873 Amir 'Ali was planning to write on the Mughals, but nothing materialized for about another thirty years.[74] Even then his output was limited to two articles on the Ghaznavid, Sultanate, and Mughal eras in a survey of "Islamic culture in India," which lacks both literary merit and historical acumen. Yet these articles, rare ventures for Indian Muslims of his period, provide a useful source for reconstructing some of Amir 'Ali's views

71. See "Tahzib aur us ki tarikh"; "Islami sultanat ka zawal."

72. For an example of Saiyid Ahmad's criticism of the writing of some other Indian and British authors on Indian history, see "Strictures upon the Present Educational System in India," reprinted in *The Aligarh Movement, Basic Documents: 1864-1898*, edited by Shan Muhammad (Meerut, 1978), 1:193-94.

73. Muhammad bin Qasim's invasion of Sind was dismissed in five lines without any discussion of the cultural effects ('Ali, *A Short History of the Saracens*, p. 104).

74. Garcin de Tassy, "Ce musulman distingué . . . a aussi l'intention de publier un ouvrage sur l'empire mogol," in *La langue et la littérature hindoustanies en 1873: revue annuelle* (Paris, 1874), p. 58.

on the Indian Muslim cultural past. A third lecture on Persian culture, subsequently published, supplements the portrayal.[75]

Omitting any reference either to the Arabs in Sind or to any of the regional sultanates, Amir 'Ali appraised in some detail the record of the Ghaznavid and Delhi Sultans in northwest India. In spite of intermittent bloodletting, and the "tyrannous" if not actually "half mad" acts of cruelty perpetrated by Muhammad bin Tughluq, he found evidence of considerable patronage to learning in the Ghaznavid and Tughluq periods. Even Muhammad bin Tughluq found favor with him as an "accomplished scholar devoted to learning and arts."[76] The reign of Firuz Shah Tughluq, who was rather quaintly depicted as "the most lovable personality in Mediaeval India," marked in Amir 'Ali's view a high peak in state patronage of Sanskrit as well as Islamic studies, facilitating urban growth, including mosques, colleges, hospitals, gardens, and canals, and schemes directed at relieving unemployment and "redressing the wrongs of the oppressed." Clearly, the Delhi Sultans, though overshadowed by the achievements of the Baghdad 'Abbasids, were responsible in his eyes for some considerable if rather intermittent cultural energy, which in some rulers' hands was inclusive also of non-Muslim achievements.[77]

"A new epoch in the history of Islamic culture," the results of which were, by implication, comparable to the highest of Arab achievements, was initiated, in Amir 'Ali's view, by the Mughal accession.[78] His identification of the role of Persian as an increasingly significant factor in the creation of "Islamic culture in India" probably reflected a very personal perception of this phase of the past, at a time when many other Indian Muslims were encouraging a "shift away from the Persianate strands of Indian Islam, towards an Arab legacy increasingly defined as central."[79] This theme he later pursued in more depth in a lecture on "Persian Culture" given to a no doubt very sympathetic audience at the Persia Society of London.

In eulogizing, in particular, the reign of Emperor Akbar, the consolidator of Persian influence, for his patronage to learning and his humanitarianism,

75. Amir 'Ali, "Islamic Culture in India," *IC* 1.3 (July 1927): 331-56; "Islamic Culture under the Moguls," *IC* 1.4 (October 1927): 499-521; "Persian Culture," a lecture delivered before members of the Persia Society, 20 June 1913.

76. 'Ali, "Islamic Culture in India," pp. 349-53.

77. 'Ali, "Islamic Culture in India," p. 353.

78. 'Ali, "Islamic Culture under the Moguls," p. 499.

79. Shackle and Majeed, *Hali's Musaddas,* p. 5; "Islamic Culture under the Moguls," p. 503. Amir 'Ali's family had settled in India, from Persia, in the wake of Nadir Shah's invasion.

Amir 'Ali was following in already well-worn tracks, probably marked out for him by the history textbooks he had read during his college years.[80] His personal sympathy for Akbar's theological liberalism was certainly displayed very transparently, concomitantly with a hostility to those conservative clerics of Akbar's reign whom, "as in Europe," he portrayed as "the persecuting enemies of non-conformity."[81] He also drew from a very recently published Urdu biography of Akbar by the Punjabi scholar, Muhammad Husain Azad. It seems that in the late nineteenth century Amir 'Ali was not alone among Muslim scholars in holding up the Akbarian ethos as the appropriate solution for India's cultural and religious complexities. In contrast, although he wasted few lines on him, the verdict on Aurangzeb was clear: his reign marked "a distinct setback to Musulman culture . . . in fifty years he undid the work of a century."[82] Some later writings show that he admitted that Akbar's "eclectic culture" and religious inclusiveness had failed.[83]

Amir 'Ali's portrayal of Nur Jahan's cultural role reflects Amir 'Ali's efforts in many of his lectures and writings to justify a public place for women in Islam. Critical, like many British historians, of the apparent weakness of Akbar's successor, Jahangir, Amir 'Ali praised his wife's cultural accomplishments to an extent that exceeded the much more measured evaluations of his college textbooks.[84] In his view, "the whole culture of India . . . bears the mark of her genius"; she "introduced into India all that is still beautiful and refined in the institutions of Mahommedan civilisation in India."[85] Nevertheless his final verdict was that "Musulaman culture in India attained its zenith under Shah Jehan" in the more "sober" atmosphere of a court where, Amir 'Ali felt, the maintaining of a cultural balance between Muslims and Hindus was an important objective.

Too much emphasis should not be placed, perhaps, on what Amir 'Ali emphasized and omitted, as the entire survey is superficial compared to his

80. See J. C. Marshman's (*The History of India,* 1:122-24) portrayal of Akbar compiled for honors students at the University of Calcutta: "Akbar was not only the ornament of the Mogul dynasty but incomparably the greatest of all the Mahomedan rulers of India . . . [he] adopted the principle not only of religious toleration, but what has been found a more difficult task even in the most enlightened Christian communities, of religious *equality*."

81. 'Ali, "Islamic Culture under the Moguls," p. 505.

82. 'Ali, "Islamic Culture under the Moguls," p. 517.

83. 'Ali, "The Modernity of Islam," *IC* 1.1 (January 1927): 1.

84. Marshman (*History of India,* pp. 126-34) had praised her "fertile genius" in the military sphere but was otherwise cautious in his evaluation.

85. 'Ali, "Islamic Culture under the Moguls," pp. 512-13; 'Ali, "Persian Culture," p. 30.

better-known historical works. While he regaled his readers with long anecdotes about the importation of tobacco in Akbar's reign, he made no mention at all of the new Jesuit presence. His comments on the period from the early eighteenth century until his time of writing (ca. 1900) were particularly random and seem to reflect mostly hearsay gleaned from literary circles in north India rather than any particularly authoritative sources. He had certainly imbibed from his student reading of European textbooks a view of the eighteenth century as "chaotic," declaring that after 1712 "Indian history is a nightmare," and likening the Marathas to "the Huns of India." The Lucknow court he cast in the role of temporary assumer of the Mughal cultural mantle in the mid eighteenth century. He saw the British achievement as a degree of cultural revival in Delhi after 1803, only to be destroyed by Bentinck's unsympathetic attitude to Islamic culture, but enjoying a final brief flowering in the 1850s under the last Mughal, the poet-king Bahadur Shah. He made no mention of cultural tendencies in Calcutta during the early nineteenth century, a reflection probably of the absence of Muslim *ashraf* participation in the Hindu-led religious and literary reassessments of that period, and perhaps also of his own family's uncertain identity as recent migrants to Lower Bengal. Yet his concluding prognostications about possible future cultural patterns do seem to reflect his own experiences in Lower Bengal. Strongly marked was a personal sense of nostalgia for what he represented as the waning of the "old culture" of the *ashraf* classes, exemplified by his memories of the gatherings of poets, sometimes attended by English officials, that had now been replaced by debating clubs. He expressed doubts, however, that his own preferred agenda of engrafting "the best part of European culture on the remains of Islamic culture" could ever actually be realized in the form of a new synthesis of "Anglo-Mahommedan culture." Always ambivalent about the "Christian" component within "European culture," he simply left the "best part" undefined.

Conclusions

Any significance of this phase of late-nineteenth-century cultural interaction beyond the literary and professional circles frequented by the three participants should be questioned. All three protagonists became well-known figures in north India, each making his mark in various spheres of administration, law, or education. Each continued to write on the relationships between culture, religion, and civilization until his death. Yet, although they met and interacted in the context of their administrative responsibilities and continued to expound their views through further publications, there was no more communication between them in the cultural and religious arena after the initial phase of riposte to William Muir in the early 1870s.

The reluctance seems to have been largely William Muir's. He failed to make any reply either to Saiyid Ahmad or to Amir 'Ali although they both mentioned him in the prefaces to their own works and drew on his statements in the course of justifying their own views. Although he revised and abridged his *Life of Mahomet* for republication in the mid 1870s and 1890s, and then produced further studies of Arab history, he seems to have made no reference in these later works to the criticisms of any of the Muslim scholars. He must have been aware of their own further contributions because, as late as 1900, he was a reviewer for the *Nineteenth Century*, one of the journals to which Amir 'Ali made frequent contributions on issues concerning Islamic society and the problems of Indian Muslims. Muir had also maintained close relations with Saiyid Ahmad over administrative matters until his own departure from India in 1876, but Muir did not correspond with him from Britain as he did with several other Indian "friends" and associates. One must conclude that Muir's stance on the understanding of a providential history, which could be read only according to Protestant Christian principles, could not admit any useful purpose in further interaction with Muslim upholders of an alternative view. Muir's *Life of Mahomet* and other histories nevertheless maintained their place in Britain as leading works of reference throughout his own lifetime and beyond. Apart from a few stylistic changes and some corrections, his views on Islamic doctrine, culture, and civilization remained in the later editions as "stationary" as he judged Muslim society.

Amir 'Ali's histories also outlived him. His earliest riposte to Christian criticism, the *Critical Examination*, reappeared nearly twenty years later, in 1891, with the new subtitle *The Spirit of Islam*, by which the book has continued to be known and influential in the twentieth century. Saiyid Ahmad, caught up for the rest of his life in affairs connected with the Aligarh College and movement, did not succeed in adding to the volume of essays that has been discussed here. They were published, however, in their original Urdu form in 1887, and, together with his many speeches, editorials, articles, and commentaries on religious and educational issues, they constitute the most important corpus of modernist thinking on intercultural dialogue in the Urdu language.

All three protagonists did share some common ground whether or not they would have recognized it as such. Each realized that pragmatically, if not ideally, the well-being of Indian Muslims demanded a degree of coming to terms with political realities, in spite of differing perceptions of the past and of each other's cultural identities. Each thus visualized and strove toward the creation of cultural bridges, crossable by Indian Muslims without any jeopardy to religious principles and cultural legacies. Muir tried unsuccessfully to achieve such engrafting pragmatically through his plans for a new university in the northwest whose curriculum would, in a last-ditch neo-Orientalist effort, resurrect the ethos of the Anglo-Oriental colleges of the pre-1857 era. The Muir Central College, and the later Allahabad University, fell short of this aspiration, but his educational ideas were partly implemented by others in educational institutions supportive of Muslim cultural interests in Lahore as well as in Aligarh. Saiyid Ahmad, the founder of the Anglo-Muhammadan College at Aligarh, and its *éminence grise* until his death in 1898, was the most obviously influential of the three in this respect. Not only did his college plan succeed, but he was primarily responsible for persuading fellow *ashraf* Muslims to realize the advantages of cooperation with the British at a number of levels. The British, too, lionized him personally, in ways that achieved leverage after his death for other Muslim spokesmen to make their weight felt on issues affecting their co-religionists. Of the three, it might seem that in spite of apparent political influence in Britain on behalf of Muslim pressure groups, Amir 'Ali was of less account among Muslims in India than his own memoirs would suggest. Other studies have suggested that his marriage to an Englishwoman, his Western lifestyle, and his appointment as a Privy Councillor had the effect of distancing him from Indian cultural concerns in spite of his undoubtedly active role in Muslim politics.[86] Possibly, in his case, the rebuttal of Christian criticism of Islamic culture and history was in the long term his most significant activity, although his readership was British rather than Indian Muslim. If so, it is perhaps a finding that is in keeping with this sequence of cultural interactions concerning understandings of Islam and Muslim culture and society that, it has been shown, drew on the Hejaz, and on London, rather more than on the north Indian site of the initial contemporary encounters.

86. Rafiuddin Ahmed, *The Bengal Muslims 1871-1906: A Quest for Identity,* 2nd ed. (Delhi, 1988), p. 14.

CHAPTER FIVE

Dalits and Christianity in Colonial Punjab: Cultural Interactions

JOHN C. B. WEBSTER

The beginning of a permanent Christian presence in the Punjab may be dated from the arrival of John C. Lowrie at Ludhiana in 1834. Lowrie and his successors in the early Protestant missions to the Punjab, unlike Alexander Duff in Calcutta, did not have an evangelistic strategy that led them to target specific groups within the population. They were, however, attracted to the Punjab by the presence of the Sikhs, whom they considered more "receptive" than others, and their use of schools and literature did betray a certain, perhaps unconscious, bias toward the literate. Their initial contacts with the Dalits seemed to have been unremarkable, confined to village itinerations and meetings with individuals. In 1859 and 1860 Mazhabi Sikhs in the 24th Punjab Native Infantry became interested in Christianity, but that movement was effectively snuffed out by government order before a significant number were baptized.[1] At about the same time and for the next two decades, the Baptists and Society for the Propagation of the Gospel (SPG) missionaries in Delhi found that the greatest response to their preaching came from the Chamars, and yet converts came in relatively slowly as individuals or nuclear families. Consequently, cultural interaction between them as a distinct social group and the missionaries was not adequately assessed at the time.[2]

It was with the rural Chuhras of the central Punjab that the missionaries

1. CMS, *Proceedings,* 1859-60, pp. 117-18; CMS, *Proceedings, 1860-61,* pp. 117-19.

2. See my "Missionary Strategies and the Development of the Christian Community: Delhi, 1859-1884" (forthcoming).

in that province had their most significant encounter with Dalit culture. Beginning in the 1870s and growing until the 1920s, when it tapered off, there was a mass conversion movement to Christianity among the Chuhras that dramatically increased the Indian Christian population of the Punjab. The decennial census reported increases from 3,912 in 1881 to 19,750 in 1891, 38,513 in 1901, 163,994 in 1911, 315,031 in 1921, and 395,629 in 1931. While conversions tended to be the result of individual and family, rather than group, decisions, the movement was so large that it created a good number of village congregations, some of which were of sufficient size to become centers of Chuhra Christian culture.

The following discussion explores the cultural interactions between the Chuhras of the central Punjab and the Protestants who created churches among them. It is divided into three parts. The first examines Chuhra culture at the turn of the century when the mass conversion movements were gaining momentum. The second focuses upon the cultural interaction between Christians and Chuhras during this time. The third attempts to move forward one generation to see what was happening in cultural interactions between missions and the children of converts — both in the rural church that conversion movements had produced and in the urban congregations of Chuhra converts who had migrated to the cities. The assumption is that conversion is a lengthy process rather than a single event, involving not only a change of religious allegiance but also some sort of inner transformation.

A word is needed about the sources on which this study is based. Most, but not all, were written by missionaries. This creates two serious problems that affect the conclusions reached. The first is that our present understanding of Christian-Dalit cultural interactions will of necessity be filtered through missionary perceptions that were themselves an integral part of that interaction. Perceptions of the Dalits will thus be more indirect and even based on speculation. The second problem is that there will be other gaps at key points. This is because the missionaries who produced the sources available to us did not provide direct evidence of the cultural interaction in which they and their "native agents" were involved. Consequently, it has become necessary to resort to more indirect, circumstantial evidence to gain some understanding of this subject.

I

The following description of the Chuhras from the 1881 Punjab Census provides a useful starting point for an understanding of their culture:

> The Chuhra or Bhangi of Hindustan is the sweeper and scavenger *par excellence* of the Panjab, and is found throughout the Province except in the hills. . . . He is one of the village menials proper, who receives a customary share of the produce and performs certain duties. In the east of the Province he sweeps the houses and village, collects the cowdung, pats it into cakes and stacks it, works up the manure, helps with the cattle, and takes them from village to village. News of a death sent to friends is invariably carried by him, and he is the general village messenger. . . . He also makes the *chhaj* or winnowing pan, and the *sirki* or grass thatch used to cover carts and the like. In the centre of the Province he adds to these functions actual hard work at the plough and in the field. He claims the flesh of such dead animals as do not divide the hoof, the cloven-footed belonging to the Chamar.[3]

This description identifies the Chuhras by locating them within the village economy and the *jajmani* system of reciprocal obligation between patrons and clients that defined economic relationships within the village. Chuhras rarely owned land, and only a small portion had a claim upon some land as long-term tenants. Usually they were hired as agricultural laborers either on an annual or, more commonly, on a daily wage basis. In addition, Chuhras received small payments as well as "gifts" for traditional services rendered and had to perform some services without receiving any payment. They were thus almost totally dependent upon their powerful patrons for survival itself, and, as H. J. Strickler pointed out in the early twentieth century, "the poverty of the Chuhra is a byword." Most were in debt to their employers or local merchants, both of whom often defrauded them:

> The poverty of the Chuhra has led to customs repugnant to the Hindu mind, thereby adding virulence to his already deep aversion to low caste people. For instance the Chuhra will eat foxes and jackals, or worse still, carrion. Whenever an animal dies in the village, the Chuhras are required to carry it away. As pay, they get the skin. But gnawing hunger often leads them to take more than the skin, choice pieces are saved for the pot. It is not uncommon to see members of several families cutting off and carrying away parts of a dead ox, while fifteen or twenty scrawny dogs and a host of vultures crowd near, waiting for their turn.[4]

3. *Census of the Punjab* [hereafter *Census*], 1881, 1:318.

4. H. J. Strickler, "The Religion and Customs of the Chuhra in the Punjab Province, India," unpublished manuscript, 1926, p. 6.

What differentiated Chuhras from others in the village was their situation of more extreme poverty, insecurity, and dependence upon others for their livelihood. In addition, other villagers considered them to be polluted people and did not allow them to use the village well. They lived in small mud houses on the edge of the village, wore simple clothes, and ate simple food. Given the conditions under which they had to live, it is not surprising that use of opium and alcohol was quite common among them. They did have their own leaders and caste *panchayats* to deal with matters internal to the caste and to negotiate matters affecting relationships with others in the village.

Their religious life, however, offers most insight into their culture. It had four important features. The first was what one observer called their "religious flexibility."[5] Chuhras tended to adopt the religion of the dominant groups within their villages. Where Muslims dominated, they became Muslims and were called Musallis; in Sikh villages they became Sikhs and were known as Mazhabis; and in Hindu villages they remained Chuhras and had their own religion. H. Griswold suggested, as late as the 1930s, that these "great traditions" provided only a "thin veneer" to their religious lives.[6] Clearly, they were adapting to the religious preferences of those upon whom they were economically dependent, either to please them, or to earn greater respect from them, or to gain their protection as co-religionists.[7] Conversion to Islam or Sikhism brought some degree of religious equality, perhaps within the confines of the mosque or *gurdwara*, but not social equality; the evidence is conflicting at those key points.[8]

A second feature was that Chuhras, regardless of formal religious allegiance, shared fully in a more generalized village religiosity or what contemporary Western observers called the "superstitions" common to the village as a whole. Most obvious was their belief in evil spirits and ghosts, one of the most dreaded of which was a *churel* or spirit of a woman who had died in childbirth. Like other villagers, Chuhras relied on *faqirs, bhagats,* and *pirs* to drive these away. Chuhras also believed in omens, in sorcery and magic, in the evil eye, in charms, and in auspicious and inauspicious times. They joined in the worship of Muslim saints, of Mata Devi who was the smallpox deity, and Gugga Pir who protected people from snake bites. They honored sacred places and objects. They had their own totems and taboos,

5. *Census,* 1921, p. 178.

6. Hervey DeWitt Griswold, *Insights into Modern Hinduism* (New York, 1934), p. 232.

7. W. P. Hares, "The Chuhras of the Punjab," *Church Missionary Review* [hereafter *CMR*] (June 1920): 118.

8. See *Census,* 1881, 1:154, 319; Hares, "Chuhras," p. 118.

which could vary according to the *gotras,* or kin groups, to which they belonged.[9]

Third, the Chuhras had their own life-cycle customs and ceremonies. There appear to have been no special ceremonies at childbirth, but *gur* (a sugar product) was given to friends when the baby was born, and ten days later relatives were invited to a meal. The mother was considered to be impure for a period of twenty-one days, after which she bathed and resumed cooking. Ceremonial surrounding betrothal and marriage was by far the most elaborate. Marriages were arranged and took place before the girl reached puberty. A bride-price was paid, gifts were exchanged, people were fed, and songs were sung that expressed the thoughts, feelings, and desires of all involved. The actual wedding was performed by a Brahmin priest, a Muslim *maulvie,* or Chuhra *gyani* (one who had memorized Chuhra lore) under a canopy of green branches. The climax came when the bridegroom walked around the bride seven times and then she walked around him seven times. After a few days at her husband's house, she returned home until called for, sometimes after attaining puberty several years later. Once again gifts were brought and songs were sung. Chuhras allowed divorce and remarriage, but only at the first marriage was there any ceremonial or exchange of gifts. At death the body was prepared for burial. A priest recited a prayer, and others followed. After the burial the women sang and beat themselves in time to the dirge, and, when the funeral was over, all those who had touched the body bathed.[10]

The fourth aspect of Chuhra religion consisted of some distinctive beliefs and practices centered around the worship of Bala Shah.[11] For this Chuhras erected dome-shaped shrines of mud or brick that had no images but had niches for oil lamps and an altar for offerings. Worship, led by Chuhras themselves, was generally weekly on Thursday evenings, with a major sacrifice being offered once or twice a year. What is not clear from the sources is whether Chuhras gave up the worship of Bala Shah upon becoming Muslims or Sikhs. Bala Shah worship was certainly prevalent in areas of Muslim dominance and

9. This paragraph is based on J. Youngson, "Chuhras," *Indian Antiquary* [hereafter *IA*]. Rev. J. Youngson, a Church of Scotland missionary in Sialkot, published his work in serialized form from March 1906 to May 1907; see *IA* (January 1907): 19-21; H. A. Rose, *A Glossary of the Tribes and Castes of the Punjab and North-West Frontier Province* (Punjab, 1970), 2:207-9; and Strickler, "Religion," pp. 50-61.

10. Based on Youngson, "Chuhras," *IA* (March 1906): 85-96, (November 1906): 302-10, and (December 1906): 337-40; Rose, *Glossary,* pp. 190-99.

11. The best source for Bala Shah worship is Youngson's Chuhra *kursinama* (genealogy), which he translated and published in *IA.*

showed clear signs of Islamic influence and, to a lesser degree, that of Sikhism. The genealogies of Bala Shah as well as the songs and prayers used in worshipping him offer important insights into some distinctive elements of Chuhra culture. Bala Shah was a devotee and priest of God whom God had exalted. Because he was such a great devotee, having worshipped God for thirty-six ages, his own followers could take refuge in him for protection and mercy, especially on the day of resurrection.

> The priest, the great Bala, commands,
> "Adorers of the Name escape God's wrath;
> The righteous hears, the rest are ignorant.
> But those that hear, and trust, shall be set free from fear of pain."[12]

Bala became incarnate ten times. Genealogies vary, but the first incarnation was Jhaumpra,[13] one of four Brahmin brothers who were all sons of Brahma. God ordered the brothers to remove a dead cow that, because he had killed it, God did not consider unclean. Jhaumpra agreed to remove it if "in the day of resurrection, when my people cross the narrow bridge that spans the mouth of hell, thou wilt have mercy on them."[14] His brothers also agreed to restore him to their company after four days, but, when Jhaumpra had removed the cow, they changed their minds and said they would accept him only after four ages. So Bala, incarnate as Jhaumpra, became a Chuhra. If Bala is thus not their primal ancestor, he at least became one of them. God will send to hell the Hindus and Muslims who distance themselves from the Chuhras, while the followers of Bala will enter heaven.

> The faith of Kalak Das [son or nephew of Jhaumpra], the Chuhra, is a perfect faith.
> If any Shahi [follower of Bala Shah] reads Muhammad's creed, an unbeliever he is branded;
> And if Baba Nanak's, he shall be rejected;
> All that do profess the creed of Bala straight to heaven shall go.[15]

12. Youngson, "Chuhras," *IA* (March 1907): 73.

13. Two others were Balmik, often to be identified with Valmiki, the legendary low-caste author of the *Ramayana*, and *Lal Beg*. Thus, those in this source who are called "Shahis" were often referred to elsewhere as Balmikis and Lal Begis. These are variants of the same religion.

14. Youngson, "Chuhras," *IA* (January 1907): 27.

15. Youngson, "Chuhras," *IA* (January 1907): 29.

As this brief description indicates, there is a close identity between Bala Shah and the Chuhras.[16] As with other Dalit origin myths,[17] this one affirms the highborn origins of the Chuhras whose subsequent fall was due both to their own virtue (devoted obedience to God in removing the cow) and to the deceitfulness of the high castes. Those who take refuge in Bala will have their vindication on the resurrection day, while others who scorn them will suffer ultimate rejection. Until then, however, the world seems to be ruled both by social custom and the unpredictable spirits; God does not intervene or interfere, rewarding devotion only at life's end. Thus there is both an important affirmation of inherent dignity and, at the same time, a passivity with regard to their present circumstances built into Chuhra religion.

The socioeconomic and religious pictures of Dalit culture offered by these late-nineteenth- and early-twentieth-century sources seem to reinforce, rather than contradict, each other. Chuhras shared much of the village culture just as they shared in the village economy. Their general religiosity and religious "flexibility" as well as the similarity of their life-cycle ceremonies and customs to those of the dominant castes all provide evidence of this. For the Chuhras, however, the central reality in the village was clearly the patron-client relationship to which almost all of them were bound and upon which they were dependent for life itself. The patron was expected to provide sustenance as well as help in time of need; to him service was rendered in exchange. This is reflected in Chuhra religion. There was much that was adopted, adapted, and borrowed from the religions of the village patrons, even though (and this is a psychologically significant variant) in the mythology of Bala Shah Chuhras affirmed not only equality of birth with their patrons but even a superiority of virtue and of ultimate destiny. In addition, the Chuhras seemed to depict God as an alternative patron in whom they took refuge. Hope in this patron, however, was confined to life beyond the grave. The obstacles posed by humans and spirits alike, which have to be overcome to attain fullness of life here and now, were enormous, and God did not offer any assistance or even guidance in that struggle.

16. For a fuller description of Chuhra religion see my *Religion and Dalit Liberation: An Examination of Perspectives* (Delhi, 1999), pp. 15-23.

17. Lynn Vincentnathan, "Untouchable Concepts of Person and Society," *Contributions to Indian Sociology* n.s. 17.1 (January-June 1993): 53-82.

II

The Chuhra mass conversion movement began at their own initiative within the territory of the American United Presbyterian Mission, the headquarters of which was in Sialkot. The person credited with starting the movement was a lame, illiterate man about thirty years old named Ditt. Unlike other Chuhras, Ditt was not an agricultural laborer dependent upon a particular patron within the village for work but an independent businessman who made a living buying hides from his own and neighboring villages and selling them to dealers. Ditt did not hear the Christian message from missionaries or mission workers itinerating around his village but from a young Hindu Jat, in a neighboring village, who had been baptized in November 1872. What he found compelling in the message we are not told, but he decided to become a Christian on the basis of what he had learned from his friend. In June 1873 Ditt was accompanied by his friend to Sialkot and introduced to the missionary, the Rev. Samuel Martin. Ditt quickly convinced Martin that he already both understood the gospel well and believed it sincerely enough to receive baptism. He then went back to his village and to his work. In August he returned with his wife, their daughter, and two neighbors whom he had instructed in the Christian faith. The following February he brought four more neighbors to Sialkot, where they were also baptized.[18] By the time of their annual meeting in 1875, the missionaries recognized that a conversion movement among the Chuhras was under way.[19]

As it happened, Ditt had begun what was to be the largest, but not the only, mass conversion movement among the Chuhras within the boundaries of the Sialkot mission. The other two, which seem to have been quite independent, began near Gujranwala and Gurdaspur. Each spread because of the efforts of Ditt and others like him. As one missionary explained in 1883, "At the first, one man made a profession of faith in Christ, and it was principally through his efforts that the work spread through the neighbouring villages, then through the friends and relatives of those who first believed."[20] In Awankha, a large village in the Gurdaspur district, the leader was Changhatta, who had been on a religious quest for some time when he first heard the Christian gospel preached by an Indian evangelist in a nearby town. In 1881

18. This account follows that in Andrew Gordon, *Our India Mission* (Philadelphia, 1886), pp. 421-27.

19. *The Seventeenth Annual Report of the Board of Foreign Missions of the United Presbyterian Church of North America Presented to the General Assembly in May 1876*, p. 19. [hereafter *UPCNA Annual Report*].

20. *UPCNA Annual Report*, May 1884, p. 85.

five men in Awankha, then eighteen more men and eleven children, and finally twenty-one more people, mostly the wives and daughters of the initial converts, were baptized.[21] By 1884 the village had an organized congregation.[22] Awankha seems to have been typical of the general pattern of conversion by male and/or family rather than group decision, even though the number of converts there was unusually large and their entry into the Church particularly rapid.[23] In 1884 and 1885 the movement spread beyond the boundaries of the Sialkot mission and the neighboring missions became involved as well.[24]

Once there was a significant number of inquirers or converts within a village, it was the practice of the missions to send a teacher (or catechist) there to instruct them. This man was generally a Chuhra who had received some training from the mission for his tasks, which included home visitation, instruction in the fundamentals of Christian faith, the conduct of daily prayers and Sunday worship, and instruction for holding a Sunday School for young and old.[25] In the beginning these teacher/catechists were resident in or near the villages they were serving. As the conversion movements continued to grow and to tax the human resources of the missions, each catechist had to assume responsibility for more villages.[26] Just before the First World War Bishop Whitehead of Madras estimated that the United Presbyterians had an average of 187 Christians, in four villages, per paid worker, and that the Church Missionary Society had 500, in six villages, per paid worker in their Christian settlements in the Chenab colony.[27] In the cultural interactions between the missions and the Chuhras, these workers played the key role as the continuing presence within the village and as cultural mediators. Unfortu-

21. Gordon, *India Mission,* pp. 437-45.

22. *UPCNA Annual Report,* May 1885, p. 38.

23. The mission statistics for 1890 indicated that there were 10,171 Christians in 525 villages, just under twenty individuals or perhaps five families per village. *UPCNA Annual Report,* 28 May 1891, p. 29.

24. For a fuller description see John C. B. Webster, *The Dalit Christians: A History,* 2nd ed. (Delhi, 1994), pp. 46-52.

25. Robert Stewart, *Life and Work in India,* new ed. (Philadelphia, 1899), pp. 262-63.

26. In 1883 the Sialkot Mission reported, "Our plan has been to place an assistant in each important village, requiring him to visit the neighboring villages within a distance of five or six miles. Owing to scarcity of helpers we have been compelled to enlarge the circuit of each one of our laborers, but this again prevents them from giving as much personal attention to each village as it requires. Some important circuits too are yet vacant." *UPCNA Annual Report,* May 1884, p. 84.

27. Henry [Whitehead] Madras, "The Mass Movement towards Christianity in the Punjab," *International Review of Missions* [hereafter *IRM*] 2 (1913): 447-48.

nately, there is no record of their interactions either with the missionaries or with the Chuhra villagers. Only the records of the missionaries and Indian pastors, who toured the districts and whose personal contact with the Chuhra residents of any one village was only intermittent and of relatively short duration, are available. These do, however, provide some useful indirect evidence concerning cultural interactions during this period.

The image of the Chuhra held by the missionaries, who worked among them, was fairly consistent. The most commonly repeated adjectives in their writings were "poor," "degraded," and "ignorant." Yet, in the eyes of the missionaries they were morally and spiritually no worse than their Hindu and Muslim neighbors; they were also seen as promising, or more promising, as the converts from other sections of Punjabi society. Moreover, the Chuhras' views of God and sense of sinfulness were close to those of the Christians.[28] Andrew Gordon described the gospel message that the United Presbyterian rural workers preached to the Chuhras as telling "the story of Jesus the Son of God, who became a poor man, wrought miracles, died for sinners, arose from the dead, and ascended to heaven."[29] It was thus no different in content or emphasis from the message preached to others, except for the simplicity of style and probably the reference to Jesus' birth into poverty, which would identify him with the Chuhras.

With regard to the requirements for baptism, the Sialkot mission had obviously arrived at a policy by 1885:

> The attainments of these people before baptism are necessarily very limited. To set up a high standard, and require them to reach it before admission, would, we think, be entirely without Scripture example. They must know Jesus Christ the Son of God, the sinless One, and the only Saviour of sinners; they must know that he came from God, became man, laid down his life for sinners, and now welcomes all, even the poorest and vilest, to come to him; they must turn their backs upon idols, and every religion but that of Jesus, heartily receiving and resting upon him alone, and promising obedience to him. If we are satisfied with them on such simple points as these, we think it our duty to receive them.[30]

28. For a good sample of such views among United Presbyterian missionaries see *UPCNA Annual Report,* 1885, pp. 26-27; S. Martin, "Work among the Chuhras," in *UPCNA Annual Report,* 1906, pp. 62-65; W. T. Anderson, "Progress in the Village Christian Communities," in *UPCNA Annual Report,* 1909, pp. 170-73.

29. Gordon, *India Mission,* p. 446.

30. Gordon, *India Mission,* p. 462. Rowland Bateman, a missionary of the neighbor-

There were three specific cultural demands that the missionaries made upon Chuhra converts as part of their obedience to Christ. The first two, observing the Sabbath as a day of worship and rest from work and giving up eating carrion,[31] required of the converts a considerable economic sacrifice, as the missionaries well knew. The third, remaining faithful in marriage, became a matter of church discipline; converts could be and were suspended for "loose views of the marriage relationship."[32]

In their turn the missionaries, and Christianity itself, became identified with the Chuhras in the countryside, especially in Sialkot district where a large majority of the Chuhra population converted to Christianity. For this reason the better-educated Punjabi mission workers were at first reluctant to commit themselves and had a difficult time adjusting to this work.[33] An initial missionary concern was that the large influx of Chuhras would make others unwilling to convert.[34] However, they quickly became convinced from their study of Scripture, especially 1 Corinthians 1:26-31, that it was God's way to begin not with those of high status but with the poor, the powerless, and the ignorant. What they found was that the higher born continued to come in at the same slow rate as before, but that the mass conversion of Chuhras did open them up to a certain amount of public ridicule. In the villages they and their workers were mocked as *Chuhra ka guru* (teachers of Chuhras); while newspapers made fun of them for having to baptize rural

---

ing CMS mission, had Chuhra converts pass through three stages: those who professed a desire to become Christians; those who confessed that they were "on the Lord's side" and had learned "the Creed, the Ten Commandments and the Lord's Prayer" and who might be baptized after a learning and waiting period, preferably with their wives and children; and baptized Christians who continued to learn so as to qualify as communicant members. H. C. Velte, "Mission Work among the Low Caste Tribes of the Punjab," *Indian Evangelical Review* 69 (July 1891): 9-10.

31. This prohibition seems to have been instituted because both Indians and Westerners considered eating carrion evidence of such human degradation that, from a missionary perspective, it was incompatible with a profession of Christian faith. Anderson, "Progress in the Village," pp. 171-72. There are reports that it was readily, even happily, accepted and enforced by the converts themselves. See also K. C. Chatterjee, "Village Missions and Village Churches," in *Report of the North India Conference of Christian Workers Held at Mussoorie, 17-25 September 1902* (Calcutta, 1903), p. 107; R. Maconachie, *Rowland Bateman: Nineteenth Century Apostle* (London, 1917), pp. 101-2.

32. The three demands are given in S. Martin, "Work among the Depressed Classes and the Masses," *Report of the Third Decennial Missionary Conference Held at Bombay, 1892-93* (Bombay, 1893), 1:23. All converts in one village were suspended for not honoring the marriage relationship. *UPCNA Annual Report,* 1881, p. 20.

33. Gordon, *India Mission,* p. 429.

34. *UPCNA Annual Report,* 1876, p. 19; 1877, p. 15; 1884, pp. 85-86; 1885, pp. 25-27.

Dalits, they also indicated alarm about their threat to the traditional social order. As one put it:

> The Hindus are wrong in deriving comfort from the fact that persons of higher castes have ceased to fall a prey to Christians, and that the poor Missionary has now to baptize sweepers and Chamars into the Church in order to lend some importance to his annual reports. They are, however, labouring under a mistake, and should remember that Christianity levels the distinction made by Hinduism between a Brahman and a Chamar. A Brahman or Chamar convert to the Christian religion ceases to be either, and is metamorphosed into a coated and pantalooned individual, who can touch, and sit on the carpet with persons of other faiths and drag every one out of a railway carriage.[35]

Chuhra perceptions of, and interaction with, the Christian missions can perhaps best be inferred from missionary statements concerning both Chuhra motivation for conversion and the problems missionaries faced in developing self-sustaining congregations among them. Apart from religious motivations that seemed focused on the dignity and respect their new religion would bring them,[36] the act of conversion itself was one of defiance. Chuhras saw in Christianity a basis for hope of improvement in this life and not just in the one after death. This was obvious in the many requests for material assistance that often accompanied an expressed interest in Christianity. These the missionaries invariably turned down, and for a good number of Chuhras that was the end of the relationship. The other form of help they sought was intervention in their conflicts with village landowners and officials. Chuhras were attracted to Christianity's egalitarian religious ideology as well as to joining a mixed community with a status higher than their own. At a deeper level, however, the Chuhras saw in the missionary and the Mission Society a new patron, an alternative patron, or at least a counter-patron to the village landlords. The evidence is that Chuhras, accustomed as they were to patron-client relationships, sought to adopt the missionaries and missions as new, more be-

35. Excerpt from the *Sat Dharm Parcharik* (24 March 1902), in *Selections from the Vernacular Newspapers — Punjab*, 1902, p. 216. See also the *Paisa Akhbar* (29 July 1897), in *Selections from the Vernacular Newspapers — Punjab*, 1897, p. 720 and *Parkash* (14 May 1912), in *Selections from the Vernacular Newspapers — Punjab*, 1912, p. 408.

36. Gordon (*India Mission*, p. 429) cites the telling case of one convert who, on hearing the gospel preached in a town bazaar, did not think it could possibly apply to Chuhras. For a general discussion of such motivations see John C. B. Webster, *The Christian Community and Change in Nineteenth Century North India* (Delhi, 1976), pp. 58-64.

nevolent patrons. It is equally clear that this was a role that the missionaries did not relish and that they resisted. Perhaps at no other point was the cultural interaction between rural Dalits and Christian spokespersons more profound and long lasting.

Missionary awareness of this patron-client relationship was not immediate. Their early reports reveal a preoccupation with the "mixed motives" of their inquirers and converts, the "material" being mixed with the "spiritual," the "temporal" with the "eternal." In one village in the Gurdaspur district Gordon explained to the Chuhras that "we were in India not to provide corporeal but spiritual bread." However, "these poor people said that we were their *mabap* (parents) and continued perseveringly to indulge the hope of our kindly performing for them, sooner or later, the duties arising from this parental relation."[37] Gordon considered *mabap*-ism a heresy to be stamped out,[38] and, like all United Presbyterian missionaries, he was a staunch advocate of self-support among village congregations. As far as I can determine, the missionaries left their converts to fend for themselves in temporal matters, giving them neither land nor employment.[39] They did, however, create a network of village, town, and city schools that provided many of the next generation with a way up and out of the oppression and poverty of the villages. Two decades after Gordon was writing, W. T. Anderson reported "a spirit of independence" among Chuhra converts, the result being not greater economic independence, although they were more prosperous, but the greater self-respect achieved by having successfully given up eating carrion. He saw such independence as a mixed blessing, however, because he thought that Chuhra converts were not always using their new-found independence wisely. They needed proper guidance.[40] That sentiment perhaps best defines the kind of paternal relationship with the Chuhra Christians that the nineteenth-century missionaries deemed necessary.

Surprisingly little is known about the details of Chuhra appropriation of Christianity during the nineteenth century. The most immediate consequence of conversion was almost inevitable persecution. The Church of Scotland mission, also at Sialkot, had to deal with thirty court cases brought

37. Gordon, *India Mission,* p. 438.

38. Gordon, *India Mission,* pp. 438, 445.

39. There were to be exceptions to both of these rules. Some converts were later trained as rural workers and became employees of the mission. When the canal colonies in western Punjab opened up, the missions were given land and settled some of their Chuhra converts there. However, no assurances of either of these were given at the time of baptism.

40. Anderson, "Progress in the Village," p. 172.

against their Chuhra converts during just one year.[41] The reports of the United Presbyterian mission are full of comments on persecution; sometimes so severe that converts either apostatized or left the village.[42] Conversion did not change Chuhra patterns of decision making. Rural churches had *lambardars* or *panchayats,* but it is not clear how these related to the preexisting caste *panchayat* or how conversion affected relations between those Chuhras who did and those who did not convert within the same village. Christian life-cycle rituals were introduced, but these probably served as supplements rather than substitutes for much that Chuhras already had. For example, conversion did not affect the age of marriage or the nature of marriage negotiations, but the Church Missionary Society did insist that Christians marry other Christians and that any existing marriage arrangement between their children and the children of nonconvert families be broken off.[43] One missionary reported a case in which a village catechist insisted that a Chuhra convert be buried face up rather than face down, and then had to deal with serious opposition from the village landowners.[44] The following hymn, composed by a Chuhra convert, perhaps best expresses their inner appropriation of Christianity.

> Bring my Jesus to me, O my God!
> To Thy door have I come, O my Creator!
> The winner of my heart, Christ the beloved!
> My Creator, my beloved Lord!
> Let me never forget Thee, my Lord, O Christ!
> 'Twas for me He came into the world;
> My Beloved lost His life for my soul,
> And saved my soul from sin.
> I wandered about astray and lost,
> But I heard His voice calling me;
> Having pity on me, a sinner.
> He bore the burden of my sorrows;
> He injured none,

41. H. F. Lechmere Taylor, *In the Land of the Five Rivers: A Sketch of the Work of the Church of Scotland in the Punjab* (Edinburgh, 1906), p. 92.

42. For some of the most serious cases see *UPCNA Annual Report,* 1878, p. 44; 1879, p. 19; 1881, p. 20.

43. Robert Clark, *The Missions of the Church Missionary Society and the Church of England Zenana Missionary Society in the Punjab and Sindh,* edited and revised by Robert Maconachie (London, 1904), p. 123; Maconachie, *Rowland Bateman,* pp. 101-2.

44. R. Thackwell, Letter to Dr. Gillespie, 12 March 1895.

Yet the cruel ones crucified Him.
O cruel ones! Why did you commit this dreadful deed?
Did not the fear of God restrain you?
We are beggars at Thy door,
Thou hast fed us all.
In Thy hand is my life,
The shadow of Thy mercy is over me.
O Beloved, show kindness to me,
Who am oppressed by many sorrows.[45]

One can see in this hymn the same basic poetic forms, the same spirit of *bhakti* (devotion), and the same theme of refuge as in the songs to Bala Shah. Where it differs is in its telling of the story of Jesus Christ rather than Bala Shah or his incarnations, in its emphasis of inner transformation, and perhaps in its revelation of some awareness that God would intervene on the devotee's behalf prior to the resurrection day.

Baptism not only established a relationship between the missionaries and the Chuhra converts but also identified each with the other. Since that was what both missionaries and inquirers wanted, the nature of their relationship and its consequences for both parties became central issues of cultural interaction. That it would be some sort of paternal relationship was a foregone conclusion. This fitted in with the "guardian" mentality of these particular Protestant missionaries in relation to "uneducated" India in particular, as well as with the patron-client relationships to which the Chuhras were accustomed. The two groups, however, did not share identical perceptions of what that parental relationship involved. During the period of mass conversion movements that established relationships between the missions and rapidly increasing numbers of Chuhras, the points at issue were bound up with assumptions about what the salvation of the Chuhras entailed. The missions that, for the most part, set and enforced the terms of the relationship saw salvation almost exclusively in terms of a change of religious allegiance leading to a change in behavior patterns, an inner spiritual transformation, and a favorable eternal destiny, whereas the Chuhras saw it, at least on first encounter, primarily in terms of improving the external circumstances of their lives. The missionaries thus perceived their own obligation in this paternal relationship as primarily one of religious leadership and guidance (with education as an important component), whereas the

45. J. F. W. Youngson, *Forty Years of the Panjab Mission of the Church of Scotland* (Edinburgh, 1896), pp. 269-70.

Chuhras expected those obligations to include a wide range of social, economic, and even political (vis-à-vis the landlords) assistance. In the ensuing period between the two world wars these two points of view would move closer together. In the meantime the Christians had succeeded in challenging the passivity, fatalism, despair, and, to a lesser degree, dependency inherent in Chuhra culture without altering very much, for the vast majority, the conditions of their struggle for survival. The Chuhras on their part had challenged the urban and literate culture of the missionaries by forcing them out into the villages and to the very bottom of rural society where, from an evangelistic point of view, the real action was.

III

The years between the First World War and Indian Independence marked a new period in the cultural interaction between the Chuhras and the representatives of Protestant Christianity in the Punjab. The political context of interaction had changed significantly. In 1917 Edwin Montagu, Secretary of State for India, committed the British to "the progressive realisation of responsible government in India," and two years later India's resulting new constitution included not only more self-government but also communal electorates not just for the Muslim minorities but for the Sikh minority in the Punjab as well. The most immediate consequence of this change for the Christians was to intensify the politicization of religious conversion. In the "politics of numbers" that ensued, the transfer of large numbers of people, even into the politically insignificant Christian community, could affect the balance of power between the major communities of the Punjab. Missionaries faced increased competition for the religious loyalty of rural Dalits from groups such as the Arya Samaj, and rural Christians felt this communal pressure most powerfully at the time of the decennial census, especially in 1931.[46]

The other important change was a shift of emphasis in missionary writings from the evangelization of the Chuhras to the development, among those already converted, of churches that were self-governing, self-propagating, and especially self-supporting. Missionaries were aware that the number of converts was outstripping their provision of adequate pastoral care, and

46. The pressure was not to convert so much as just to enroll themselves as having the same religion as their landlords. See, e.g., *The 97th Annual Report of the Punjab Mission of the Presbyterian Church in the U.S.A. Co-operating with the United Church of Northern India for the Year 1930-31* [hereafter *Punjab Mission*], p. 10.

that unless the rural church were put on a solid footing it would not survive the nationalist attacks and communal competition to which it was being subjected. Missionary and pastoral attention was therefore directed increasingly toward the transformation of the converts already won and the creation of viable Christian churches among them. As a result, the primary locus of cultural interaction between Christianity and Dalit religion during this period was within the Christian community itself. There were three crucial points of interaction: the rural church, the education of the children of Chuhra converts, and the Chuhra Christians within the urban churches.

The Rural Church

The conversion of the Chuhras had been more rapid than the missionaries had anticipated. The fourfold increase of the Indian Christian population in the Punjab between the census of 1901 and that of 1911 had caught them by surprise, as the total was larger than they could account for from their own records. By 1921 the total had almost doubled again. Missionaries speculated that a large number of Chuhras might simply have declared themselves Christians without having undergone either instruction or baptism.[47] In addition, there were some "free-lance missions" that had exacerbated the problem by performing baptisms wholesale, giving no instruction about Christianity but assuring people that by becoming Christians they could get land from the government, and "by reason of these hopes fleecing the people and well lining their own pockets."[48]

The result of such rapid and uncontrolled expansion, far surpassing the missions' capacity to provide pastoral care, was a rural church that was, to missionary eyes, insufficiently Christian. A change of allegiance of varying degrees had indeed occurred, and some changes in behavior were becoming more apparent. The missionary lament was that no profound change of heart had yet taken place (with a few exceptions) and that the general level of ignorance concerning the basics of Christian religious life was dangerously high. Old beliefs and superstitions lingered. Christian life-cycle rituals did not completely replace those practiced of old, and the participation of converts in the rituals of Chuhra relatives and neighbors, while forbidden, could not be entirely prevented.[49] In 1932 the Church Missionary Society (CMS) mission

47. C. F. Hall, "A Suggested Policy for Mass Movements," *CMR* (May 1914): 280.

48. These freelance missions are described in W. P. Hares, "Mass Movement Work in the Central Punjab," *CMR* (September 1918): 318.

49. B. Nesbitt, a Presbyterian missionary, enunciated the following principle, which

in Narowal claimed that "all our marriages are according to Christian rites, numbering about eighty a year."[50] Other missions could not make such claims. In fact, marriage practices were a source of considerable missionary frustration. It was the Chuhra practice to pay a bride-price, and it seems that Christian girls fetched a higher price in the marriage market than did other Chuhra girls. Some unscrupulous fathers were not above arranging marriages with, and collecting engagement payments from, several different parties at the same time, thus causing endless quarrels.[51] Missionaries disapproved of the relative frequency of divorce among Chuhras and were happy to bring converts under the stricter Christian marriage law. They were also upset at the high costs of marriage festivities, which often left fathers deep in debt for the rest of their lives.[52]

It is worth noting that in 1914 reports from two of the four major missions in the Punjab indicated that there were far more men than women among the Chuhra converts, that women did not take much part in worship, and thus that Christianity was largely a man's affair.[53] In order to rectify this imbalance as well as to build up Christian families, a special effort was made to recruit foreign single women missionaries for rural work.[54] Women's work focused largely upon visitation and instruction in Christian faith and the preparation of women for baptism or confirmation as communicant members of the church. Discussions were also held on such subjects as hygiene, sanitation, nutrition, and child care. Literacy classes were less common, but

---

was accepted by virtually all of his missionary colleagues: "the Christians must come out of their old bondage to superstition and sin, and in order to do this must make a clean break with their old Chuhra customs, and even with their relatives and friends in so far as these stand in the way of denying the old life and accepting the new." *Punjab Mission,* 1924, p. 26.

50. L. N. Meredith, "Narowal, 1868-1932," *C.M.S. Mass Movement Quarterly* [hereafter *MMQ*] (March 1932): 3.

51. Hares, "Mass Movement Work," pp. 321-22; Digby R. M. F. Creighton, "Facing Facts, Dark and Bright," *MMQ* (October 1922): 13-14; R. B. Nesbitt, "Engagement and Marriage among Village Christians," *National Christian Council Review* (July 1925): 278-85; C. L. Richards, "A Mass Movement Church and Its Ethical Needs," *MMQ* (December 1927): 59, and "The Average Village Christian," *Church Missionary Outlook* [hereafter *CMO*] (April 1931): 72-73.

52. For example, Nesbitt, "Engagement and Marriage."

53. Hall, "A Suggested Policy," pp. 286-88 and "Village Christians in North India," *Indian Standard* [hereafter *Standard*] (January 1914): 14.

54. The assumption was that Indian women could not do this because if married they had domestic responsibilities, and if single it would be unsafe for them to visit and live in villages alone. See, e.g., Hall, "Suggested Policy," pp. 286-88.

where they were introduced the primary aim was to enable women to read the Bible.[55]

Economic realities as well as religion shaped cultural interaction within the Christian community. While there is evidence that a considerable number of Chuhra Christians migrated from their villages to the cities, to canal colonies, and even to the northwest frontier, there is mixed testimony about improvements in the economic conditions of their lives in the villages. Improvement seems to have been greater in the canal colonies of western Punjab, where the demand for agricultural labor led to an increase in wages, than in the central Punjab, where poverty was still rampant. Degrees of oppression also varied. In 1926 R. B. Nesbitt published the results of an informal survey that indicated that mistreatment of village Christians by their landlords was frequent. The reasons were many and varied, but underlying them all "the Zamindar feels instinctively that the Christian is escaping from the control which has been exercised over him and his ancestors for generations."[56] Toward the end of the interwar period, however, E. D. Lucas and Frank Thakur Das made a very detailed economic survey of 159 Christian families in eighteen villages in the Sialkot district and found them to be both very poor and deeply in debt. Landless agricultural laborers made up 66 percent of the sample in the twelve villages around Pasrur and 72.2 percent of the sample in the six villages around Narowal. Those who had yearly contracts as tenant farmers constituted 19 percent and 11 percent, respectively, while the rest did semi-skilled or unskilled labor. Monthly income was less than two rupees per person, well below the subsistence level. In the Pasrur area 82 percent of the families were in debt, the result primarily of marriage expenses, and around Narowal, 92 percent. The average debt was equivalent to the family's entire income for nineteen months, and the annual interest often exceeded the family's cash income for the year.[57]

In this socioeconomic context of poverty, indebtedness, and conflictual relationships with village landlords, the rural missionaries made special efforts to promote self-support among the rural churches. The aim of self-

55. Rebe M. King, "Women's Work in the Jhang Bar," *MMQ* (January 1918): 7-9 and (July 1923): 1-3; A Lady Missionary to the Punjab, "Talking to Women," *Standard* (May 1919): 137-39; E. A. Russell, "Women's Work in the Punjab," *MMQ* (June 1926): 27-29.

56. R. B. Nesbitt, "Disabilities of Village Christians," *National Christian Council Review* (June 1926): 330.

57. E. D. Lucas and Frank Thakur Das, *The Rural Church in the Punjab: A Study of Social, Economic, Educational and Religious Conditions Prevailing Amongst Certain Village Christian Communities in the Sialkot District* (Lahore, 1938), pp. 28-39.

support was an independent church.[58] As one missionary put it, "real independence of spirit is fostered by independence in finance."[59] In this respect the United Presbyterians, among whom a revival had spurred giving, had made the most progress by the beginning of this period. In 1922 thirty of their seventy-five organized congregations were listed as self-supporting, but a dozen or so qualified because of the contributions of resident missionaries.[60] They also had their pastors raise their own incomes from their parishioners, whereas the other missions paid their rural pastors fixed salaries from a central fund to which all churches contributed. Appeals were made to the villagers' devotion to Christ, to their pride and self-respect, and to their desire to have their own pastor. Methods of giving more appropriate to the largely noncash economy of the village, such as "the Lord's pot" in which handfuls of flour were placed at regular intervals, were devised, and regular training in stewardship was given to rural church leaders.[61] Some rural reconstruction schemes were introduced, but these were most helpful only where the Christians either owned land (as in the Christian villages within the canal colonies) or held it as long-term tenants.[62] According to C. H. Loehlin, who conducted a three-month survey, the key was for the missionaries, mission workers, and the people themselves to believe that, despite the obvious poverty, self-support could be achieved.[63] This effort did increase the number and proportion of pastors that the churches alone supported, but in some areas the number of villages the pastor then had under his charge grew to the point where the quality of pastoral care suffered, especially in the villages in which the pastor was nonresident.

58. Hares, "Mass Movement Work," p. 326; and Harris J. Stewart, "The Problem Contained in the Relation of the Mission to the Indian Church," *Women's Missionary Magazine* (November 1922): 227.

59. H. J. Strickler, "Organizing the Village Church," *United Church Review* [hereafter *UCR*] (July 1933): 219.

60. Stewart, "Problem Contained," p. 230. By 1929 this had increased to 64 out of 100 organized congregations. J. G. Campbell, "Self-Support in Village Churches in India," *Standard* (July-August 1929): 194.

61. Campbell ("Self-Support," p. 194) linked women's work to self-support because it was women who held the purse strings in the village. See also W. P. Hares, "A Church Council Meeting in the Punjab," *MMQ* (April 1924): 13-14; C. H. Loehlin, "Self-Support in Village Churches: A Report of a Survey," *Standard* (April 1929): 89-93; W. P. Hares, "Self-Support in Village Churches in India," *Standard* (May 1929): 124-27; and R. B. Love, "A Self-Supporting Church," *Standard* (May 1929): 130-31.

62. See, e.g., J. C. Heinrich, "Rural Reconstruction and Village Self-Support," *UCR* (June 1939): 166-69.

63. Loehlin, "Self-Support," p. 90.

At the end of this period there seems to have been little change among rural Dalit Christians with regard to marriage customs and the selling of brides.[64] The same could be said of dependency, although there were exceptions.[65] Literacy was estimated at 20 percent, a disappointment to the missionaries but a significant improvement nonetheless.[66] Poverty persisted, as did oppression, but there were changes in the living conditions of village Christians. Sanitation had improved, houses were better ventilated, general health standards had risen, more children were attending school, women's groups and youth groups were being organized, and women were more skilled and more active in church life.[67] Progress toward self-support had been made, but the goal had not been attained. Lucas and Thakur Das found that in the Narowal area (CMS) none of the rural churches fully supported their pastors, whereas in the nearby Pasrur area (United Presbyterian) all of them did. According to their analysis the degree of concentration or dispersion of the local Christian population was primarily responsible for this difference. Presbyterian pastors had a wider area to cover than did their counterparts associated with the CMS.[68] Another variable was whether pastors and missionaries lived up to what their Dalit parishioners considered to be their obligations as patrons.[69] In 1945-46 S. N. Talibuddin conducted a survey of self-supporting churches within the Punjab Synod of the United Church of Northern India. He found that the number of self-supporting village churches, while still small, had increased, but that pastors were being so thinly spread over large numbers of villages that the quality of pastoral care and the resulting quality of congregational life was a source of serious concern. As in the Lucas and Thakur Das study, and J. W. Pickett's earlier study of the mass movements that drew some of its data from the Punjab,[70] church life showed most vitality in those villages where pastors were resident.[71]

64. W. F. Hawkes, "A Challenging Situation," *CMO* (January 1940): 4-5; I. D. Parasar, "The Christian Mission Field at Narowal," *MMQ* (June 1945): 15-16.

65. Parasar, "The Christian Mission Field," p. 16; Christopher Cox, "Gojra Village Mission," *MMQ* (June 1945): 14; L. Woolmer, "Church Consciousness," *MMQ* (June 1945): 20; the exception is in Clarence Falk, "Progress and Decay," *UCR* (April 1946): 50.

66. R. Chalk, "Man Shall not Live by Bread Alone," *MMQ* (June 1945): 19.

67. D. M. Corton, "Montgomerywala: Past and Present," *CMO* (May 1938): 103-5; Falk, "Progress and Decay," p. 50.

68. Lucas and Das, *Rural Church in the Punjab*, p. 47.

69. Lucas and Das, *Rural Church in the Punjab*, pp. 50-51.

70. J. Waskom Pickett, *Christian Mass Movements in India* (New York, 1933).

71. S. N. Talibuddin, "A Study of Self-Supporting Churches in the Punjab," *UCR* (May 1947): 278-81, (June 1947): 300-306, (July 1947): 325.

Schools

The cultural interaction that occurred in the schools was probably more profound but certainly more limited in scope than that in the churches. The first schools the missions introduced into the villages were designed to provide instruction in the Christian faith and, as a means to that end, some basic literacy. In places where there was a sufficient concentration of Christians to make the effort worthwhile, they introduced schools that provided a formal education following the curriculum and examinations of the school system overseen and subsidized by the government. They also had town boarding schools for the more gifted and committed students who could advance beyond the primary level. What limited the influence of these schools was the fact that not all rural Christians sent their children to school.[72] Lucas and Thakur Das found that in the 159 families from the eighteen villages they studied the literacy rate among adult males was 11.3 percent, and among adult women, 1.9 percent. Of the 270 children between the ages of six and fourteen, sixty-seven, or 24.8 percent, were literate. They also found that the proportion of children attending school was much higher in villages that had Christian schools than in those that did not.[73]

The nature of the cultural interactions in the boarding schools may best be illustrated by reference to two that were set up specifically for the rural Chuhra Christians. The Narowal Christian Girls' Boarding School was started by CMS missionaries in response to the requests of village converts during the 1890s in the heart of their largest "mass movement area." About twenty-five years later, in 1918, it had eighty boarding and nine day students. "Many are very wild and untamed at first, and it seems impossible to do anything with them, but patience and perseverance do much; and after the first rule, which is obedience, has been mastered, the rest becomes comparatively easy."[74] The aim was not upward mobility but to prepare the girls to become good wives and mothers in a village setting. "They have no idea of order and cleanliness when they come to us, so besides teaching them to read their Bibles, we try to inculcate habits of cleanliness, thrift, and economy, so that they may be able to order aright the homes of their husbands."[75] It was also hoped that the girls would spread the light of faith in

72. W. P. Hares, "The Narowal Mission — A Ten Years' Retrospect," *CMR* (November 1916): 557; Creighton, "Facing Facts," p. 14.

73. Lucas and Das, *Rural Church in the Punjab,* pp. 42, 44.

74. M. W. Morrison, "A Girls' Boarding School in the Punjab," *MMQ* (January 1919): 11.

75. Morrison, "A Girls' Boarding School," p. 12.

their villages. What the school therefore offered was "a simple vernacular education."

> They are taught reading, writing, arithmetic, elementary geography and grammar. They cut out, make, mend, and wash their own clothes, spin, sew and knit — do a little grinding, and all the cooking. They also do bead work of different kinds, and gold and silver embroidery. Every morning they do physical exercises in the courtyard, and this helps to keep them in good health. But the principal study, and the one to which most time is given, is the study of the Bible.[76]

The Moga Training School for Village Teachers, started by Ray H. Carter of the Punjab Mission of the Presbyterian Church in the U.S.A. in 1908, was raised to a middle school in 1917, and in 1923 a two-year teachers' training course was added.[77] The school was a daring educational experiment that attracted considerable attention, not only from the Punjab Government but from other parts of India and abroad, when W. J. McKee introduced the project method of teaching in 1919. Each class had a project for the year (for example, the village home, the village farm, the village bazaar, the village's relations with the outside world) around which all classroom learning was organized. Each child had his or her own plot of land to cultivate and worked on the school farm. The aim was to develop character, initiative, persistence, self-reliance, organizing ability, cooperation, a spirit of service, and a sense of responsibility so that they could become committed and effective village "uplift" workers. The school also published a small monthly, the *Village Teacher's Journal,* to keep teachers up-to-date on information and methods being used at the school.[78]

Both schools were Christian and emphasized religious education and Christian witness. Both taught new skills, enhanced the students' sense of personal competence, and through the residential experience exposed them to some cultural values that challenged and potentially transformed, at least, the Dalit sections of the villages. Where the schools differed was in their ped-

76. M. W. Morrison, "Education in a Mass Movement District," *India's Women* (November 1917): 126.

77. *25 Years: Moga Training School for Village Teachers* (Lucknow, 1937), pp. 126-28.

78. "Village Schools and their Teachers," *Standard* (September 1921): 268-72; W. J. McKee, "Rural Education in India: Moga Training School," in *Standard* (August 1923): 243-46; W. J. McKee, *New Schools for Young India: A Survey of Educational, Economic, and Social Conditions in India with Special Reference to More Effective Education* (Chapel Hill, 1930), pp. 140-84.

agogy. Irene Harper, who with her husband served at Moga for many years, argued that the prevalent pedagogy that relied on memorization, docility, and conformity fostered dependence and competition, whereas "learning through doing" in individual and social projects developed habits of independent thinking, self-reliance, and cooperation.[79] Thus, this pedagogy was far more radical in its social and psychological implications for the rural Dalit Christian student.

The Urban Church

The sources consulted provide remarkably little discussion of Dalits in the urban churches, but some of what is there is highly suggestive. In an assessment of the impact of the rural mass movements on the city churches, a Presbyterian report had this to say:

> The trend of these people, ever since the mass movement began, has been to the city, and it is in the cities where large numbers of these people are to be found today. . . . Recently some one condemned the mass-movement in strong terms and in the course of his remarks pointed to a self-supporting Church in a city, not associated in his mind with mass-movement work, as an argument that other types of work were more profitable. Yet the pastor of that Church, the majority of its officers, and at least 80% of its members had come out of the mass-movement. If you are tempted to disparage mass-movement work, make a study of the Churches of North India, and you will find in all of them large groups who trace their origin back to the mass-movement. And so for a true evaluation of this work, we must not only make a study of the villages where the people live, but go to the Railway shops, to Government offices, to the Courts, to Hospitals, to Schools and Colleges, to Churches and Parsonages, to Homes of culture in the cities, and there we shall find many of these people once despised, and now honoured and respected. Little do we realize what the Church in North India owes to the mass-movement.[80]

79. Irene M. Harper, "The Religious Education of Village Christians," *Standard* (May 1925): 137-41.

80. *Survey of the Evangelistic Work of the Punjab Mission of the Presbyterian Church in the USA 1929*, p. 30.

The inference here is that the Dalits in the urban congregations were not conspicuously Dalits any more. By virtue of having become skilled or white-collar workers they had "blended into" the older, socially mixed, urban congregations and into their culture in such a way as to make their own Dalit caste origins either invisible or irrelevant.

That was not the entire picture, however. CMS missionaries working on the northwest frontier discovered that quite a large number of Punjabi Christians (an estimated 2,000 in twenty-one stations in 1927)[81] had migrated to the towns and cities in the region in search of work. In a couple places they had a virtual monopoly on municipal and cantonment sweeper jobs, and in others they worked as laborers. Only a few who had moved away from their Punjabi villages had also moved up in the social scale. The missionaries found these Christians cut off from and very ignorant of their faith; they therefore took steps both to train them and to organize them into congregations. Since there were very few Afghan converts and thus no preexisting church to "blend into" on the frontier, these Christians retained their distinctive identities both as Chuhras and as Punjabis. Among them the missionaries encountered some of the same problems as in the Punjabi villages: their religious "flexibility" and reluctance to give up old religious practices, their intermarriage, and their eating with Chuhra relatives. In starting schools among them, the missions had to face competition from the Arya Samaj to function as their religious patrons and beneficiaries.[82]

An important study of Dalit Christians in the Punjab, published in 1937, which drew upon urban as well as rural data, is J. C. Heinrich's *The Psychology of a Suppressed People.* He found among the oppressed an almost insatiable desire to assert their own superiority over others. Dalits emerging from oppression felt freer to express this — sometimes in constructive ways (for example, as in an evangelistic campaign in Rawalpindi Presbytery where they played a leading role)[83] and sometimes in destructive ways. Among their favorite targets for abuse were the pastors and mission employees who worked among them. The result was that both these workers and the supervising missionaries found relationships with urban Chuhra Christians extremely stressful.[84]

81. Olive Elwin, "Echoes of the Punjab Mass Movement on the North-West Frontier of India," *CMR* (December 1927): 365.

82. Elwin, "Echoes," pp. 358-67; Lilian A. Underhill, "The Afghan Frontier: Its Problems, Progress, and Possibilities," *CMR* (June 1927): 114-24; (Mrs.) O. Elwin, "Punjabi Christians in Dera Ismail Khan," *MMQ* (September 1929): 36-38; J. S. Dugdale, "A Channel for God on the North-West Frontier," *CMO* (January 1933): 5-7.

83. J. C. Heinrich, *The Psychology of a Suppressed People* (London, 1937), pp. 123-28.

84. Heinrich, *The Psychology of a Suppressed People,* pp. 65-89.

The information available on Dalits in urban churches raises more questions than it answers. It seems important to differentiate the upwardly mobile from the horizontally mobile among them. The former seem to have "blended in," taking on urban ways and probably being more individualistic or nuclear-family centered in outlook, whereas the latter seem to have transferred most of their village culture to their urban *basti*s. Judging from Heinrich's largely anecdotal data, however, both groups bore the psychological scars of past oppression. This affected their cultural interaction with other representatives of Christianity, foreign and Indian, in the cities.

IV

The interaction between Dalits and other Christians in the Punjab during the years following the First World War does not lend itself to neat, coherent generalizations. Superficially there was too much diversity. The range of cultural issues involved in the interactions had expanded and deepened too much. Both the pace and the degree of change varied much from village to village, or village to town, or class to class in the urban areas. At the same time one can also see profound commonalities. Maybe the Chuhras had not really changed all that much, and neither had the missionaries. Conditions were changing, however; converts were becoming more independent and self-supporting, although they remained dependent upon the missions. Chuhras experienced some freedom of opportunity in the wider society as well as within the churches. The result was that pain and resentment, long suppressed, came increasingly to the surface. Relationships within the Christian community became more volatile, less bound by tradition, less predictable, and thus more stressful. Caution is necessary, however, about such conclusions when the evidence is so thin.

This chapter has focused primarily upon the Chuhras and particularly upon those who converted to Christianity. It has sought to understand how they were affected by cultural interactions with other representatives of Christianity. In the analysis an attempt has been made to inquire into the inner psychological (for example, predispositions, attitudes, perceptions, emotional meanings) dimensions of culture as much as into its more outward, behavioral manifestations. It was the missionaries who not only set the terms for those cultural interactions but also framed their major concepts and concerns for the historical record. We have thus been forced to see that interaction almost exclusively through missionary lenses. Would the Chuhras then have described it any differently? Probably so. To what extent would their prior religion have shaped the record that they might have produced, just as Christian religion has so obviously shaped the missionary record? Maybe very little, for at the heart of it interaction seems to have been shaped on the Chuhra side by a deep ambivalence about traditional patron-client relationships, as well as by a burning desire for dignity and respect, which were certainly expressed in their religion but did not seem to have been derived from it.

CHAPTER SIX

Revival from a Native Point of View: Proselytization of the Indian Home Mission and the Kherwar Movement among the Santals

PETER B. ANDERSEN

Srimati Sona Murmu (ca. 1862-1918), a Santal lady and Christian convert, later baptized around 1876, is known from the biography that the Rev. P. O. Bodding published soon after her death.[1] In it he conveys his regard for one of his collaborators from the time of his arrival at the Santal Parganas in 1890 and gives Danish and Norwegian mission friends an account of a deeply religious young girl. She strove for acceptance as a Christian, and, eventually, when the missionaries were satisfied as to her seriousness, she was baptized. Bodding portrays her life as governed by an increasing depth of religious understanding and feeling.

The portrait is convincing. Bodding had persuaded Sona to write down

1. P. O. Bodding, *Sona: En kristen Santalkvindes Liv og Gjerning* (Copenhagen, 1919).

Major parts of this chapter are based on the late P. O. Bodding's folkloric collections, held in Oslo, and thanks are due to Santosh Soren, Copenhagen, and Marine Carrin, EHESS-CNRS, Toulouse (with whom I am preparing selections from the archives for publication), and Harald Tambs-Lyche, University of Picardy-Jules Verne, Amiens, who, with Marine Carrin, is working on the anthropology of the history of the Danish-Norwegian mission to the Santals. I also wish to thank Tove Tybjerg and Carin Laudrup, of the Department of History of Religions, University of Copenhagen. For the Indian Home Mission my main sources are the works of Johan Hodne and Olav Nyhagen. I have had some difficulty reconciling Nyhagen's text to his statistical tables, but this has little bearing on the general picture.

some of her memories, and he often quoted her writings or what she had told him.[2] At the end of the book he included a series of her letters to her son Johan, who was a leper. For the mission friends at home, in Scandinavia, Sona's concerns and admonitions, together with her profound Christian persuasion in the tradition of the Pietist Danish and Norwegian lay movements, were evidence of the successful spread of their own kind of Christianity among the Santal people in the jungles of interior India.

In what follows I try to put Sona's story within the context of the general social and religious changes among the Santals from the middle of the nineteenth century to the publication of Bodding's Danish book: *Sona: The Life and Deeds of a Christian Santal Lady.*[3] The account will touch upon the Santal insurrection, the famous Santal "Hul" in 1855, and comment on the Kherwar movement. Sona's story is open to a reinterpretation of the religious life of the Santals in the last part of the nineteenth century, when it is seen in relation to the other movements. The Hul, as well as the somewhat later Kherwar movement, has been described by social historians.

The suppression of the Hul and its social background are central to most histories of the events from the time of W. W. Hunter's (1868) early account in his *Annals of Rural Bengal.*[4] Until the 1980s there was general agreement that the Hul was a Santal insurrection, and some scholars, mainly anthropologists, assumed that it was a general insurrection comprising all of the Santals, or at least backed by them.[5] In 1983 Ranajit Guha put forward a Gramscian interpretation of the events, in which he argued for the construction of a Santal identity as opposed to a peasant identity in the legal aftermath of the insurgency.[6] This may, however, be understood as evidence of a fluid state of alliances between different social groups rather than evidence of an original peasant identity broken up into different tribal and caste identities in the aftermath of the rebellion. There is, in fact, ample evidence of Santals identifying themselves as a group from the end of the eighteenth century.

2. Modern ethnographers might term the book a "life history" — see James P. Spradley, *The Ethnographic Interview* (New York, 1979), pp. 21-24 — or perhaps an autobiography. Bodding's division of voice and authorship between Sona and himself seems appropriate because he may have had different intentions from those Sona had when she wrote. Spradley stressed this problem; see his *Guests Never Leave Hungry: The Autobiography of James Sewid, a Kwakiutl Indian* (New Haven, 1969).

3. Bodding, *Sona.*

4. W. W. Hunter, *The Annals of Rural Bengal,* vol. 1 (London, 1868).

5. See, e.g., Joseph Troisi, *Tribal Religion: Religious Beliefs and Practices among the Santals* (Delhi, 1978).

6. Ranajit Guha, *Elementary Aspects of Peasant Insurgency in Colonial India* (Delhi, 1983).

Here the existence of a Santal identity among those people considered as Santals is taken for granted. However, it would be interesting to investigate the Kherwar movement from the point of view of identity formation since the few figures identified as Kherwars seem to have come into existence during census operations, thereby indicating that the "Kherwars" so recorded had reported other identities at other times.

Whereas the Hul has been dealt with in a great number of publications on the Santals, the Kherwars have received relatively less consideration. The reasons may be that they were less colorful, and indeed more difficult to label, even if they forwarded demands for *Santal raj.* Some scholars have considered the Kherwars to be more religious than political,[7] although at least one of the early Christian missionaries to the Santals, L. O. Skrefsrud, viewed their activities as a direct continuation of the Hul. He warned in an article in the *Statesman and Friend of India* that they propagated "a rabid, socialistic, political agitation, the religion being only a means towards an end."[8] This formed part of his argument that the authorities should take severe action against them. Much of the discussion on the Kherwars has, however, been more concerned with whether they were under the influence of Christianity or Hinduism. Skrefsrud's biographer, Olav L. O. Hodne, argues that they were not influenced by Christianity,[9] and it is clear that some later Kherwars undoubtedly were influenced by Hindu ritual practices. My understanding, however, is that this discussion is generally based on the impressions of external observers, such as the Christian missionaries, and "official" reactions to the Kherwars.

In all of this it is not easy to discern the voice of the Santals, but my intention is to allow them to speak for themselves. Even if nearly all Santals were illiterate at the time of the Hul, and the Kherwars of the 1870s had left no statements of their own, except in court proceedings, it would still be possible to enter the minds of some of the Santals of the time via Bodding's collections. Sona's "autobiography" constitutes only a very small part of his folklore collections. Bodding published a number of other volumes: studies in Santal medicine and witchcraft and linguistic works such as grammars and a dictionary of Santali. All his works formed a background for his translations of the Bible into Santali. His publications on Santal folklore seem to reflect his personal love of the folktales, and they constitute a major part of the material.

7. Johan Nyhagen, *Santal Misjonens Historie med Særlig Henblikk på Utviklingen i India og Norge 1867-1967,* Bind 1-2 (Oslo, 1990), 1:283.

8. 8 November 1880.

9. Olav L. O. Hodne, *Skrefsrud Missionary and Social Reformer among the Santals of Santal Parganas: With Special Reference to the Period between 1867 and 1881* (Oslo, 1966), pp. 265-86.

We are told that Bodding, whenever he heard a new story, requested that the storyteller tell it to one of the Santals who collected and recorded stories for him.[10]

Many publications have appeared on the Bodding material, but the archives have not yet been fully used. As a historical source they must be seen as the statements of those Santals who were willing and able to talk to Bodding's assistants. Some of the informants, who were mostly anonymous, were Christian of course, but not all, and Bodding went a long way to find reliable informers on rituals and events. The period of the recordings is evident; dated letters show that the collections were already underway by 1893 and continued up to at least 1925.[11] When discussing earlier events such as the Hul and the Kherwar movements, Bodding's informants are not any better than other sources. They must be seen as persons who represent a line of tradition. Sometimes they state that they were present; sometimes it is evident that their knowledge is, at best, secondhand. As statements of the religious mood and social changes in Santal society in the period around the turn of the century, however, they speak for themselves. The manuscripts reflect different positions among the individual Santals, and one has to consider how far they can be seen as representative of Santal society at large. They may be representative only of those Santals who befriended the missionaries. These considerations must be kept in mind when considering the different issues dealt with by the narrators. Some of the differences and homogeneities between those Santals who joined the Christian and the Kherwar movements, respectively, will be considered below.

My argument is that there was an ongoing reinterpretation of religious thought and practices, on the part of the Santals, in an attempt to come to grips with social events from the middle of the nineteenth to well into the twentieth century. The Santals conceptualized the events at a much higher analytical level than that indicated by most social histories and anthropologists. They were active and independent in their reactions to the Christian missions, to representatives of British rule, and to surrounding Indian society. Bodding's biography of Sona may be seen as an early example of giving voice to the Santals even if he never states this explicitly.

10. Sagram Santosh Kumar Soren, comp., *Catalogue of Santalia Manuscripts in Oslo*, Nordic Institute for Asian Studies Report Series, no. 41 (Copenhagen, 1999), pp. 3-5.

11. Soren, *Catalogue*, pp. 3-5.

Sona

The Indian Home Mission to the Santals was founded in 1868 by the Dane Hans Peter Børresen (1825-1901) and the Norwegian Lars Olsen Skrefsrud (1840-1910), together with their wives, of whom the German Mrs. Caroline Børresen (1832-1914) was the most famous. They had come to India with the Gossner Mission and worked for it from 1863 to 1865 among the Cols in Chotanagpur, a little to the south of Santal Parganas.[12] As a result of conflict with the mission they left, and after three problematic years, later known as "the Exile," Børresen and Skrefsrud were appointed as helpers to a Baptist missionary in Santal Parganas in 1867. The next year Skrefsrud was baptized as a Baptist. In 1871 the Baptist missionary had to return home because of ill health, and over the following years Børresen and Skrefsrud gradually established an independent mission, moving more and more toward a Lutheran position. This was the result, in part, of the founding of support groups of Pietist mission friends in Denmark, Norway, and other European countries.

It is evident that the mission to the Santals had a slow start. The two first converts, baptized in 1867, soon lapsed, and the next three were not baptized until 1869. Gradually, however, the mission was established. A major breakthrough came in 1873 when an influential local village leader *(pargana)*,[13] Matru, was baptized by Skrefsrud. Matru had been broken by eight months in jail, and after that Skrefsrud had cured him from dropsy and prepared him for baptism. Skrefsrud informs us that a delegation of five hundred village leaders met him and that 111 asked for baptism, a number that may be reflected in the available figures of baptism.

During the period the mission undertook social work and established itself as a buffer between the Santals and Hindu moneylenders. It rented the right to collect land revenue in its neighborhood, and the missionaries were on good terms with some of the government officials. Børresen used such official contacts when he established a government relief program under his own leadership during the famine of 1873-74.

Børresen took upon himself the task of distributing the famine relief, which was given only on the conditions that the recipients did a day's work in return and that he was allowed to preach the gospel to them. This was part of his arrangement with the District Commissioner, and was in this way legal, but it gave rise to a number of critical voices. The reporter of the *Times* (of

12. Hodne, *Skrefsrud*, pp. 64-68.

13. A *pargana* is a chief of a hundred villages.

Calcutta) for 31 August 1874, Mr. George Kerry, who had been freed from his work in the Baptist mission to make the report, admitted that he had allowed himself to be caught up in the spell of Børresen's eagerness to help the Santals with the well-run program. Nevertheless he wrote:

> The Commissioner conceded M. Boerresen's claim to preach daily, either himself or by some of his agents, to the people employed — many thousands at one time, now about 1,700. It may be granted that the missionary had a right if he gave his time without recompense, to make his own conditions, and in this case, perhaps, the government were in the right in acceding to them; but the example cannot safely be followed. . . . Mr. Boerresen exercises his right in the fullest extent. . . . Altogether, I am describing an exceptional station under an exceptional man, who is not above using wiles and stratagems against Satan, but who is an entity and an individuality among men. He lately had the audacity to dismiss a committee which he thought useless — fancy a missionary dismissing a committee. . . . But his good work remains. He is worthy of support. He will not flinch from Brahmin or zemindar or Maharajah or civil officer or the crown. I think this is a quality that Denmark has good reason to be proud of, and that England has good reason to be proud of too.[14]

Mr. Kerry ends his comments with a warning: "Mr. Boerresen is, I fear, an ambitious man," and says, "What I heard with the greatest dislike was that [Børresen said] there had been a great revival among the Santals due to the famine. . . . Boerresen stays in the dam and often he baptises hundreds during a day, but remember, it is he who hands out the food."[15]

According to Johan Nyhagen, *The Church Book (Dåbsregisteret)* counted 1,592 baptisms in 1874-75. This was a revival indeed, and it helps explain why the Danish and Norwegian lay Christians decided to back the mission with funds a little later. Ever since, however, the quality of the conversions has been debated. Had the newly baptized understood the faith or did they act for food? Later, the official historian of the Norwegian Santal Mission, Johan Nyhagen, allowed himself to question the quality of the conversions, even if tried to adopt a positive position. In his interpretation the Rev. Vilhelm Beck, leader of the Danish Inner Mission, saw a parallel to the Danish Church in Børresen's strategy:

14. *Times,* 31 August 1874, Calcutta, cited in Nyhagen, *Santal Misjonens,* 1:204.
15. Nyhagen, *Santal Misjonens,* 1:205.

> When the heathens asked for baptism, it had to happen immediately, the teaching could be added at a later point. Then — according to Beck — there would be a lot of Christians by name only, who had at the utmost reached the elementary class, and who would conduct their lives much like the heathens. But in such a Christian population, there ought to be an Inner Mission. That was the way Europe had become Christian, and that was what he thought would be the right thing to do in Santalistan.[16]

Against this background one can read Bodding's biography of Sona as a contribution to the argument for the depth and seriousness of the conviction of the Santals converted by Skrefsrud and Børresen.

The biography deals with Sona's family background, her education in Mrs. Børresen's girls' school, her marriage to Gulu Murmu, and their life in the service of the mission as schoolteacher and catechist. In addition it communicates what information Bodding had on the life of all her children.

Sona relates her memories about how people were frightened by the missionaries in the beginning, as they were thought to abduct people and sell them to the fearsome *Gormuha*s and *Ekaguria*s as food. Bodding added the soothing comment to the readers that, by 1919, this fear had long disappeared.[17]

During the famine of 1873-74 Sona, together with her family, participated in the construction work of the great pools, and during that time she heard Børresen preach for the first time. She did not understand the message, but the episode as she remembered it reflects the reactions of an eleven-to-twelve-year-old girl. According to the account, Børresen said, "'Come, come, join us to Heaven,' but all knelt down. Then I thought," Sona writes, "He says, 'Come, come, join us to Heaven.' Why do they not go up to Heaven? Why do they kneel down?"[18] Another childlike reflection is her thought on how great the *bonga* of the Christians must be when a man who had been bitten by a snake was cured after the prayers of the Christians. This episode may, one should note, have been especially relevant to Bodding's audience in Denmark and Norway since it is parallel to the episodes of intercession and miracles systematically stressed in the narratives of the early missionaries.[19]

In her biographical writings Sona does not reveal her theological and per-

16. Nyhagen, *Santal Misjonens,* 1:296.

17. Bodding, *Sona,* p. 9.

18. Bodding, *Sona,* p. 11.

19. For example, Matru's imprisonment; see Harald F. Jørgensen, *Evangeliet blandt Santalerne, den Nordiske Santalmissions Historie* (Copenhagen, 1940), p. 65.

sonal religious reflections much beyond the level of simple statements of her staunch Christian position. In a story she wrote about Mr. and Mrs. Børresen, but which focuses on her own life, she starts: "When Papa [Mr. Børresen] was in Scandinavia, the Christian Santals became unfaithful. They did not come to church and began to fall off. They did not send their children to school; and the pupils did not stay, even if they were brought by force to the school."[20]

In another episode she relates that she and her husband, who were then leaders of a mission station, were ordered to stay at the headquarters in Benagaria for five or six months and were reprimanded for their wrong kind of faith. "According to their understanding, we were almost like excommunicated persons. . . . Then they sent us back (to our respective places) when they gave us the highly religious teachings."[21]

Exactly what teachings they deemed necessary for Sona and her husband she does not say, and the context leaves no doubt that she felt that they were accused on false pretexts. It is difficult to know exactly when this took place. The only time Sona and her husband were ordered to stay in Benagaria according to Bodding's account was in 1899, when Skrefsrud accused a number of mission leaders of abusing the power and money that came with their positions. Bodding comments: "However well the intention [of Skrefsrud] might have been, there were bad elements who exerted their influence and prospered by it to the harm of the good intentions."[22] This story shows Skrefsrud in a unflattering light, and it could have been counterproductive if it had influenced the Danish and Norwegian laymen who supported the mission.

It is in her correspondence with her son, who was hospitalized for leprosy, that Sona's faith is displayed to the full and in a way that must have an appeal to modern and less religiously minded Danes and Norwegians.

Dumka, 16 July 1918

My Dear son Johan!

I have sent your book and I have got your letter. Take your medicine. How we pray every day, we pray for you, for the family, for all Christians. At that time of the day, remember your mother's prayer, and pray as

20. Sona Murmu, *Papa ar Mama* [Papa and Mama], ms. fol. 1686, file IX, pt. 3 (*Santalia,* no. 2949).

21. Sona, *Papa ar Mama.*

22. Bodding, *Sona,* p. 22. Bodding's account of the context may reflect Sona's own information in her manuscripts.

well. Jesus loves you. By this severe pain he draws our hearts to him. We shall come him nearer and nearer. Do not growl. Praise God. He looks after us, my beloved child. . . . Do not forget to read in the Bible and sing! No more, my son. With love.

Your Mother[23]

Bodding's biography must have shown the lay people that there was no doubt about the quality of Sona's moving, religious, and motherly statements of faith and her devotion to Jesus.

As to the situation of the mission in 1919, when Bodding wrote Sona's biography, some of his comments on her early life show that he was resigned to the problems: "She never forgot what she experienced then. The zeal and love was great among the first Christians. God give that it had never cooled off."[24] Whether this mood was caused by an isolation of the Christian cause or by the early national agitation in India, or whether it was only a reflection of developments within the mission itself, is difficult to tell. There was a conflict over the leadership of the mission, and in 1922, a few years later, Bodding was overthrown as its leader in a plot, the origins of which may date back to his conflicts with the late Mrs. Børresen.[25] Perhaps a hint of this conflict is to be found in Bodding's remark on Mrs. Børresen's severe Prussian discipline during Sona's days in the girls' school of which Mrs. Børresen was head.[26] What is important is that Bodding was right in his analysis of Sona's religious life: she was a deeply devout Christian from her youth, and she bears witness to the seriousness of at least some of the early converts of the mission. The question is whether her conversion to Christianity is representative of a general religious fervor in her lifetime. It seems likely that this judgment may be supported from the materials collected by Bodding.

Aftermath of the Hul and the Kherwar

There is agreement that the Hul must be understood as a reaction to ruthless exploitation of the Santals by non-Santals in the context of a particular agrarian system. The Santals were low-level workers employed in groups under a village leader, the *manjhi*, to clear forests so that cultivation might be intro-

23. Bodding, *Sona*, p. 86. The Santali originals of Sona's correspondence are not among Bodding's manuscripts. They have, presumably, been lost.

24. Bodding, *Sona*, p. 11.

25. Hodne, *Skrefsrud*, pp. 66-103.

26. Bodding, *Sona*, p. 18.

duced. Under the agrarian system they were afterward allowed to harvest the land that they had cleared, but in many cases they were soon "disinherited" or reduced to the status of poorly paid landed workers devoid of any right to leave the land because of their mortgages.[27]

In 1854 conflicts broke out in an area called Damin-i-Koh, in the northernmost parts of the Rajmahal Hills (south of the Ganges River), where more than eighty thousand Santals had settled from the early nineteenth century.[28] During 1854 the houses of moneylenders were plundered and burned down, and petitions were sent to the government to seek justice and a rearrangement of agrarian relations. Since the government took no serious action, a demonstration to the Calcutta authorities was arranged under the leadership of the brothers Sidhu and Kanhu, and Chandhu and Bhairab, who said that they were acting according to the orders of God Thakur. The demonstration is estimated to have comprised about ten thousand persons, mostly Santals, and it soon took to looting. A police officer who tried to arrest the leaders was killed, and the government took severe action against what was considered an insurrection. About thirty thousand Santals took part, but not as a regular army. When between twelve thousand and fourteen thousand of the Company's soldiers attacked at the end of the rainy season in 1855, the uprising was crushed.[29]

After the Hul the East India Company began to remedy a number of the grievances of the Santals. A district, the Santal Parganas, centered around the Damin-i-Koh, was created. This was the district where the Danish-Norwegian mission to the Santals later settled and had its headquarters. Here the Santal village headmen were given special powers, and the Santals were allowed to process their court cases with the Company's British personnel without intermediaries.

In Bodding's collections an otherwise unknown Santal, Durga Tudu, voiced the grievances of the time before the Hul in a story titled "The Old Time before the *Hul*."[30] In his narrative the time before the Hul is characterized by a long list of social problems. The Santals are exploited by other groups, and, out of fear, they either run away or lose when taking up a fight;

27. The term "mortgage" is used in the contemporary literature on the Santals. It is unclear exactly what debts led the Santals to mortgage their farmlands.

28. Estimated at no fewer than 83,265 in the Damin-i-Koh in 1851 alone. L. S. S. O'Malley, *Bengal District Gazetteers: Santal Parganas* (Calcutta, 1910), p. 99.

29. There are many accounts of those events in the specialist literature. The references for the present account can be found in Nyhagen, *Santal Misjonens,* 1:37-42.

30. Durga Tudu, *Sedae hul pahil rea katha* [The Old Time Before the *Hul*], ms. fol. 1686, file VI, pt. 2 (*Santalia,* no. 2467).

they even start fighting among themselves. What he adds to the usual analysis, however, is not only an understanding of the atmosphere of fear of the people in power but also a statement on the breakdown of age-old forms of social solidarity due to the exploitation: "In this way their mutual help among themselves disappeared when they fought against others." This narrative of a change from a collectively based solidarity to no solidarity can be understood as a comment on the introduction of individual forms of debt instead of collective forms.

As a Santal statement it conveys a kind of contemporary social analysis that supports a general "modernization" thesis. This seems unique for the time. So, for the dating of the experienced "individualization" it is necessary to consider the date of the statement. It may well be a comment on the changes in Santal society around 1900 rather than on the background of the Hul almost fifty years earlier. Even so it sheds light on Santal understanding of social change.

In the aftermath of the Hul there were two important reactions that may have been common to many Santals of the Santal Parganas. Both are found in the narratives of several anonymous narrators. One is that the two leading brothers, Sidhu and Kanhu, were in fact acting on the orders of God, but they sinned, and for this reason they could not create a *Santal raj.* (In this version the political intentions of the formation of a *raj* are quite explicit.) The thought was that God had ordered Sidhu and Kanhu to stay "clean," but when they came to power they took beautiful girls, daughters, daughters-in-law, and wives of other men. This is an interpretation, which is most properly understood as a reaction to the lost case, following the lines of a common Indian hierarchical interpretation of cleanness versus sin. (As to the rapes, they seem to be a historical fact established beyond any reasonable doubt.)

The other common element, which is stated several times, is that the Hul was before the time of the arrival of the Sahibs, which indicates that the post-Hul situation was better than the one before their arrival. Whether the Sahibs who are mentioned are missionaries or colonial administrators is not known: both were present before the Hul. The statement, as it appears in relation to its date and setting, indicates that some Santals in the Santal Parganas found the colonial administration legitimate because it was righteous. Others, who were not Christian Santals, agreed with this position (the anonymous informants evidently do not reflect Christian points of view in any simple way). However, it is impossible to argue who, or how many, considered the colonial power legitimate. In this regard the Kherwars inform our discussion since they took another religious and political position in relation to the colonial power.

The Kherwars

The Kherwars appeared in 1868 under the leadership of a Bhagrit Manjhi. He demanded that a *Santal raj* should be introduced and that the Santals should stop their sacrifices to the "evil *bongas*" for the adoration to Ram(a) or Chando, that is, Sin Chando, the Sun.

Bhagrit Manjhi was arrested in 1868 as an instigator of disturbances. He was active again up to the time of the 1871 census, continued his activities during the great famine in Bengal in 1874, and was sentenced to two years imprisonment. Besides him, his brother Ram and several Hindu leaders participated and were, every now and then, placed under arrest. There were further activities during the census period of 1880-81. Extra troops were stationed in the main town of Santal Parganas, Dumka, from 1874 to 1877 because of the Kherwars, and again during the period 1880-81.

Joseph Troisi reflects a common assumption when he sees the Kherwars as being almost assimilated into Hinduism as more and more Hindu cult elements and the concept of "cleanness" were introduced by the leadership. This development, according to Troisi, was only checked as the result of a new and different kind of tribal mobilization, the Jharkhand movement, in the 1930s.[31] Whether the Kherwars were so numerous among the Santals that they could ever have had that impact is difficult to judge, but during the 1881 census operations 40,960 people insisted on being recorded as Kherwars, not as Santals.[32] However, there is an argument, based on an often implicit assumption that religions constitute separate entities, and that these will break down from within at the introduction of foreign elements.

In the case of the Kherwars, the assumption has blinded people to the other possibility: that the Kherwars are just another example of the same kind of religious fervor among the Santals that the Christian converts demonstrated with their religious feelings. If one thinks about it, some elements in the Kherwar movement point to this, the most evident being the rejection of the traditional *bongas* in the religion of the Santals as wicked. This dogma cannot be found anywhere in Santal or Hindu religion before the condemnation of the *bongas* by the missionaries.

That there are themes common to the Christian and the Kherwarian revivals is demonstrated in the story, told by an anonymous Santal, about the

31. Troisi, *Tribal Religion,* pp. 255-59, and his "Social Movements among the Santals," in *Social Movements in India,* vol. 2: *Sectarian, Tribal and Women's Movements,* edited by M. S. A. Rao (New Delhi, 1979), pp. 123-32.

32. Cited in Hodne, *Skrefsrud,* p. 273.

Bhabajii, the leaders of the Kherwars.[33] The narrator tells us that he hurried to attend Bhagrit Manjhi's sermons as soon as Bhagrit appeared, and one gets the impression that he had attended the sermons of most of the other Kherwars even if he is not specific about all cases. In general terms all the *babaji*s could heal nearly all kinds of physical illness. They saw illness as a sign of sin, and they explained again and again that the healing did not come from them but from God. Their followers would meet them in the evening, and the *babaji*s would promise the ailing that God would help them, but the ill would be required to believe in him.

The story about the sins of Sidhu and Kanhu, who lost because they could not control their own lust, is repeated as part of Bhagrit Manjhi's presentation of his own demands against the colonial power. From the narrator's point of view the reason that the colonial power sent for rice from Burma, for famine relief, was their fear of him, a fear that was justified, the narrator implies, since Bhagrit was clean and could easily establish the *Santal raj* if he so wished. In spite of the fact that Bhagrit Manjhi was arrested, the narrator expresses no doubt of any sort about the powers of the *babaji*s, for in a number of cases their healings worked and people regained their health. In addition, all of the *babaji*s said that their deeds would only last for three years, and then the effect would be over. According to the story, each of them died three years after they had appeared, which must be understood as a kind of narrative proof of their claim of God's mandate.

Exploitation, Lost Fight, and Spiritual Fervor

There is no way of knowing whether the last narrator did, in the end, come to the "right" kind of faith, from Bodding's point of view, and convert to Christianity. It may be that he did. We can, now and then, detect disturbing stories underlying his narration about the *babaji*s: for instance, when he tells how they demanded money from their adherents even if they "sat" on a heap of money in an almost literal sense. What happened to the narrator does not concern us here. What matters is that he described the religious mood of the Kherwars as a kind of fervor similar to that observed earlier among the Christian converts.

Generally it seems that quite a number of the Santals in Santal Parganas tried to interpret what they understood as the social breakdown of Santal so-

33. Anonymous, *Babajuiko reak* [The Babajis], ms. fol. 1686, file II, pt. 5 (*Santalia*, no. 2203).

ciety under what they conceived as foreign exploitation. Some described the breakdown as a kind of "individualization" using analytical terms similar to those of sociologists. They saw the reasons in the breakdown of old social exchange systems. Few, of course, used such terminology. Most framed their understanding in terms of "cleanness" versus "sin" and explained the defeat of the Santal Hul as the result of sin. On the personal level that might lead them toward one religious persuasion or another that addressed the problem of sin.

The Christian interpretation of a just and harmonious society, put forth by the Indian Home Mission, was connected with an understanding of the colonial hegemony as just and legitimate. The mission itself tried to establish justice and legitimacy through relief efforts to the poor and in social reconstruction. In the case of the Kherwars the "solution" was, in the main, connected to demands for social reconstruction.

As religious revivals, the Christian mass movements and the Kherwars movement may both be seen as related and similar responses to the same social and religious problems of the late nineteenth century.

CHAPTER SEVEN

Entering into the Christian Dharma: Contemporary "Tribal" Conversions in India

BENGT G. KARLSSON

> For me, conversion is a free, personal, and consequently responsible act. A *forced conversion* is therefore a contradiction in terms. In the Christian belief, conversion is a gift of God. It is not something that can be acquired by right, still less can it be acquired by inducement, or by the offer of rice and jobs.
>
> Alan de Lastic, Archbishop of Delhi,
> Interview, *Frontline,* 1 January 1999

I

Christian conversion among tribal or indigenous people, during 1998 and 1999, reached the main arena of Indian politics. The Hindu fundamentalists, or *Hindutva* organizations, rallied over what they describe as a "Christian conspiracy" to wipe out Hinduism from the country. Christian missionaries are thus charged with organized proselytization of the lower sections of Indian society, something that is described as a major threat to Hindu cultural values and the integrity of the nation. Changing religion is to some Hindu fundamentalists the same as a change of nationality, and to them only a Hindu is a rightful or "true" Indian. Backed by accusations of "forced conversions" of tribal peoples, the Hindu fundamentalists have intensified a campaign of terror and hatred against Christians, instigating violence, burning churches, beating priests, preachers, and ordinary church members, raping nuns, and killing people.

The campaign reached a peak in December 1998, and the most spectacular event a month later was the killing of the Australian missionary, Graham Stewart Staines, and his two young sons, who were burnt alive in their car.[1] As many critics have pointed out, the government, dominated by the Bharatiya Janata Party (BJP), failed to a large extent to stop the violence and protect the Christian communities in vulnerable areas. The prime minister, Atal Behari Vajpayee, refuted any allegations that the BJP itself had been involved in, or had in any way instigated, these attacks. Others, mostly independent observers, argued for a rather more direct relationship between BJP rule and the anti-Christian campaign. Vajpayee's call for a national debate on religious conversion appears to suggest, as the historian K. N. Panikkar points out, "that the blame, in fact, rests with the victims."[2] Other BJP, Rashtriya Swayamsevak Sangh (RSS), and Vishwa Hindu Parishad (VHP) leaders have been much more outspoken and have more or less explicitly justified violence against Christians, often describing it as a spontaneous, popular reaction against the missionaries' unlawful activities, that is, their "forced conversions."

Linked with the recent controversy are cases of conversion among tribals or *adivasis* in the Dangs, an interior hilly part of the state of Gujarat. Activists within the VHP, Bajrang Dal, and a local *Hindutva* organization (Hindu Jagran Manch) claim that the Christian missionaries have forced, bribed, or pressured people into becoming Christians. The Church is thus said to have taken advantage of, or exploited, the ignorance of tribal people.[3] The Church

1. The Wadhwa commission investigated Staines' murder. It identified Dara Singh as the main suspect and described him as an individual fanatic. Singh has, however, been described as connected to BJP and RSS and as an activist in Bajrang Dal, all of which deny any connection to him. The National Council of Churches claim there is evidence of Singh's association to the Sangh Parivar (see *Times of India,* 11 August 1999, and *Frontline,* 24 September 1999). In a recent BJP news report (http://www.bjp.org), journalist and party ideologist Arun Shourie criticizes those who claim that Dara Singh was affiliated to organizations linked to BJP and RSS. Shourie argues that Staines was not the innocent social worker the church and the media have made him out to be, and that he did carry out conversions. In the Australian missionary journal *Tidings,* Staines and his wife describe how they participated in baptisms of tribals. Shourie concludes that Staines's concerns were those of "a typical missionary." In no instance had the conversions been approved by the local authorities as they should by Orissa law. (So, Shourie argues, the responsibility for the deaths had nothing to do with any Hindu organization; Staines indulged in illegal conversions and was at fault.)

2. *Frontline,* 12 February 1999, p. 20.

3. Interview with Jayantibhai Kewat, BJP leader in the Dangs and founder of the Hindu Jagran Manch, an organization with the explicit goal of halting Christian conversion and bringing people back to the Hindu fold (Rediff Interview, 31 December 1998,

agrees that there have been conversions among the tribals in the area, but says that these were of free will and thus a matter of conviction or belief.[4] Government investigation (by a special bench of the National Commission for Minorities) has not found any proof of force behind the conversions in the Dangs.[5] Ghanshyam Shah, Professor of Social Science at Jawaharlal Nehru University, New Delhi, has for a long time carried out research in Gujarat, and he disputes the statements by the BJP government in Gujarat that forced conversions have been carried out in the Dangs. Shah, writing for one of India's most prestigious and independent journals, maintains that the government has been unable to produce any evidence of such acts. During a field trip in early January 1999, Shah heard from converts their various personal reasons for accepting the gospel; most commonly "curing of diseases, relief from tension related to day-to-day problems, (and) faith in prayer which helped them in personal crises."[6] The use of force clearly came from various Hindu organizations, mainly Hindu Jagran Manch, which have been harassing and pressuring the Christians who did not follow their advice to "reconvert." Shah's findings are unequivocal: "The events in the Dangs are a part of organised persecution of Christians in Gujarat."[7] His accounts of peoples' conversion narratives are also significant, and, as we will see, they are more or less identical to those I have recorded among the Rabha people and to other researchers' accounts of indigenous or tribal peoples' conversions. Generally speaking, Shah's article also points to a more general conclusion, or, rather, point of departure: that in trying to make sense of people's change of religion one is bound to investigate how this action relates to the converts' own projects and desires and, further, to their overall life situation. For any person or group to convert, we can assume that the new religion makes sense or, in one way or another, resonates with the interests of the individual or people in question.[8]

---

www.rediff.com). Kewat argues that the *adivasis* would never accept Christianity willingly and that it is a question of either force or bribery, and he says that by becoming Christians they endanger Hindu culture and religion.

4. The United Christian Forum for Human Rights has also stated in relation to the Gujarat conversion that all Indian citizens have the right to choose what religion they want to practice (see, e.g., *Times of India,* 12 January 1999).

5. I have been unable to obtain any report or formal statement on the Gujarat case by the National Commission for Minorities, and I rely here on press reports.

6. Ghanshyam Shah, "Conversion, Reconversion and the State — Recent Events in the Dangs," *Economic and Political Weekly* (6 February 1999): 315-18.

7. Shah, "Conversion," p. 318.

8. Consider, e.g., Dr. Ambedkar's and his followers' conversion to Buddhism and other controversial conversion movements, such as the Muslim conversions in Meenakshipuram in Tamil Nadu in the early 1980s. There are rather well-conceived mo-

I use "interest" in a broad sense here, to include both conscious and partly conscious motivations or aims for human action. One can, of course, think of a situation where direct force or methods of "brainwashing" are used to make people join a sect or become members of a religious congregation.[9] It appears, however, that arguments about "forced conversions" in India have not pushed it to this extreme. As a general rule, then, I take it to be a question of people choosing conversion rather than being converted.

This is not to deny that there are organizations that promote and encourage people to join their religious fold. In the Dangs, according to Shah, almost twenty church organizations are working. These organizations work closely with the locals. With compassion, but also with medicine and welfare programs, they try to reach the *adivasis*.[10] There are great differences in how churches function today. Some churches emphasize dialogue and understanding between religions and do not see their task as one of spreading the gospel to others. There are, however, a number of Christian churches that pursue a rather aggressive form of evangelization, using modern media techniques and well-orchestrated mass meetings with charismatic preachers. Not long ago I discovered, on the internet, the Joshua Project 2000 of the A.D. 2000 and Beyond movement. This global network of Christian churches, established in the early 1990s, had the goal of "a church for every people and the gospel for every person by the year 2000." They claimed "Joshua 2000 [was] an evangelism plan" focusing on "unreached" or the "least evangelized" peoples in the world.[11] The Joshua Project 2000 also had a special plan for northern India, an area that, as they say in their document "To The Uttermost Part — The Call to North India," is "strategically important in completing the

tives behind these (to escape caste discrimination). See E. Zelliott, *From Untouchable to Dalit: Essays on the Ambedkar Movement* (New Delhi, 1999); J. Ali Khan, "Mass Conversions of Meenakshipuram — A Sociological Inquiry," in *Religion in South Asia*, edited by G. A. Oddie (New Delhi, 1991).

9. There are reports of the use of threat and force by *Hindutva* organizations, such as the Hindu Jagran Manch in Gujarat, which carry out so-called "reconversion" or "home-coming" camps where Christian tribals are made to "return" to the Hindu fold.

10. Shah, "Conversion," p. 315.

11. Such peoples are registered in a special "Untargeted List," and for every sixteen hundred people listed so far a special "People Profile" has been established. Information is collected and ordered in a highly systematic way. Records are kept on whether those in question have access to the Bible (complete, New Testament only, or other parts), a Jesus film, Christian broadcasting, and audio recording of the gospel. With this information a "priority ranking," from 1 (highest priority) to 9, is worked out for each person. The Untargeted List includes the Rabha, whom they interestingly enough give a priority ranking of only 8.

unfinished task of world evangelisation."[12] The entire nature of the Joshua Project 2000, and the language or terminology used in documents, made the spread of Christianity sound like a well-planned military operation. Obviously, those who invest time and money in the project find these methods instrumental to their goal of world evangelization. I would still claim, however, that regardless of the activities of some missionary societies or single missionaries, agency is finally in the hands or heads of the converts themselves. Even in colonial contexts it would be misleading to discuss religious conversion in terms of its being forced upon "native" subjects. The latter need, in one way or another, to embrace or appropriate the new religious identity for conversion to come about. But the convert, like all other human subjects, is not free or detached from the historical and social circumstances.

Jean and John Comaroff's much discussed historical anthropology of the Tswana people in southern Africa provides an important example of how we can approach Christian conversion in colonial (and postcolonial) contexts.[13] The Comaroffs describe how the Tshidi, a Tswana people, initially found the mission useful and tried to attract missionaries to work among them. They did this in competition with chiefs of other groups, who also found the mission a "priced resource," as the Comaroffs put it.[14] Missionaries were, among other things, looked upon as a source of valuable goods as well as of technical skills. Once in place, however, the mission "forced" the people into a dialogue very much on its own terms, a dialogue that in the end resulted in a "subtle internalization" of the categories and values of Protestant ideology.[15] The missionary encounter is here part of a larger cultural dialectic set about by

12. This and other citations and information on the Joshua Project 2000 came from http://www.ad2000.org.

13. See Jean Comaroff and John Comaroff, "Christianity and Colonialism: The Tswana Case," *American Ethnologist* 13.1 (February 1986), and *Of Revelation and Revolution: Christianity, Colonialism and Consciousness in South Africa* (Chicago and London, 1991); Jean Comaroff, *Body of Power, Spirit of Resistance: The Culture and History of a South African People* (Chicago and London, 1985). Other examples of similar anthropological research are J. Clifford, *The Predicament of Culture* (Cambridge, Mass., 1988); G. M. White, *Identity Through History: Living Stories in Solomon Islands Society* (Cambridge, Mass., 1991); R. M. Keesing, *Custom and Confrontation: The Kwaio Struggle for Cultural Autonomy* (Chicago and London, 1992); R. W. Hefner, ed., *Conversions to Christianity: Historical and Anthropological Perspectives on a Great Transformation* (Berkeley, 1992); and B. Meyer, "Modernity and Enchantment: The Image of the Devil in Popular African Christianity," in *Conversions to Modernities: The Globalization of Christianity*, edited by Peter van der Veer (New York, 1996).

14. Jean and John Comaroff, "Christianity and Colonialism," p. 3.

15. Jean and John Comaroff, "Christianity and Colonialism," p. 14.

the incorporation of the Tshidi into colonial society and economy. To the Comaroffs it is clearly not a question of people being forced or pressured into becoming Christians, but neither was it something freely chosen. Adopting Christianity in situations like this is, as Jean Comaroff argues, a response on the part of the oppressed "to regain a sense of control" (a sense of self) in troubled times.[16] Some element of choice and agency is nevertheless clearly there. It is also significant how the Tswans mold or create their own form of Christianity rather than merely adopting a ready-made Western type of church.[17]

The Comaroffs' work, like that of others (including my own), is grounded in a theoretical and political attempt to claim historical agency for dominated or subaltern people. An aspect of this is to represent such people as, at least partly, in control of their engagement with the larger world. Such a position needs, of course, to be scrutinized. In his contribution to the book *Conversions to Modernities: The Globalization of Christianity,* the anthropologist Talal Asad does this.[18] Asad asks why it is so important in recent work on religious conversion "to insist that the converted are 'agents,' and that their conversion is based on a free and informed individual decision."[19] To him conversion is "rarely the result of an entirely 'free choice,'" but rather "a consequence of forces beyond their [the converts'] control."[20] Although in his critique he overstresses the level of freedom in this choice (few would argue it is entirely free), he has a point. Emphasizing agency and resistance in accounts of conversion in another epoch or society runs the risk, as Asad argues, of being more a reflection of our time and modern ideological assumptions about the individual as an independent moral subject. These accord humans with the capacity to initiate, choose, and act (consciously) on their own. But in other places and times, and for the religious-minded person today, conversion, according to Asad, is more the work of God or the divine than an act of human will. The initial citation of the Archbishop of Delhi,

16. Jean Comaroff, *Body of Power,* p. 253.

17. This situation can be analyzed in terms of a "contact zone," where even situations of unequal power relations offer some space for action and negotiation on the part of the weak or subaltern; see M. L. Pratt, *Imperial Eyes: Travel Writing and Transculturation* (London and New York, 1992); J. Clifford, *Routes: Travel and Translation in the Late Twentieth Century* (Cambridge, Mass., 1997).

18. Talal Asad, "Comments on Conversion," in *Conversions to Modernities: The Globalization of Christianity,* edited by Peter van der Veer (New York, 1996), p. 271.

19. See Talal Asad's introduction to his *Genealogies of Religion: Discipline and Reasons of Power in Christianity and Islam* (Baltimore and London, 1993).

20. Asad, *Genealogies of Religion,* p. 263.

Alan de Lastic, is an example of how conversion in the Christian tradition often is perceived as a "gift of God." Here then we are entering the difficult domain of belief and faith, a domain largely absent from the agenda of present-day social science. Gauri Viswanathan argues in *Outside the Fold: Conversion, Modernity, and Belief* that there is a general lack of language and terminology to talk about beliefs in terms other than "fundamentalism" or the "pre-modern."[21] She takes the example of the Subaltern Studies project, arguing that researchers also fail to come to terms with belief systems as essential to the "subaltern consciousness."[22] The main point of the book, stated at the outset, is that change of religion is one of the most "unsettling political events in the life of a society."[23] This is clearly the case in India today, but it is also, as Viswanathan shows, true for other societies and other epochs. Trying to write about such politicized matters is a minefield. Any account is bound to be read as a plea in favor of one side or the other.

The section that follows will consider why people change their religious belonging and how conversion is narrated. It is necessary to break out of the "forced-free" dichotomy and address the issue of religious conversion in different terms. The empirical case I deal with is the contemporary conversion movement among the Rabhas, or the Kochas, as they prefer to call themselves, a tribal community in West Bengal.[24]

The Rabha comprise a set of rather loosely connected groups, the main ones being Pati, Rangdania, Kocha, and Maitori Rabha. Linguistically the Rabha belong to the group of Bodo languages, within the Tibeto-Burman language family. Culturally they are close to people like the Bodo and the Garo, and like them they are officially recognized as Scheduled Tribes. In official statistics Rabhas number in total just above two hundred thousand people, but their own organizations claim at least double that number. The majority live in Assam, but there are Rabha communities in Meghalaya and West Bengal (possibly also in Bangladesh and Nepal). The Rabhas in West Bengal belong to the Kocha section and commonly refer to themselves as Kocha; they number between fifteen and twenty thousand. Of these the majority live within the "forest villages" (forest reserves), and it is among them that the conversions have taken place.

21. Gauri Viswanathan, *Outside the Fold — Conversion, Modernity, and Belief* (Cambridge, Mass., 1998), p. xvi.

22. Viswanathan, *Outside the Fold,* p. xvi.

23. Viswanathan, *Outside the Fold,* p. xi.

24. I was engaged with the Rabhas in West Bengal throughout the 1990s, with about one year's fieldwork in villages in the Jalpaiguri area. I have also conducted shorter field trips to Rabha settlements in Assam.

Since the late 1970s, the Rabhas, living in the forests in the very northern part of the state (close to the Bhutan and Assam border), have started to convert to Christianity. Today about two-thirds of the community are Christian and belong to the Rabha Baptist Church. The question arises why they "chose" to become Christian, and why at this particular juncture in their history. After all, the Rabhas had been exposed to Christianity for at least a century without converting (with the exception of a few individuals).[25] I argue that the Rabhas' conversion on one level has to do with rather pragmatic reasons, similar to those mentioned by Shah. As the people themselves often put it, "Their old religion had become both ineffective and too costly in today's world." On another level, the change of religion also related to a more implicit agenda of modern "identity formation." By becoming Christian, a tribal community like the Rabhas could construct themselves as both different and modern. Their conversion was a form of "cultural strategy" by which the community struggled to establish a new sense of self. Making use of recent theories of agency, identity formation, and subaltern resistance, I understood the Rabhas' conversion to Christianity to be part of a larger project of ethnic mobilization and a struggle for survival in the forest.[26] I still subscribe to this analysis but have nevertheless found it urgent to return to the issue and to concentrate on one aspect of their conversion. Before addressing the Rabhas' change of religion, however, let us recall earlier controversies regarding tribal peoples' conversions to Christianity. This was a highly contested matter long before the *Hindutva* forces came into political power in India.

II

Most Indian and Western scholars have discussed the spread of Christianity among tribal and indigenous people in India in terms of cultural destruction and political submission. The Church is thus often perceived as a partner in the colonial penetration of new territories. Undeniably the mission and the colonial state often did work in close collaboration. The former often received support and protection from the government and, in turn, helped the government to consolidate its power in the peripheries of the empire. Education was a subject in India where government and mission interest coincided, and

25. Other tribal groups in the area, mainly the Bodos (or Meches), did convert in large numbers at the end of nineteenth century and the beginning of the twentieth century.

26. B. G. Karlsson, *Contested Belonging: An Indigenous People's Struggle for Forest and Identity in Sub-Himalayan Bengal* (Lund, 1997; rev. ed., Richmond, 2000).

in the northeastern hills missionaries had government support in organizing and running the entire school system. As is well known, education and health were key instruments of missionary influence.[27] It is important to bear in mind, however, that government and missionary interests often clashed. In this context one should recall the East India Company's initial reluctance to allow missionaries at all into their territories, fearing that their activities would create disturbances. William Carey and his fellow pioneers from the (British) Baptist Missionary Society, arriving in Bengal at the end of eighteenth century, had to work "underground" and seek protection from the Danish Crown.[28] It was only in 1813, after strong pressure from churches at home, that the Company's charter was modified to allow missionaries legal entrance into India. Support for missionary activity was, however, never as straightforward and wholehearted as is commonly believed, and throughout the colonial period the government placed various restrictions on it. Some colonial officers were strongly critical of Christian missionaries being allowed to intervene in the life of tribal peoples. Richard M. Eaton gives an example in his article on Christian conversion in the Naga Hills. A serious controversy between the Baptist mission and the government developed over the issue of Western clothing. The mission made the Naga converts wear Western clothing, such as trousers, shirts, blouses, and long skirts. This was strongly opposed by J. P. Mills, the local government official. In 1925 Mills prohibited further missionary work in the Naga Hills unless the missionaries changed their policy.[29]

Later Verrier Elwin, who himself set out to India as a Christian worker but became a "barefoot anthropologist" and later a government adviser on tribal affairs, was among the more outspoken critics of the missionary involvement with the tribals. He also took the step, shocking at the time, of leaving the Anglican Church, saying that the "entire missionary enterprise" had become "distasteful" to him.[30] In *A Philosophy of the NEFA,* Elwin argues in favor of the independent government's policy (which he himself has been engaged in formulating) of not allowing missionaries to interfere with the affairs of tribal people in NEFA (the present-day state of Arunachal Pradesh).[31] Elwin

27. F. S. Downs, *History of Christianity in India,* vol. 5, pt. 5: *North East India in the Nineteenth and Twentieth Centuries* (Bangalore, 1992), pp. 53-63.

28. H. C. Vedder, *A Short History of Baptist Missions* (Philadelphia, 1927), pp. 29-31.

29. Richard M. Eaton, "Conversion to Christianity among the Nagas," *Indian Economic and Social History Review* 21.1 (January-March 1984): 13-14.

30. Verrier Elwin, *Leaves from the Jungle: Life in a Gond Village* (Oxford, 1958 [1936]).

31. Verrier Elwin, *A Philosophy of the NEFA* (Shillong, 1958).

was upset with the missionaries' attempt to impose their values and lifestyle on the tribals. All that he celebrated among the tribals — their freedom, their songs, dances, festivals, and institutions such as youth dormitories — were opposed by the missionaries. But as Ramachandra Guha writes in his recent biography on Elwin,[32] his movement against Christian missionaries also had a tactical side to it. Indian independence was becoming a possibility, and by distancing himself from the Church, Elwin could thus reaffirm his Indian identity. By this he hoped that the new Congress leadership would become a powerful ally in protecting the tribals. Elwin was disturbed also by interference from puritan Hindu reformers, but he found it best not to take issue with them. Instead he invited or urged the Hindu community to take a more active role in protecting the rights of the aboriginal communities.[33]

Christoph Furer-Haimendorf, a well-known Western anthropologist of a later generation, took a similar stance and argued that, although missionaries brought good things like education and medical facilities to the tribals and, for example, helped preserve and develop tribal languages, their influence was largely negative and "eroded much of the tribes' cultural heritage."[34] Above all, he argued, Christianity has divided the tribal communities and destroyed their social unity.

This view of missionary activity as mainly a force of cultural imperialism is still dominant among anthropologists working among indigenous people in different parts of the world. While not contesting such a position, I would argue for a more sophisticated approach. Alongside the story of missionaries imposing Christianity on the tribals, I advocate that a parallel story be told: a story in which people are seen as agents who for various (conscious and partly conscious) reasons choose to become Christians and make Christianity part of their own political and cultural projects and struggles. This other story is largely absent in the literature of tribal India. There are, however, some interesting examples worth mentioning, such as Julian Jacobs's reinterpretation of the Naga ethnography. He argues, for example, that Christianity offered the Naga groups a common language, English, which became a "powerful force for promoting the overall sense of Pan-Naga ethnicity."[35] Robbins Burling claims in his classic monograph *Rengsangrii* on the Garos in Meghalaya that Christianity helped the Garos to maintain a separate identity toward the en-

32. Ramachandra Guha, *Savaging the Civilized: Verrier Elwin, His Tribals, and India* (Delhi, 1999).

33. Guha, *Savaging the Civilized,* pp. 164-71.

34. Cristoph Furer-Haimendorf, *Tribes of India: The Struggle for Survival* (Delhi, 1982), p. 319.

35. Julian Jacobs, *The Nagas: Hill People of Northeast India* (London, 1990), p. 156.

croaching population of the plains.[36] Besides a distinct identity, Christianity has, through its educational institutions, also provided the Garos and other communities in northeast India with political leaders.[37] It is through this well-educated elite that the Garos, together with the Khasis, have been able to establish Meghalaya as a separate Indian state. The same can be argued for both Nagaland and Mizoram. It is this aspect of Christianity that renders it so controversial. In general, Christians are seen, if not as antinational, at least as not fully in favor of India as an independent state. Ethnic separatism in northeast India is often taken as an example of how Christian organizations strive to undermine the unity of India. It is thus claimed that separatist movements are supported by foreign (Western) interests and are part of a missionary-led master plan to divide India.[38] This is the reason why the Indian government in the 1960s expelled all foreign missionaries from the northeastern region and other parts of the country. In the case of more recent ethnic movements there are reports of involvement by a "foreign hand" in the form of Christian organizations and Western missionaries. Chandana Bhattacharya, in her book on the Bodoland movement in Assam, mentions how such involvement was viewed, as expressed in the headlines of a national daily: "[M]issionaries inspiring tribal stir for Bodoland."[39] In relation to the present conflict over conversions in the Dangs, Hindu fundamentalists state that the hidden motive of the churches is to make Gujarat an autonomous Christian state.[40] In the case of the Rabhas' conversion to Christianity, considered below, it was initially suggested that an "unholy alliance" of foreign, Christian welfare organizations, Naxalite groups, and the Kamtapuri movement demanded a separate state for northern West Bengal to destabilize the region.[41] In all these cases there is an underlying assumption that links Christian conversion with foreign involvement and ethnic separatism. The *Hindutva* organizations use or evoke this assumption to gain popular support.

36. Robbins Burling, *Rengsanggri: Family and Kinship in a Garo Village* (Philadelphia, 1963), p. 316.

37. B. G. Verghese, *India's Northeast Resurgent: Ethnicity, Insurgency, Governance, Development* (New Delhi, 1996), pp. 283-85.

38. See, e.g., RSS publications, such as *RSS — A Vision in Action* (1988), compiled and edited by H. V. Seshadri, which is available on their home page on the internet (http://www.rss.org).

39. Chandana Bhattacharya, *Ethnicity and Autonomy Movement: Case of Bodo-Kacharis of Assam* (New Delhi, 1996), p. 19.

40. Shah, "Conversion," p. 312. See also *The Rediff Interview* with Jayanthibai Kewat, of the Hindu Jagran Manch (31 December 1998) (www.rediff.com).

41. See Karlsson, *Contested Belonging*, p. 188.

III

The Rabhas follow their own religious faith, which they refer to as the *Kocha dhormo.* It is a form of indigenous religion that for centuries has developed by incorporating various Hindu traditions and other religious influences in the region.[42] Rabhas have their own deities (although some are shared by other tribal communities in the area, above all by the Bodos), and these are known under various names. *Mahakal* and *Thakur bai* are often referred to as the most powerful deities. *Rundthuk Basek,* represented by two clay pots filled with rice and one egg, is also commonly claimed to be the main deity of the community. Some argue, in fact, that *Rundthuk Basek* is synonymous with *Kocha dhormo.* The religious practices are mainly carried out by the *huji,* a person who through secret knowledge can communicate with the spirits *(bai).* In most cases, a ritual performance *(bai tangi)* by the *huji* would contain animal sacrifice and consumption of rice beer *(jokot).* The Rabhas often refer to themselves as Hindus, although as some put it, "Hindus in their own way." Obviously, their religious performances have little in common with those of caste Hindus. Few Rabhas would, for example, celebrate Durga puja, which is perhaps the most important Hindu festival among Bengalis. With the conversion to Christianity, people have come to be identified as either "Hindu" or "Christian." The category "Hindu" is anything but homogenous. It includes above all those who practice the traditional *Kocha dhormo,* but also followers of a local Buddhist-inspired sect called *Janayogi* (what the followers describe as a *Prakiti dhormo,* i.e., "nature religion") and those who have joined various Hindu sects. It is important to keep this complexity in mind as one approaches the issue of conversion. Clearly this is an environment in which multiple religious choice has become possible.

A few Rabha families converted to Christianity in the late 1940s and early 1950s, under the influence of the Swedish mission with its center in the town of Cooch Behar. These converts were not only few in number but seem soon to have returned to the old faith.[43] It was not until the late 1970s that the

42. The sub-Himalayan region, referred to as the Duars, is a cultural frontier where people of different faiths and religious traditions interact. Apart from Hindu influence, there are Buddhist peoples from the hills, Muslims from the plains, and various "folk" or indigenous religions.

43. I have been able to locate only one of these early converts, and he, who at the time was a young boy, told me that they received some plots of land through the mission, but that this land was flood prone and was deserted after some years of crop failure. As people left the land, they appear to have given up Christianity and, as in his case, to have returned to the *Kocha dhormo.*

Rabhas in West Bengal started to become Christians in larger numbers. By that time there were two competing denominations, the Seventh Day Adventists and the Rabha Baptist Church, based in Assam. Besides differences in their religious practices, the most important difference between the two denominations is that the Seventh Day Adventists are organized as a nonethnic church and try to reach all communities, whereas the Rabha Baptist Church is ethnically, or communally, organized. The Baptist Church was established by Australian missionaries in the late 1950s. When they were expelled from India in 1967, an Indian missionary couple from the well-established Baptist Church in Mizoram took over. In spite of the initial role of the Australian Baptists, who are still active through contacts and limited financial support, and the work of a Mizo missionary, the Rabha Baptist Church is entirely a Rabha affair. The staff and members are all Rabhas. They use their own language, *Kocha krau,* for their sermons, and their hymns are either translated into Kocha, or hymns in Kocha are composed by the Rabha themselves. The Bible is being translated into Kocha, but meanwhile the Rabha in West Bengal use the Bengali Bible.

In opposition to this, the Seventh Day Adventists are organized as a "nonethnic" or multi-ethnic church. They have their center in Ranchi, in Bihar, and most of the staff are either Christian *adivasis* from Bihar or people from other parts of India. Hindi is the main language of communication in the church, and the Bible and hymnal are in Hindi. To some extent they also use Shadri, the local creole language, mainly spoken by the tea garden tribals, and in their schools English is the preferred language. The congregations contain people from different communities. In one village church, for example, the preacher was a Santal and the members were Santals, Bodos, Rabhas, and Garos. The Adventists seem to have had considerable money to spend on their campaigns in the late 1970s. Some Rabhas have said that they had been promised money if they converted, but that in the end no such money was distributed. The Adventists could afford to build "nice" churches and schools and to employ professional teachers from outside, without raising any money from the converts themselves. The Adventist Church, however, failed to secure involvement from below and did not manage to integrate the community into its organization. In this way the local Adventist churches failed to become self-reliant and self-regenerating and were constantly dependent on initiatives and support from the church outside the district. The expansive phase of the Adventist Church proved to be very short, and since the mid 1980s their numbers have fallen drastically, reducing them to only a few scattered families. During the same period, the Rabha Baptists markedly increased in number. Today about two-thirds of the Rabhas in the forest villages of West Bengal are members of the Baptist Church. Most of the earlier Adventist converts have become Baptists, or, as in one village, they have returned to their "traditional" religion. The experience of this particular village, known as Kodal Bustee, provides important clues as to how the conversion process worked on the ground.

Kodal Bustee was the Adventists' center among the Rabha. Here they established a school, appointed a teacher, and constructed a large church. When I first visited the village in December 1989, the process of reconversion was in full swing. The teacher, from Meghalaya, complained that the villagers had stopped sending their children to the mission school. The *mondol* or headman reported that only fifteen out of the eighty-five families in the village were still Christians. The others had returned to their old faith and did not want to have anything to do with the Adventists. Earlier, in about 1978, the whole village, except the *huji* and his family, had become Christian. The *mondol* gave a rather straightforward explanation for their reconversion. First of all, as Christians, they were not allowed to drink *jokot,* their traditional brew used in all social and religious events, and some villagers could not abstain from drinking. Others had difficulty observing the strict diet prescribed by the Adventists, particularly staying away from pork, which is the Rabha's favorite food. The Adventists considered many items of their diet unclean, among them tea and fish without scales. People were constantly breaking the rules and therefore could not become true Christians, the *mondol* said. Nor were they following their own religion. They belonged nowhere, and all sorts of problems began in the village. People became sick. They became frightened and finally decided to become "Hindus" again. The *huji,* who never became a Christian, performed rituals for their reentry. Everything has improved since, the *mondol* explained. Elephants had, for example, stopped attacking their paddy fields. Rice beer was brewed again in every house, and people could eat whatever they liked. Later I heard similar stories from people who had left the Adventist Church, saying that they had problems observing the food regulations and abstaining from *jokot.* Religion is in other words closely connected to how one lives, and not just to belief. The Adventists' special dietary rules[44] did not go well with the traditional Rabha way of life.

The Baptists have no restrictions regarding food, but like the Adventists they strongly object to the drinking of *jokot.* Being a Christian, in fact, is

44. The Adventist preacher, who worked among the Rabhas at the time, told me that they did not demand a fully vegetarian diet as this was associated in rural India with Hinduism. They made instead a distinction between pure and impure animals, allowing, for example, chicken but not pork.

talked about among the Rabhas as being a "non-*jokot* drinker." This is not only the case among the Rabhas but appears to be a universal sign of the Baptist Churches in this part of India. In relation to the Garo in Meghalaya, Burling notes that both for the Christian Garos and the Songsareks, that is, the nonconverted Garos, the "shunning of rice beer" is "the primary sign of Christianity."[45] This is also true of the Naga. The Baptist missionaries working among them were so concerned with banning rice beer that "non-drinking became popularly accepted as the outstanding mark of a Christian."[46] Similarly, the Mizo Baptists had to give up their beloved *zu* (rice beer), and tea became the social drink of the community instead.[47] Roman Catholic missionaries seem, however, to have a much more permissive attitude to alcohol.[48] The point to stress here is that becoming an Adventist Christian demanded a more complete break with previous life. Becoming a Baptist also implied radical changes in everyday life, but it nevertheless appeared to offer more space for cultural continuity and, as will be shown, for a new sense of ethnic belonging.

Australian Baptists had started to work among various tribal peoples in Goalpara district, in upper Assam, in late 1940. The Rev. Rex Glasby and his wife Peggy established, in 1957, a mission station in Debitola. The Rabhas did not particularly welcome the Glasbys. As the missionaries describe it, the first small group of Christian Rabhas had to face all sorts of hardships: physical assault and discrimination such as not being allowed to draw water from the village well or share food with others. After some time, however, these attitudes started to change, and this, as the Glasbys themselves put it, was to a large extent a result of Peggy's skills as a pharmacist and Rex's enthusiasm and social capacity. By the time the Glasbys were forced by the government to leave Assam, they had made some progress. Their success, however, was not numerically impressive, and they left only "three small congregations."[49] It was later, during the time of the Mizo missionary, the Rev. Rokhama, and his wife, that the Glasbys' work started to bear fruit, and in the early 1980s the number of churches had increased to twenty-three, with a total Christian community of about twenty-five hundred.[50] Since then the expansion has largely stopped in Assam, and center of gravity has shifted to the Rabhas in West Bengal.

45. Burling, *Rengsanggri,* p. 314.

46. Eaton, "Conversion to Christianity," p. 14.

47. C. R. Nag, *The Mizo Society in Transition* (New Delhi, 1993), p. 207.

48. Cf. Jacobs, *The Nagas,* p. 153.

49. J. Redman, *The Light Shines On* (Hawthorn, 1982), p. 128.

50. Redman, *The Light Shines On,* pp. 121-28, and Australian Baptist Foreign Mission, *Our Heritage* (Melbourne, 1951), pp. 37-41.

Interestingly, it took about two decades from the start of the missionary work for the Rabha Baptists to cross the Assam–West Bengal border and come in contact with the Rabhas in the forests of northern West Bengal. This has long puzzled me. One would imagine that from the beginning the Baptists would try to reach the entire Rabha community, or at least all those who spoke the same language, that is, *Kocha krau*,[51] which the missionaries had adopted as the working language into which they had started to translate Christian texts and songs. I have been told several times by Rabhas in West Bengal that it was one person, an influential Rabha leader from Assam, who took the first steps to spread the gospel among them. It was said that as he traveled through the area (going to Darjeeling), he by chance met some Rabhas and thus discovered that there were Rabhas living in northern West Bengal. After this he started to visit different villages and teach about Christianity. The Rabha Baptist mission became involved only later and sent preachers there. Could it really be the case that the Rabha Baptist Church did not know about the existence of fellow Rabhas in West Bengal prior to this "discovery" of the mid 1970s? I found this hard to believe, but, after meeting those in charge of the mission work at the Rabha Baptist Union in Assam and hearing their same story, it appears the most likely explanation.

When the Rabha Baptists started to approach the Rabhas in West Bengal, they seem to have been well received, and within a short time they established themselves in a number of villages. The first conversions took place, and the first church was established, in Mendabari village in 1977. Mendabari is still the center of the Rabha Baptists in West Bengal, and the only pastor in the state lives there. From the first conversions in Mendabari, the expansion of the Baptist Church appears to have been a largely self-generating process. Rabha Baptist preachers carried out evangelical work, but, as I understand it, it was to a large extent the villagers themselves who took the leading role and invited the preachers to their villages. Kurmai was the second village where conversions took place and a church was established. Christianity then spread to other villages such as Khoyerbari, Gosaihat, Mela Bustee, Kuklung Bustee, and Gadadhar.

Initially the general pace of conversion appears to have been rather speedy, with several families being baptized at the same time. Furthermore, as in the case of Kurmai, it was often an influential person who took the lead. In Kurmai, for example, the initial convert was a powerful *huji*. Today, however, the process seems to be more gradual. In the recent cases of conversion that

51. The different Rabha groups have their own rather distinct dialects. Some sections have lost their own language and mainly speak Assamese or Bengali.

have taken place during my stays, those who are most active and eager to become Christians are youngsters (teenagers) and women. When the first people or families in a village become Christians, and thus break the ice, the process takes off. Once there is a substantial number of Christians in the village, they will form a separate congregation, build a church, and elect people to the various offices in the congregation. As a part of this process, the Baptist Union appoints a "master," or evangelist teacher, whose main responsibility is the education of the children. This is a special arrangement for the churches in West Bengal since the Union has found that very few Rabha children in Duars attend school and most Rabha lack basic skills in reading and writing. The Baptist teachers use the Kocha language as the medium of instruction, as opposed to the state schools, in which only Bengali is used. Once this stage has been reached, it is relatively easy for other people in the village to join the church. Many Rabha villages have become entirely Christian.

Conversion is, in most cases, an individual decision, and I have never heard of any cases of forced or involuntarily conversion. Indeed, such allegations have not been raised by anyone, including the "Hindu" Rabhas who are most critical of the Christian conversions. Commonly, someone in the family takes the initial step of becoming Christian, and the rest of family follows. It is relatively rare for a family to remain divided for very long. In many narratives of conversion, there is someone in the family who initially strongly opposes the decision to convert, but in the end he or she also accepts it, and, often, along with others in the family, finally also takes baptism. The baptism ceremony takes place in a nearby river and is carried out by either the Rabha preacher, who lives in Mendabari, or by someone from the Rabha Baptist Church in Assam.

Building a church is vital to the new congregation. The church buildings are simple, constructed of bamboo, with walls of mud and straw.[52] When the congregation grows and it has managed to collect money from members, a new, wooden church building is constructed. Money for the church is always raised in the village itself. Moreover, the congregation must contribute a fixed amount of money yearly to the Rabha Baptist Union in Debitola. In addition to overall administration, the Church Union has responsibility for the appointment of pastors and the evangelist teachers. These teachers, or "masters" as they are called, are in most cases young, educated Rabhas from Assam (all are men). Besides being responsible for the education of the children in the

52. It is interesting to note that in the attacks on Christians in the Dangs it was questioned whether the bamboo-straw-and-mud constructions that were destroyed were actually churches.

village and the running of the church activities, they have many other social functions in the village. For example, if someone falls ill, the master is called, and he often decides or suggests what is to be done. If the case is serious and the patient needs a doctor, the master probably will accompany him or her there. In other cases, relatives, together with the master, often sing for the sick in the evening, and if the patient has consulted a doctor and received medicine, they will sing to give the medicine the strength to cure. As an educated person, the master also helps villagers to fill out government forms, make applications, and write letters. He often leads the Sunday service and the other weekly gatherings in the church, preaching, saying prayers, and leading the singing, though his role in this depends on the other leading church members. All congregations have their own officials: a *pallok* (local preacher), a church secretary, and a treasurer. There are also a women's church and youth organizations; they hold separate meetings and have their own elected officeholders. Except for the officials of the women's organization, all church officials are men. The pastor baptizes, and he also performs weddings and funerals. Every village congregation also sends representatives to the various meetings and conferences held by the Rabha Baptist Union. The village selects one or two children to be sent to the mission school at the compound in Debitola, in Assam, where they receive a small grant from Baptist families in Australia.

When discussing their reasons for conversion, the Rabha often told a sort of standard story. It is said that as a Christian one does not have to perform costly rituals in which rice beer and meat (chicken, pork, or goat) must be provided for the *huji*. If someone is taken ill, one just buys some medicine, sings with others, and gives the medicine to the person. The money saved can be used for other things. To give up drinking rice beer is also mentioned as beneficial, both for the economy and for the peace of the family and community. Christianity brings *shanti* (peace) of mind, as one old man expressed it. Most would point, also, to the enormous expenses of the various ceremonies that one must perform as a Hindu, expenses people no longer can bear. However much money they have today, more is always needed. Interestingly enough, such explanations also appear central to other people becoming Christians.[53] C. L. Hminga's study of the first generation of Mizo Christians

53. In other contemporary ethnographies similar accounts of Christian conversion appear. C. A. Kammerer, for example, in her fieldwork among the Akha people in Thailand, was surprised at the uniform answers to questions about why people had converted. They said either that they no longer knew their "traditional religion" or that they no longer could afford to practice it. "'I had no chickens; I had no pigs,' an old woman told me to explain her conversion" (C. A. Kammerer, "Custom and Christian Conversion among Akha

shows that they explain their conversions in terms of "cost-effectiveness": not having to perform costly and frequent sacrifices if someone becomes ill. Not only was the missionaries' medicine cheaper and simpler to take, but it also proved more powerful or successful in curing the patients.[54] Barbara Boal, a missionary and ethnographer among the Konds in Orissa (in the 1950s and 1960s), gives the following standard answers to the question why the Konds had started worshipping the Christian God: "We are wearied of the never ending sacrifices." "So much ritual-observance was destroying us; we couldn't afford it any longer." "We exhausted our money without any profit whatever." "The priest kept on telling me to sacrifice a pig. I sacrificed every pig in the village, and still I was sick." "The cost of appeasing the spirits was ruining us — and our children still died anyway. So we came to try 'the new laws.'"[55]

Most Rabhas also describe their conversion in terms of a radical change in their life, and indeed as a change to a new and better life. People often point to the Christian Rabhas in Assam and argue that since their conversion they also enjoy a better standard of living. They are better dressed, more educated, and many are in government service or have other employment. Concerning dress, great emphasis is put on the fact that all women in Assam wear Rabha dress — *lufun* (skirt) and *kambang* (shawl). Being a Christian seems to imply being more oriented toward the "modern." This is the opinion of both the Christian and the Hindu Rabha. A middle-aged *mondol* in a "Hindu" village, for example, said that those who have become "Christians" have become more "developed" (using the Bengali word *unnuti*). Education is given a high priority among Christian Rabhas, and the same is true of the use of modern medicine. Even if the traditional herbal doctor is still called in for certain cases, the Christian Rabhas do not consult the *huji*, and therefore to a greater degree use modern medicines. To the Christian Rabhas, being "developed" does not appear to mean becoming less Rabha; most would argue the opposite. The only way for the Rabha to survive today, they say, is to become educated and to learn about the rights and the facilities available for their development, particularly about government funds that, it is claimed, are likely to

---

highlanders of Burma and Thailand," *American Ethnology* 17.2 [May 1990]: 283). Birgit Meyer argues in the case of the West African Ewe peoples' conversion to Christianity in the early twentieth century that there were economic motives behind them, but importantly also a disappointment with the "efficacy of the old religious practices" (see her "Modernity and Enchantment," p. 210). As she explains it, conversion was both a quest for the new and a "deliberate turn away from the old" ("Modernity and Enchantment," p. 212).

54. Cited in Downs, *History of Christianity*, p. 185.

55. Barbara Boal, *The Konds: Human Sacrifice and Religious Change* (Warminster, 1982), p. 194.

be snatched away by the Bengalis. Without education there is no future for the Rabha, it is argued. Similarly, Christian Rabhas say that with education people become prouder of themselves as Rabhas (pointing again to the fact that most women wear Rabha skirts in Assam). Others take the Rabhas in the Kamakhaguri area, a village area outside the forest where an earlier Hindu-reformist movement has had big impact, as a warning: "they are all Hindus and they no longer know their own Kocha language, and all women wear saris — they are ashamed of being Rabhas," Christian Rabhas argue. As noted above, within the category of "Hindu" Rabhas there are great differences, and it contains above all the traditional *Kocha dhormo.* It is interesting, however, that the Christian Rabhas stress their difference from those who practice traditional Rabha religion. The Christian songs, for example, refer to the time prior to conversion as "confusion," "wandering in the dark," and being "lost in the jungle without direction"; they claim that Christianity brought direction, light, and truth. To become a Rabha Christian means, in other words, to discard actively "the old ways"; or, to put it differently, Christian identity is constructed in opposition to the traditional *Kocha dhormo* as well as to the larger Hindu society.[56]

In summary, becoming Christian means giving up rice beer and other alcoholic beverages. This act alone, I would argue, makes a big difference and initiates other important changes in the daily life of a person. These very concrete differences in lifestyle, or way of being, are what count most when a person decides to convert. He, or she, has seen how others have changed by becoming Christians. All traditional Rabha worship includes the consumption of rice beer, and thus becoming a Christian and shunning it makes a radical break with all previous religious practices. One could say that becoming Christian creates a radically new way of being Rabha. Of course, Christianity is not the only religion where some movements demand abstinence from alcohol; many major (world) religions or religious reform movements take a stand against it. Many social protest movements condemn the use of alcohol and other intoxicants, and it appears that tremendous political energies can be set free just by getting people to shun alcohol. The Devi movement among the Bhils in Western India, during British rule, is a good example of this.[57] In the Hindu reform movement among the Rabhas, giving up drinking was central

56. Today there is also an increased interest in the old ways, largely propelled by the Rabha Hasong movement in Assam. This movement strives to unite all Rabhas, to revive old cultural practices, to create a common Rabha language, and to establish an autonomous Rabhaland.

57. David Hardiman, *The Coming of the Devi: Adivasi Assertion in Western India* (Delhi, 1987).

to the required purification. The *Janyogi* movement put a ban on the use of alcohol as well as other mind-altering items such as tobacco and betel nut. However, even if giving up alcohol is part of various religious and social projects, among the Rabhas it has become the prime marker of Christian conversion.

IV

Rabhas' narratives of conversion suggest that it, above all, is a question of adopting a more "appropriate" way of being in the world. The conversion is not narrated in terms of a spiritual revelation or as the work of God's grace. Neither have I detected coercion or inducement behind people's decision to become Christians. Christian worship is described as simpler, less costly, and more secure. As Christians many Rabhas say they no longer are in the hands of the *huji,* who seems to inspire fear and anxiety. Resources that earlier had to be allocated for worship can now be used to improve the social and economic situation of the family, for land, education, and modern medicine. This type of reasoning is also common in other people's conversion stories, but it appears as an almost universal narrative of Christian conversion.

Entering into the Christian dharma is indeed a serious matter, and the change of religious belonging radically transforms a person's "sense of the self." It is not so much a question of giving up one set of beliefs and adopting another new "cosmology." After all, most Rabhas know very little about Christian belief at the time of conversion. With the passage of time, as a person becomes active in the church, Christian beliefs and ideas will be grafted on to the old or previous ones. The dramatic change is instead, as I have argued above, in the lifestyle or way of life of the convert. Religion in the Indian context is often talked about as dharma. This Hindu concept means the spiritual-moral order or duty, or the rightful social norm. Dharma has, in other words, a wider meaning than the Western term "religion." Rabhas also use the term "dharma," although pronouncing it as *dhormo,* and thus, for example, talk about their traditional *Kocha dhormo* and refer to Christianity and Hinduism as being different *dhormo*(s). To them, it appears as if both beliefs or cosmology and lifestyle (modes of acting and ordering one's practical life) are evoked by the term. To change *dhormo* is thus a matter of changing behavior as well as of adopting new beliefs.

CHAPTER EIGHT

Theology and Authority, Constitution and Improvisation: The Colonial Church in India

GERALD STUDDERT-KENNEDY

I

The Christian churches in India were an important site of cultural interaction. Investigation of this interaction within churches and their structures in late imperial India, however, raises the problem of locating a specific approach in a notoriously amorphous field. The evidence presents a plurality and diversity of "structures." One needs to acknowledge the complexities while at the same time developing a conceptual basis for subsequent exploration. My earlier study, *British Christians, Indian Nationalists and the Raj,*[1] attempted to open up the large theme of "Christian imperialism" in the last decades of the Raj, and inevitably reflected on the colonial Church, broadly conceived as including both the Anglican Church in India and the other post-Reformation denominations associated with it. Specific lives touched on in that book will be contrasted here as exposing erratic but intelligible linkages between colonial Church organization in general and the larger domain of an enclosing imperial process.[2] The central theme pursued through the sample

1. Gerald Studdert-Kennedy, *British Christians, Indian Nationalists and the Raj* (Delhi, 1991; new ed. 1999).

2. For recent work on specific missionary organizations, see Steven Maughan, "Imperial Christianity? Bishop Montgomery and the Foreign Missions of the Church of England, 1895-1915," North Atlantic Missiology Project (hereafter NAMP) *Position Papers* 31 (1997), and Peter Williams, "The CMS and the Indigenous Church in the Second Half of

of individuals and groups, variously architects, agents, beneficiaries, and victims of Church "structures" is of a complex division of authority among domains interlocked by inescapable conflicts.

An incidental intention here is to highlight a significant connection between the argument and the setting of the conference for which this paper was originally prepared, for the comparisons raise some formidable ghosts of Oxford and Balliol College past, from the years of Balliol's notoriously "effortless superiority" — the phrase was Asquith's — in all walks of life.[3] It was within the University of Oxford's square mile, and with notable density in Balliol College's few acres, that the preponderance of the Empire's intellectuals learned to interpret their purpose in life.[4] Balliol was itself an important institutional player in a complex imperial encounter.

In the chapter's title — "Theology and Authority, Constitution and Improvisation" — large abstractions appear that identify significant aspects of the amorphous landscape of imperial and postcolonial Christianity. These features regularly seem to be seeping into or collapsing onto each other, and therefore the formal structures and organizations of the Anglican Church and other denominations in India are less than helpful as a point of departure.

A well-informed official critic before the turn of the century bluntly described the Anglican Church's intimate dependence on government as "prejudicial to the interests and advancement of religion," hampering, limiting, and misdirecting pecuniary resources through elaborate annual budget appropriations, grants-in-aid, and capitation grants, controlled by minute rules and regulations. Its bishops were appointed in diverse and anomalous ways. Their primary responsibility, for Christian civil and military servants of the state, was ambiguously linked to the political expediency of maintaining the repute of those communities and avoiding danger to the Empire. The Indian Ecclesiastical Establishment (IEE) involved government in the enrollment of clergy, their distribution, and their ministrations.[5]

Increasingly careful attention was given, however, to the selection of bishops. Sir Arthur Hirtzel, Secretary to the Political Department at the India Office from 1909 to 1917 and Permanent Under Secretary of State until 1930, himself a prominent Anglican, corresponded anxiously with appropriate

---

the Nineteenth Century," NAMP *Position Papers* 67 (1998). These are located in the Henry Martin Library, Westminister College, Cambridge.

3. John Jones, *Balliol College: A History, 1263-1939* (Oxford, 1988), ch. 16, "Effortless Superiority."

4. Richard Symonds, *Oxford and Empire: The Last Lost Cause* (London, 1986).

5. Sir Theodore Hope, *Church and State in India* (London, 1893), p. 41.

clerics and others.[6] Candidates were always limited in number and in quality. Furthermore, the most confident expectations could be disappointed. It was impossible to make an entirely dependable match between an incoming bishop and his established clergy. Though the padres of the IEE could generally be relied upon to identify appropriately with their dispersed expatriate communities, the bishops also exercised a degree of local control over missionaries. The latter, however, had very different responsibilities and perspectives, and their immediate "line management" consisted of missionary society officials based in London or Edinburgh who represented a historical diversity of denominations and tendencies. While in some respects the imperial context encouraged interdenominational cooperation, in others, and quite unpredictably, it could sharpen sectional conflicts within a broad church that exported its theological and ideological diversities at the episcopal no less than at the missionary level. Collectively the bishops represented an imperial church establishment; individually they engaged with very different circumstances with diverse consequences.

This discussion is organized around a comparative reflection on three contrasting networks of churchmen. First, and handled at some length, there is Edwin James (E. J.) Palmer, Bishop of Bombay from 1908 to 1928, and the configuration associated with him; second and more briefly, since I have also discussed it at some length elsewhere, is the basically Free Church of Scotland network that established the Madras Christian College under William Miller, its principal from 1877 to1907;[7] third, and also briefly for the same reason, is the network of the Westcott brothers, George, Bishop of Lucknow, who died in 1928, and Foss, Bishop of Chota Nagpur, subsequently the Metropolitan of India, Burma, and Ceylon.[8] They were in India from their joint appointment to Allahabad in 1889. The "Met" retired to Ranchi in 1945. The discussion will touch on some others, including one maverick, Roland Allen, who was in his day, one comes to suspect, a missiological "pain in the neck" for a succession of bishops.

The argument is that one can recognize the coherence underlying these very diverse contributions to an extended missionary process in the light of a general theoretical perspective. The perspective itself is supported by an extensive and diverse literature of comparative history, but it was most certainly *not* shared by any of the disinterested, able, sometimes brilliant, and occa-

6. Studdert-Kennedy, *British Christians,* p. 46.

7. Gerald Studdert-Kennedy, *Providence and the Raj: Imperial Mission and Missionary Imperialism* (Delhi, 1998).

8. Gerald Studdert-Kennedy, "The Broad Church Idea of the British State," in *British Politics and the Spirit of the Age,* edited by Cornelia Navari (Keele, 1996), pp. 17-39.

sionally heroic individuals who are considered here. It is possible to be very summary about the essentials of the historical argument, but it has been developed rigorously, with extensive empirical reference to nineteenth-century Europe, Africa, India, and elsewhere, by John Breuilly in his *Nationalism and the State* (1993).[9] Here I reflect on the incessant process of the reformulation of religious belief and its institutional expression in the context of the colonial situation. The chapter is not concerned with the strengths and weaknesses, from the point of view of evangelistic mission itself, of the structures and strategies of the established Church or of the missionary organizations. The primary concern is the implications of such structures and strategies for a much larger political and cultural process.

II

Breuilly's point of departure is an unqualified rejection of a set of assumptions to which all my players were for various reasons deeply committed, namely, the familiar, essentialist assumption that nationalism emerges "naturally" from preexistent entities under certain evolving circumstances, for instance, "Westernization." All but one of my subjects, Roland Allen, were much given to a rhetoric of "organic" historical change, in each case conceived in providentialist terms. In the imperial context such concepts served to separate what Partha Chatterjee ironically labels "good nationalism" from "bad nationalism," that is, to distinguish one's own or correspondingly certified variants of nationalism from "would-be nationalisms" promoted by interests not in tune with the authentic spirit of the thing.[10] This usage, however, empties the concept of nationalism of any analytical value. Indeed, it prevents the observer from seeing the obvious circularities it entails, and it discourages looking at the processes that actually take place. Specifically, it endorsed a view of the structure of Indian society as containing rigidities of caste, religion, and ethnicity and as lacking any "authentically" integrative community and identity.

Churchmen, understandably, shared an entrenched Orientalist orthodoxy and pervasive construction. Romila Thapar, for instance, has highlighted a retrospective construction for early Indian history of a *brahmana*-dominated

9. John Breuilly, *Nationalism and the State* (Manchester, 1993, rev. paperback ed., 1995).

10. P. Chatterjee, *The Nation and Its Fragments: Colonial and Postcolonial Histories* (Princeton, 1993), p. 236.

Hinduism supposedly presiding over a variety of sects, though "these multiple sects were seldom viewed in their social and historical context even though this was crucial to their understanding." A standard suppression of the constructive potentialities of "multiple communities identified by locality, languages, caste, occupation and sect" was encouraged by missionaries intent on underlining the inadequate theological and philosophical characters of Islam and Hinduism.[11] They were primarily concerned with South Asian faiths as contestable systems of ideas. For later periods, C. A. Bayly has detailed the indefinite range of political linkages and divisions available in a multifarious society, and also the functionally related social mobility over time of specific castes and *jatis* in response to economic and political change.[12] Scholars have pointed out, in various contexts, processes of "Sanskritization" as modes of Indian social mobility. Susan Harper, in her study of the work of the first Indian Anglican bishop, has shown the hazards of wishful thinking in reading a collective shift toward temperance, for instance, as a response to Christian teaching. It was rather a recognizable ritualized bid for enhanced status by a subordinate but economically buoyant group in the context of India's social hierarchies. Bishop Whitehead's optimistic comments on such groups in Bishop Azariah's diocese may well have been incautious.[13]

The monumental simplifications, assailed by subsequent scholarship, conditioned clerical and missionary attitudes toward the social and religious communities they encountered in South Asia. This is reflected in the descriptive ethnographies of the literature, in such books as Bishop Copleston's *Buddhism, Primitive and Present in Magadha and in Ceylon* (1892) and *The Village Gods of South India* (1921) by Bishop Whitehead of Madras, as well as in other studies in the Farquhar and Macnicol series on "The Religious Life of India." In 1920 and 1921, Richard Dyke Acland, Palmer's successor at Bombay, wrote in the *Bombay Diocesan Magazine* a long series on Hinduism in the same idiom for the benefit of his expatriate churchgoing community.[14] G. U.

11. Romila Thapar, *Interpreting Early India* (Delhi, 1992), pp. 60-88, "Imagined Religious Communities? Ancient History and the Modern Search for a Hindu Identity."

12. For example, C. A. Bayly, *Rulers, Townsmen and Bazaars: North Indian Society in the Age of British Expansion, 1770-1870* (Cambridge, 1983), and C. A. Bayly, ed., *The Raj: India and the British, 1600-1947* (London, 1991).

13. Susan Billington Harper, "Azariah and Indian Christianity in the Last Years of the Raj," D.Phil. thesis, University of Oxford, 1991, p. 260; Susan Billington Harper, *In the Shadow of the Mahatma: Bishop Azariah and the Travails of Indian Christianity* (London, 2000); Sir George Anderson and the Rt. Rev. Henry Whitehead, *Christian Education in India* (London, 1932), p. 96.

14. Studdert-Kennedy, *British Christians*, p. 101.

Pope, the venerable Tamil and Telugu scholar, was Palmer's immediate predecessor as chaplain at Balliol. Writing in 1974, Bishop Stephen Neill dismissed Pope's "quaint speculations as to possible Christian influences" *upon* ancient Tamil texts, which Pope believed might explain their "Christian" content. In phrases that nicely blend respect and postcolonial condescension, Bishop Neill refers to the "powerful and pious imagination" of the "Cornish sage (which spreads) its wings beyond the limits of what sober scholarship will underwrite."[15] For Muslim India, Bishop Lefroy, a uniquely learned episcopal Islamist, thought of his convert groups and their cultural contexts in corresponding "theological and philosophical" terms.[16] He was highly regarded by Lahore's learned Muslim exponents of the Quran; he even had the famous conversion of an intermittently backsliding blind *moulvie* to his credit. From the same perspective, Palmer himself, before his Bombay appointment, corresponded with Oxford's Boden Professor of Sanskrit about the concept of atheism in Buddhism.[17] He wrote to his cousin "Willie," the second Lord Selborne, just after accepting the Bombay appointment, that he "was not averse to philosophizing with, and for, Hindus."[18] As a preliminary illustration of the category of improvisation, Bishop Acland was the unwitting patron of a remarkably liberated clerical improvisation on behalf of India's nationalist movement. His own chaplain, Guthrie Michael Scott, was the contact provided by the London communist party to Michael Carritt, the one known English communist in, however briefly, the Indian Civil Service in the 1930s. Carritt had been a classical scholar at The Queen's College, Oxford. Scott, no Oxbridge man, was educated in and returned to a notable ministry in South Africa. He describes in his memoir an exhausting hill walk with Acland, unsuccessfully devoted to the demolition of his own naive and unrealistic "liberation theology."[19]

The oversimplified structural model of Indian society was reflected in government policy: for example, in the supposedly "objective" classification of ranked communities in the decennial census.[20] By objectifying a caste hi-

15. Stephen Neill, *Bhakti, Hindu and Christian* (Madras, 1974), p. 44.

16. H. H. Montgomery, *The Life and Letters of George Alfred Lefroy* (London, 1920).

17. Oxford, Balliol College, Palmer Papers [hereafter Balliol Palmer], A. A. Macdonnell to Palmer, 25 February 1907, Box 1.

18. London, Lambeth Palace, Palmer Papers [hereafter Lambeth Palmer], ms. 2851ff., 82-85.

19. G. M. Scott, *A Time to Speak* (London, 1958), p. 75.

20. Bernard S. Cohn, "The Census, Social Structure and Objectification in South Asia," in his *An Anthropologist among the Historians and Other Essays* (Delhi, 1987), pp. 224-54.

erarchy, successive censuses endorsed the model and provided a basis for the subsequent politics of caste "reservation" in employment.[21] "Objectification" fortified assumptions about the interface of Christian faith and indigenous community. In the eyes of supporters of mass caste conversions, such as Bishop Whitehead, successful group conversion meant the extraction from the structure of oppression and error of an integral, enumerated community, and its social and moral reconstitution.[22] In the political reading of nationalism to which I now turn, such events are necessarily seen in a different light.

The Anglican Church in India operated in the context of a nationalist politics, in Breuilly's sense, from well before the formation of any self-conscious nationalist movement. The nationalist movement was a development of Indian politics under an alien state. Conscious nationalist politics began with the attempt by some to infiltrate and then claim the state structure in the name of the nation. Once that has been achieved, once perceived political community and state successfully fuse — when it is no longer *my* community and *your* state — then nationalism in this analytically useful sense ceases. However, in many specific situations, certainly in South Asia, but also elsewhere — for example, in the lower Congo basin in Africa, where the Bakongo peoples developed a nationalist movement out of an alliance between missionaries and local intellectuals[23] — the nationalist fusion of community and state is too insecure to survive and is open to challenge, and thus the contest will continue. Since Indian nationalism had to contain such a diversity of competing energies, it could only hang together around the most fundamental of common denominators: namely, removing the British. It had to include radicals and collaborators and a mosaic of thousands of distinctive grassroots communities, but the nationalism of "Quit India" survived independence only at the level of rhetoric. Subsequently, differently constituted interests, including commercial, criminal, and reconstituted caste, *jati,* and "religious" interests, have competed for possession of the Indian state and its "national identity." In this competi-

21. Francine Frankel and M. S. A. Rao, eds., *Dominance and State Power in Modern India,* vol. 2 (Delhi, 1990).

22. Henry Whitehead, *Indian Problems in Religion, Education, Politics* (London, 1924). "Looked at upon the surface, it would appear that this great movement is social rather than religious. . . . I think that most people, who know about the condition of the outcastes and their past history, would certainly agree with the Census Commissioner that it is a very laudable thing for them to try to escape from their lot of misery . . . there is another fact that also needs to be borne in mind, and that is that there is always a very strong spiritual side to the movement" (p. 50).

23. Breuilly, *Nationalism,* p. 203.

tive postimperial context many Indian Christian communities are less well placed than they once were.

Both winners and losers are part of the nationalist process itself: those who are not among the winners have been excluded or have excluded themselves. Furthermore, *any* cultural, credal, or material characteristic or combination of characteristics can constitute a basis for inclusion or exclusion, and outcomes are not inevitable. The histories of nationalism, despite their differences, share the process of the pursuit of state power by coalitions competing to achieve a dominant critical mass. Any interests associated with the colonial state were no less part of the process. Bishops and missionaries, like expatriate civil servants and soldiers, were directly or indirectly locked into the highly competitive political process of inclusion and exclusion, through conversion and education,[24] or collaborative administration,[25] or army recruitment.[26]

The first of these groups, religious functionaries, brought to this process varieties of theology and complex patterns of authority including religious institutional authority, commitment to the colonial state, and commitment to one reading or another of a *metropolitan* nationalist formula in its imperial expression. They also brought constitutions, that is to say, decision-making rules that were designed to outlast their own authoritative presence, although they could find themselves reduced at times to my residual category of "improvisation."

III

Improvisation within the formal church-state structure could have political consequences. An improvisatory tendency in clerical appointment is a familiar figure in the comedies of Anthony Trollope, and an effective one precisely because it depends on no extreme exaggeration of real life. In neither fiction nor reality are the consequences for its victims necessarily amusing. In 1901 the Anglican Metropolitan, J. E. C. Welldon, resigned. He had been in office barely three years. This followed a crisis, which had infuriated and deeply distressed the man who had appointed him, and whose closest friend he appears

24. See chapters by Forrester, Oddie, Fischer, and Downs in G. A. Oddie, ed., *Religion in South Asia* (Delhi, 1991).

25. This has been a focus of interest of the so-called Cambridge School of South Asia historians. For a brief assessment and full bibliography see Sumit Sarkar, *Modern India, 1885-1947* (Madras, 1983), pp. 4-9, 457.

26. David Omissi, *The Sepoy and the Raj: The Indian Army, 1860-1940* (London, 1994).

to have been since their days together at Eton, namely, George Nathaniel Curzon, of Eton and Balliol. Curzon and Godley, the Under-Secretary of State at the India Office, with suave bureaucratic brutality contrived Welldon's resignation. The incident is ignored or lightly passed over by all of Curzon's biographers.[27]

One cannot easily laugh off this affair as the just reward of cronyism, however, because Welldon had been a formidable headmaster of Harrow, perfectly capable of keeping public school clergy in line. Curzon, as his almost panic-stricken response demonstrated, was deeply anxious about the Christian mission of empire; and manifestly for both men the *raison d'être* of Etonians was to run the empire, and who better to handle both sides of the providential equation than they themselves? But Welldon, who knew far too little about India, had been shaken to the core by what he saw as its physical and spiritual squalor. His response, with a frantic lack of reflective consultation, was to threaten to improvise an episcopate of aggressive proselytizing. This delighted some high churchmen in India and back home. It infuriated Bengal expatriates and generated alarm in the India Office. As an appointment to a highly visible and sensitive government position Welldon's was a disaster, doubly trying because high church militants simultaneously embarked on a campaign to convert the Calcutta Metropolitan into an independent Archbishopric. This would have drastically altered the ground rules linking government and church. Aspects of that Erastian constitutional understanding were criticized even by its defenders, but it worked, as long as one kept to the formal and informal rules. On this occasion, the "banana-skin" looks to have been carefully aligned to make the worst of a complex conjuncture of top person misjudgments, misperceptions, and sheer ignorance, and of conflicts and confusions internal to the structure of the Church and its authority.

Such crises could blight less hysterical episcopal initiatives. In the course of defending established episcopal authority from a theologically conservative but earnestly missionary perspective, the brilliant Bishop Copleston of Ceylon had earned the hostility of Church Missionary Society (CMS) missionaries in his Ceylon diocese.[28] W. R. Pym, Palmer's immediate predecessor at Bombay, was a broad churchman who annoyed government and outraged his own quota of militant high church clergy by coming down with a heavy

27. See Studdert-Kennedy, *Providence*, p. 87; J. E. C. Welldon, *Recollections and Reflections* (London, 1915).

28. R. C. Moberly, *An Account of the Question Which Has Arisen between the Bishop and the CMS in the Diocese of Colombo* (Oxford, 1876).

ANGLICAN CONNECTIONS
The Palmer Family

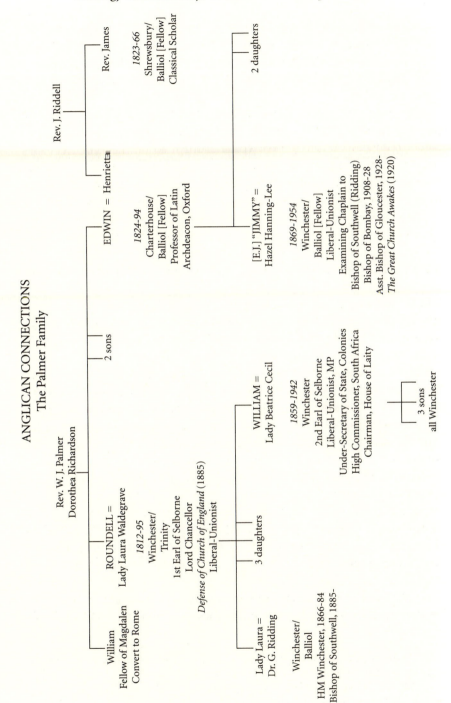

Rev. W. J. Palmer
Dorothea Richardson

William
Fellow of Magdalen
Convert to Rome

ROUNDELL =
Lady Laura Waldegrave

1812-95
Winchester/
Trinity
1st Earl of Selborne
Lord Chancellor
Defense of Church of England (1885)
Liberal-Unionist

2 sons

Rev. J. Riddell

EDWIN = Henrietta

1824-94
Charterhouse/
Balliol [Fellow]
Professor of Latin
Archdeacon, Oxford

Rev. James

1823-66
Shrewsbury/
Balliol [Fellow]
Classical Scholar

Lady Laura =
Dr. G. Ridding

Winchester/
Balliol
HM Winchester, 1866-84
Bishop of Southwell, 1885-

3 daughters

WILLIAM =
Lady Beatrice Cecil

1859-1942
Winchester
2nd Earl of Selborne
Liberal-Unionist, MP
Under-Secretary of State, Colonies
High Commissioner, South Africa
Chairman, House of Laity

3 sons
all Winchester

[E.J.] "JIMMY" =
Hazel Hanning-Lee

1869-1954
Winchester/
Balliol [Fellow]
Liberal-Unionist
Examining Chaplain to
Bishop of Southwell (Ridding)
Bishop of Bombay, 1908-28
Asst. Bishop of Gloucester, 1928-
The Great Church Awakes (1920)

2 daughters

hand, in his Primary Visitation Charge, on unauthorized ritual practices, which were a rather frequent aggravation in Britain at the time.[29] Following his own appointment to Bombay, however, Palmer observed that he, at least, was less likely to offend government than "poor Bishop Pym."[30] He was right. Palmer's selection, which began with Bishop Gore first offering himself for Bombay and then agonizing, before withdrawing and urging that Palmer should undertake it, was skillfully handled by Arthur Hirtzel, the conservative mandarin but quite forward-looking churchman at the India Office.[31] Over time, Palmer was to do more than anyone to transform and stabilize the structure of the Indian Church.

IV

Why was Palmer the right man for the job at the time? One has to consider a dense concentration of formative circumstances: an intensely devout high church extended family, close to some of the greatest in the land and steeped, through three generations, in the theory and practice of law, national and ecclesiastical; schooling at Winchester and a career at Balliol, where he was student, tutor, university proctor, and chaplain. Here was an exceedingly able product of a distinctive elite, from whom a great deal was expected, not least by himself. This provenance throws light on his response to the missionary bishopric of Bombay, in a country he had never visited and about which, as he acknowledged twenty years later, he knew little.[32] He was a personality simultaneously representative and distinctive, and a highly integrated intellectual, in a Gramscian sense — churchman, imperialist, nationalist, and, crucially for the Indian Church, constitutional lawyer.

It is a striking feature of much clerical biography that the wives, sisters, and mothers tend to be shadowy figures. Although this was generally true of the prolific Palmer and Westcott families, in both cases their women were of fundamental importance. Palmer had two admiring sisters, one of whom married a Balliol contemporary and cleric. There were also sundry admirable

29. W. R. Pym, *Charge Delivered by Walter Ruthven Pym, DD, Bishop of Bombay on the Occasion of His Primary Visitation of the Diocese on 6 February 1907,* with *A Pastoral Letter Addressed to His Clergy on Certain Points Arising out of the Charge* (London, 1907); *The Times,* 2 April 1907, p. 4; *Church Times,* 22 November 1907.

30. Lambeth Palmer, ms. 2851, ff. 82-85.

31. Studdert-Kennedy, *British Christians,* pp. 46-53; G. L. Prestige, *The Life of Charles Gore, a Great Englishman* (London, 1935), ch. xviii, "Knight Errant."

32. Lambeth Palmer, "My Twenty Years as Bishop of Bombay," 3010, f. 177.

cousins and his aunt, Lady Laura Waldegrave. His long-lived mother is a central, silent presence in the record. It was to her that an astonishing series of letters from school at Winchester, now in the Palmer Papers at Lambeth, were addressed. He had taken the top scholarship to Winchester from Oxford's Dragon School in 1882. His last few years were spent in Norham Road, almost within a well-struck "six" of the Dragon School playground, a curiously fitting closure to a socially and intellectually compact life.

During his own Balliol fellowship, Palmer twice, but unhappily, contemplated matrimony, a transition in those days regarded by Balliol's senior Fellows with sour disapproval. At Bombay, however, and with his mother's blessing, he contracted a sustaining marriage in the Palmer pattern. His mother, Henrietta Palmer, was the daughter of a tractarian cleric, and sister of another, the Rev. James Riddell, the intimate friend and Balliol contemporary of Palmer's father, Edwin. Like Edwin, Riddell was a brilliant classical scholar and Fellow of Balliol. Palmer's father, Edwin, became Professor of Classics at Corpus Christi College, and then Archdeacon of Oxford, whence Gladstone tried but failed to tempt him with vacant deaneries. He was a meticulous and efficient administrator, as was his son.

Working outward from this nuclear family, Edwin Palmer was the favorite younger brother of the formidable Roundell Palmer, first earl of Selborne, twice Lord Chancellor. Unlike Edwin, who went to Charterhouse, Roundell was a Wykehamist. He was also the father-in-law of his nephew Jimmy's first Winchester headmaster, the reforming Dr. Ridding (in a colleague's phrase, "the strong, reliable, strange and original Ridding," himself a Winchester and Balliol man). Ridding's second wife, and biographer, was Lady Laura, first daughter of Roundell Palmer and Lady Laura Waldegrave. Her cousin "Jimmy," in consequence, emerges from early boyhood referring initially to "uncle George," advancing to the more accurate and more intimate "cousin George," before becoming examining chaplain to George, Bishop of Southwell, and, finally, in 1907, writing the celebratory chapter on "Ridding's Mind and Thought" in cousin "Lolly's" memoir, just before leaving for India.[33]

Ridding's objective at Winchester was the formation of a national moral elite,[34] and "Jimmy" never for a moment doubted his vocation to belong to it, as his letters home at times make almost too clear. His second headmaster at

33. Lady Laura Ridding, *George Ridding, Schoolmaster and Bishop* (London, 1908).

34. J. D'E. Firth, *Winchester College* (London, 1949). Peter Gwyn, "The 'Tunding Row': George Ridding and the Belief in 'Boy-Government,'" in *Winchester College: Sixth Centenary Essays*, edited by Roger Custance (Oxford, 1982).

Winchester, Dr. Fearon, informed Palmer's parents that "I never knew a clever boy more docile."[35] Other dons recognized the competitive aggression behind the docility. As examinations approached, they noted that his stammer, a lifelong affliction, deteriorated.[36] He advanced to the seemingly inevitable Balliol Scholarship and election to a Fellowship.

For a clear view of the purposive content of his energy we must turn to his uncle Roundell and his father, Edwin, for E. J. Palmer was not an original thinker but a lucid articulator of their shared "truth," which was authoritatively condensed in Roundell's *The Catholic and Apostolic Church* (1899).[37] His nephew never strayed on any significant point from the high church doctrine of this family manual, which originated in letters to Roundell's son William. "Willie," a Wykehamist and Liberal-Unionist MP, would probably have succeeded Lord Curzon as Viceroy in 1904 had Curzon not stayed on. He became, after Lord Milner, the leading proconsul in South Africa and was prominent thereafter in the Round Table movement of Milner's protégés.[38] He was married to Lord Salisbury's daughter, Lady Beatrice Cecil.

The Selborne family had emerged from the early tractarian movement with an evangelical commitment tied, however, to a view of the Church as an organic historic institution, and repudiating the later excesses and accretions of the Oxford Movement. Roundell's chapter headings to his credo of 1899 read like an agenda for his nephew's subsequent management of Church reunion in South India. The final outcome of *that* restructuring accommodated concessions in relation to "heresies" (one of the chapter headings), which would have distressed Roundell, however, and did stretch his nephew and account for the troublesome passage toward reunion legislation.[39]

If the first Lord Selborne saw himself, in the first instance, as a member of the true Church, and as a public figure only thereafter, as a public figure he was in the first instance a lawyer, and as Lord Chancellor the embodiment of

35. Balliol Palmer, Box 1.

36. E. D. A. Morshead, an outstanding division master, notes on 7 August 1884, that by the end of term he gets pale and his stammer increases as exams approach. He is "old enough to learn his work should not be done in a purely competitive spirit" (Balliol Palmer, Box 1).

37. Roundell Palmer, *The Catholic and Apostolic Church,* Letters to his Son, by Roundell, First Earl of Selborne (London, 1899). Chapter titles: "The 'Ecclesia' or Church"; "Organisation of the Church — the Episcopacy; Ordinances of the Church — the Sacraments"; "Divisions of the Church — Heresies; Separation of East and West — the Reformation — The Church of England."

38. Studdert-Kennedy, *Providence,* p. 157.

39. Roundell Palmer, *Memorials, Part 1: Family and Personal (1766-1865)* (London, 1898), 1:208-11, 2:476.

the distinctively English variant of constitutional law. One must stress the rooted and intricate connection in his own mind between positive law and his faith, between the authority of law and the authority of the Church: the authority of a "national" church that sanctioned and guided national and imperial integrity and purpose. This nexus of convictions is rigorously developed over nearly four hundred pages in his *Defence of the Church of England against Disestablishment* (1887), with its long introductory letter to Gladstone. It was common ground for his brother Edwin and his nephew E. J. In an essay on Edwin Palmer printed in the final volume of Selborne's *Memorials,* Oxford's Regius Professor of Ecclesiastical History refers to Edwin's mind as at once "legal" and "logical," and rooted in "the supreme reality" of the Christian Faith "as held by the Church of England."[40] Through the Indian Church Measure (1927), and in England through the 1930s and 1940s until his retirement, E. J. Palmer was, conformably, the constitutional theorist for the Church in South India.

So what, in essence, are the connotations of the category of constitution? Under its "written" Constitution, American history provides a transparent partial answer. Particularly up to the Civil War, wrote Robert McCloskey, "the dominant judicial value, underlying the (Supreme Court's) drift of decision in widely different areas, was the value of preserving the American Union." More generally, and acknowledging that the Constitution was "conceived in ambiguity as well as liberty . . . the framers had said in effect: with respect to certain questions, some of them very momentous, the Constitution means whatever the circumstances of the future will allow it to mean."[41]

Both these principles, the preservation of organic national unity and the constitutional acknowledgment of legal history or precedent, and of lawful change, or legislative process, were incorporated in the masterpiece of Albert Venn Dicey, Oxford's Vinerian Professor of Law, *Introduction to the Study of the Law and the Constitution* (1885).[42] This highly original book, by a Balliol man, went well beyond the hints and snatches of his predecessors in applying "an analytic method to Britain's 'unwritten' constitution, so as to identify its guiding principles."[43] Dicey's work was an *eclaircisement*

40. W. Bright, Regius Professor and Canon of Christ Church, in Selborne, *Memorials, Part 2: Personal and Political, 1865-1895* (London, 1898), 2:460.

41. Robert McCloskey, *The American Supreme Court* (Chicago, 1960), pp. 26, 15.

42. A. V. Dicey, *Introduction to the Study of the Law and the Constitution* (London, 1885). Richard A. Cosgrove, "The Life of a Unionist," in his *The Rule of Law: Albert Venn Dicey, Victorian Jurist* (London, 1980).

43. Colin Munro, "Dicey on Constitutional Conventions," *Public Law,* Special Issue (Winter 1985): 637-51.

for lawyers that is still productive because it related, for the first time, the mountains of case law to half a dozen general principles.[44] Dicey and Selborne, incidentally, were allies in the reform of the legal training and professional organization.

Dicey's clarifications also fed into the wholesale recruitment of Oxford's academic lawyers and others behind one of Oxford's great "lost causes," the Liberal-Unionist Party from 1886 and its rejection of Gladstone's Home Rule thinking for Ireland, which it saw as threatening a constitutionally intolerable assault on the organic nation.[45] The Palmer family went Liberal-Unionist *en bloc.* Selborne's devastating repudiation of Gladstone, after years of devoted loyalty, seethes with wounded affection and the humiliation of misplaced admiration. In a phrase Selborne used publicly as well as privately, Gladstone had gone "morally colour-blind."[46] "Constitutional morality" is a recurrent phrase in Dicey and Selborne discourse, and as a partisan Dicey has been found guilty of assimilating constitutional morality to his own.

E. J. Palmer's illuminated Liberal-Unionist registration card, dated April 1893, three years before his ordination, is signed by Dicey, as chairman of the Oxford branch. Other Balliol men among the eleven party officers listed on it are: Sir William Anson, Warden of All Souls, Vinerian Reader of Law, and Dicey's friend and rival; G. C. Brodrick, Warden of Wadham, also a lawyer; A. G. V. Harcourt Professor Nettleship; and Sir Harry Verney, the Whig estate owner of Claydon House, Buckinghamshire.[47]

Another lawyer who was important to E. J. Palmer was Sir William Markby, formerly a Calcutta High Court judge, Balliol Fellow, tutor to the Indian Civil Service (ICS) Probationers at Balliol, and Reader in Indian Law from 1898 to 1900. The Probationers had first been welcomed to Balliol by Benjamin Jowett (Master of the College) in the mid 1870s, and by 1879 "more than half the lCS Probationers in the country were studying at Balliol."[48] Markby was also College Bursar, and Palmer was his zealous and efficient Assistant Bursar.

Palmer was to remain a liberal imperialist in this tradition while he engaged with India's ramshackle Church organization in the light provided by

44. R. H. Graveson, "Philosophical Aspects of the English Conflict of Laws," *Law Quarterly Review* 78 (July 1962): 337-70.

45. Christopher Harvie, *The Lights of Liberalism: University Liberals and the Challenge of Democracy, 1860-1886* (London, 1976), p. 219.

46. Selborne, *Memorials,* vol. 2: Letter to the Earl of Camperdown, 26 November 1886, pp. 236, 341-60.

47. Balliol Palmer, Box 1.

48. Jones, *Balliol,* p. 218.

Dicey's more durable analysis of constitution and law. His translocation of those ideas will be considered below. He did not make heavy weather of this task, as he said; he had simply inhaled the intellectual and political oxygen of family, college, and university.

V

In 1907 Palmer spent some months observing imperial management in South Africa as the guest of his cousin "Willie" Selborne (second earl of Selborne), by now High Commissioner and Governor of the Transvaal and Orange River. He reached Bombay in 1908.

Palmer was certain to be politically docile. He looked forward, indeed, to drawing on Balliol's ICS connection. His attention as bishop, however, was concentrated initially less on questions of Church management than on theology, on the condition of Christian faith in his diocese. He was appalled by what he encountered. The matter of the Congregationalist American Marathi mission at Ahmednagar particularly outraged him. His Oxford farewell sermon at St. Mary's had recognized the urgent call for Church reunion in South India, and he had learned, as Chairman of the Junior Clergy Missionary Association, that the pressure came from the grassroots.[49] In Bombay he pointed out to Ferrand Corley, who had written from Madras Christian College in its prestigious *College Magazine*, that "the claim of plenary inspiration for each congregation is incomprehensible to anyone not a congregationalist . . . a concession of authority to the most obviously unauthoritative persons." In a later issue of the *Bombay Diocesan Record* he stated that "those who present Christianity in a vague 'undogmatic' way are, I believe, steering straight towards this horrible absorption of Christianity by Hinduism."[50]

The amiable and widespread recognition by historically disparate denominations in South India "of the validity of each other's ordinances, ministry, membership and discipline" was, for Palmer, a giveaway, conceding the equivalence of faiths, acknowledging indifference to the corporate life of Christians and the revealed nature of the Godhead. Yet for the dispersed Indian Christian communities pressure for union was a political response to the threat or,

49. E. J. Palmer, *Parting Words: A Sermon Preached to Undergraduates of the University of Oxford in the Church of St Mary-the-Virgin, on 18 October 1908* (Oxford, 1909). I have not succeeded in locating records of the Junior Clergy Missionary Association. Lord Salisbury presided at its Exeter Hall meeting on 2 December 1904.

50. E. J. Palmer, *Re-Union in Western India: Papers and Articles by the Bishop of Bombay* (Bombay, 1910), part 1, iii, xi.

for some, the temptation and opportunity of the nationalist movement. In 1885, for instance, the year the Indian National Congress was founded, Dr. Pullney Andy had founded the National Church of India, with a nonsectarian and inclusivist invitation: it was "a sign of the times . . . expressing aspirations of a certain section of Indian Christian leaders."[51]

It was 1914 before Palmer identified himself with the reunion project, with the realization that the indigenous, congregation-driven demand for "union," on whatever terms, could not be resisted but might possibly be met within a coherent constitutional accommodation. This accommodation would have to protect "constitutional morality" by not fudging principles. It would have to underwrite two complementary organic unions, that of the Protestant Christian Church in India, but also, for Palmer and those sympathetic to his vision, that of the evolving imperial union within which the Church of England was both an historic and a living presence. The anxious voice of the Anglo-Catholic Whig imperialist sounds through a letter home to his sisters, during a political strike in Bombay in 1920: "I wish George Lloyd [Governor of Bombay, and a leading Tory diehard over constitutional "advance" for India in the 1930s] had carte blanche to settle this business. He has courage, special knowledge, integrity and commonsense and he is a Christian and a statesman at once. The combination exists in no one else so far as I know."[52] Palmer looked forward to an indigenous Church but could not foresee an independent India.

The constitution he devised was certainly conceived in doctrinal and political "ambiguity" — to recall McCloskey's phrases on the American Constitution — and it could only be an act of faith on Palmer's part to believe that "the circumstances of the future" might "allow it to mean" what he believed God wanted it to mean, namely, the eventual emergence of the "Great Church" into which all others must die in order to be born again.[53] In any event, he had a clear grasp of what kind of intellectual contrivance the constitution itself had to be. He understood, to borrow a phrase from a 1966 appreciation of Dicey by an Oxford lawyer, that "law as an academic discipline is closer to theology than to the social sciences whose subject matter it shares."[54]

51. B. Sundkler, *The Church of South India: The Movement towards Union, 1900-1945,* rev. ed. (London, 1967).

52. Lambeth Palmer, ms. 3005, ff. 34.

53. E. J. Palmer, *The Great Church Awakes* (London, 1920).

54. O. Kahn-Freund, "Reflections on Legal Education," *Modern Law Review* (March 1966): 123 reads: "Authority is a concept which looms large in the thinking and in the practice of lawyers everywhere. All legal reasoning is based on established norms the existence of which cannot be questioned by the lawyer. In this sense law as an academic discipline is closer to theology than to the social sciences whose subject matter it shares. . . . Our

In 1944 the report entitled *Dispensation in Practice and Theory: with special reference to the Anglican Churches,* of an Archbishop's Commission which Palmer had chaired, was published.[55] A dull document, it embodies Dicey's basic analytical gambit, a distinction between rules and customs, or, for the Palmers as ecclesiastical lawyers, rules and "dispensations." McCloskey could point to an analogous transatlantic distinction in relation to historical variations accommodated under states' rights. Laws embody the union's fundamental principles. They can, of course, be changed through structures of representation as circumstances and public perceptions shift. The law can support customs, which emerge over time for local historical reasons, or customs can simply die out as circumstances change, though they can also be abolished by law. But customs, conventions, and dispensations are, in their relation to fundamental principles, "vague and indefinite," in Dicey's crucial phrase, "both because statesmen feel that the matter is one hardly to be dealt with by precise rules, and because no human being knows how far and to what extent the nation wishes that the voice of the reigning monarch should command attention . . . the practice of the Crown and the wishes of the nation have from time to time varied."[56]

Palmer applies this analytical acknowledgment of locally permissible, historically conditioned variation, of custom or dispensation, to a politically restless and ambiguous situation. A claim for dispensation should test actual practices and claims against fundamental principles taken to sustain church authority. At the same time, it should test current sentiment through a representative machinery, of congregations, assemblies, or synods. In the Indian context, however, the "tests" clearly had to be widely interdenominational, exposed as they were to abrasive horizontal pressures and to pressures from below. What emerged in the 1920s and 1930s was a constitutional federation that found reasons for accepting that issues which had seemed, and which still seemed to many in England, to require regulation under the controlling authority of theologically exclusivist principles should be accepted as areas for "dispensation," local variation, in "vague and indefinite" relation to fundamental principles.[57] They should be formally recognized as contemporary

---

so-called 'science' is still and will for ever be based on the interpretation of sources the validity of which is assumed and not an object of our study."

55. *Dispensation in Practice and Theory: With Special Reference to the Anglican Churches, Being a Report of a Commission Appointed by the Archbishop of Canterbury in 1935, under the Chairmanship of Edwin James Palmer, D.D., Sometime Bishop of Bombay* (London, 1944).

56. Dicey, *Law,* ch. 15.

57. On subsequent resistance to the reunion proposals by High Churchmen see

ambiguities awaiting rejection or endorsement in the unpredictable "circumstances of the future." The question was where to draw the line between permissible variation and intolerable deviation or heresy.

B. Sundkler's detailed narrative account of these developments takes the reunion process largely at Palmer's own valuation. Palmer was belligerent about not fudging fundamental convictions, and about his hostility to the pragmatism for which he criticized Whitehead.[58] He was, for instance, uncompromising about the "false and distorted view on the character of the episcopacy" of his leading Congregationalist protagonist, Vernon Bartlet.[59] In the end, however, what he called "our boldest step" depended on an entirely unambiguous ambiguity over bishops and the commissioning of priests. He had clearly recognized the dilemma: "Can it be thought consistent with the reverence due to holy things that the same (commissioning) prayer should be used by two parties in the same service with a different intention?"[60]

The answer was that it had to be. Palmer is lucid, learned, and urgent on the historical Anglo-Catholic arguments for the direct transmission of authority from the Apostles to the Early Church. He was forced, however, to recommend an episcopal structure to the Indian Church on the functionalist and "Orientalist" grounds that Indians are used to Rajahs. This was entirely acceptable, but for political not theological reasons, to Indian Church leaders such as K. T. Paul: Paul had announced that he "had no use at all for history."[61] So the post-Reformation denominations in India settled for the historic and constitutional episcopate as the basis for Church organization, while hastening, in Palmer's own words, "to assure us that they rejected our view of history while accepting our practical proposals."[62] A larger political process of communitarian fission and fusion, with its own intrinsic modalities, had precipitated an evacuation of the domain of theology and moved the Christian communities in South India, and eventually more widely, toward a

London, British Library, Templewood Papers, XVII:14, Minutes of a Meeting of the General Council of the Church Union held at S.P.G, 6 June 1945, and Meeting with the Archbishop at Lambeth (Confidential), 14 January 1947.

58. See n. 50 above; for E. J. Palmer's instructions on the "admission to our pulpits of men not episcopally ordained" and the "admission to Communion of Christians who have not been episcopally confirmed" see his *After Kikuyu: A Pastoral Letter from the Bishop of Bombay to the Clergy of His Diocese* (Bombay, 1919).

59. E. J. Palmer, *Great Church Awakes*, p. 86 and ch. 7 (originally in *Bombay Diocesan Magazine*, January 1920). R. Tudor Jones, *Congregationalism in England, 1662-1962* (London, 1962).

60. Sundkler, *Church of South India*, p. 152.

61. Sundkler, *Church of South India*, p. 181.

62. Lambeth Palmer, "Memorandum on Reunion Negotiations," 2978.

structure that was doubtfully heading toward the development of Palmer's "Great Church."

In 1934 Bishop Neill wrote that communally based national elections had "immensely strengthened the sense of unity in the Church: pressure from the outside has made the whole Church throughout India conscious of itself as a separate political entity."[63] Clearly communal "unity" is seen here as desirable. In his judgment of 1970, however, he found that the emerging national constitutional structure had created an arena for the competitive proliferation of a factional postnationalist politics of communal alliances and subdivisions. In the Christian communities themselves, he could see no perceptible development of "spiritual vitality."[64] More recently, Chris Sugden has referred to the ministry of Vinay Samuel in South India in connection with Samuel's "tense relationship with the Church of South India, particularly in the light of the corruption with which it has been engulfed."[65] Episcopal authority had itself been compromised. Undeniably, "corruption" is ubiquitously allowed by the subcontinental circumstances of the present. As every Church historian knows, it is also a powerful solvent of stable belief.

VI

One can pursue another expression of the political theme in the Madras Presidency that William Miller, the famous Principal of Madras Christian College, had left in 1907, the year before Palmer's installation at Bombay. The theme is well focused by R. E. Frykenberg's image of the "white ants in Guntur,"[66] drawn from the words of a faculty member of the Andhra Christian College in Guntur who had observed the "white ant principle" in action: "A remarkable feature of local influences in Guntur is the ability seemingly to submit to high authority while at the same time achieving their own ends."

Frykenberg documents in this representative district a process by which,

63. Stephen Neill, *Builders of the Indian Church* (London, 1934), p. 142.

64. Stephen Neill, *The Story of the Christian Church in India and Pakistan* (London, 1970; Indian ed., 1972), p. 175.

65. Chris Sugden, *Seeking the Asian Face of Jesus: The Practice and Theology of Christian Social Witness in Indonesia and India, 1974-1996* (Oxford, 1997), p. 420.

66. R. E. Frykenberg, *Guntur District, 1788-1848: A History of Local Influence and Central Authority in South Asia* (Oxford, 1965), p. 230. Also his "Village Strength in South India," in *Land Control and Social Structure in Indian History,* edited by R. E. Frykenberg (Madison, Wisc., 1969), p. 245.

while established authority appears to be intact, it is relentlessly mined from within by competitive, locally coordinated agencies, which gradually appropriate the structures of central authority behind a fragile show of collective collaboration. I have examined this process at work at a later stage in Madras itself, by moving via the classic studies of D. A. Washbrook and C. J. Baker to an analysis of Principal Miller's most successful students.[67] By the 1920s the more ruthless and adroit cohorts of white ants had worked their way from locality to center, and the leaders were controlling the ministerial positions open to Indians at Fort St. George. Nearly all of them had degrees from Madras Christian College, rather than the government Presidency College, which disproportionately fed the ranks of dissidents and Gandhians. A high proportion from both institutions proceeded to further qualifications in law, the essential weapon in an elite politics concerned with land, tax, temple property, and patronage.

Miller's generation in the Free Church of Scotland was already forgetting the religious exclusivism of its schismatic "Disruption" of 1843. In Scotland the new project was reunion. In Madras Miller collaborated comfortably at the College with Anglicans and Wesleyans. Together they pursued Alexander Duff's strategy, fiercely criticized by Bishop Whitehead and others,[68] of avoiding religious confrontation and playing down proselytizing, in order to communicate Western knowledge, supposedly intrinsically Christian, to the Presidency's elites. Miller himself concentrated on historical and literary insights, drawing warnings for his pupils from Scotland's past against the premature pursuit of national "freedom" and presenting a vision of authentically organic national community in the course of his curious, but by every account memorable, interpretations of Shakespeare's tragedies. The liberal theology and modern biblical criticism introduced in Scotland by, among others, Principal Tulloch, who was Moderator of the General Assembly a few years before Miller, accompanied an increasingly sympathetic and informed response to Hinduism and Islam in Madras. The still sympathetic but more rigorous and critical comparative theology of A. G. Hogg, College Principal in the 1920s, was published in the *College Magazine.* Yet Hogg's resistance to the "fulfillment theology" of Farquhar and Andrews, which became modish in

67. C. J. Baker and D. A. Washbrook, *South India: Political Institutions and Political Change, 1880-1940* (London, 1975); D. A. Washbrook, *The Emergence of Provincial Politics: The Madras Presidency, 1870-1920* (Cambridge, 1976); C. J. Baker, *The Politics of South India, 1920-1927* (Cambridge, 1976).

68. Whitehead, *Indian Problems*, pp. 182-83. *Report of the Commission on Christian Higher Education in India* [A. D. Lindsay Commission] (Oxford, 1931), part 2, ch. 2 (3), "Bishop Whitehead's Criticisms."

missionary circles, was exceptional.[69] Miller's College was an outstanding success, though Miller had been reprimanded in public by Bishop Gell, though to no effect, for his doctrinal laxity.

One has to consider the institution from the point of view of its students and their networks. They were constantly reminded of their responsibilities as "natural leaders" in an organic nation, a burden they were more than willing to take up. They were urged to reform the oppressive rigidities of caste, and so, as high, but not always the highest caste, the more partisan among them enthusiastically attacked a supposedly Brahman monopolization of opportunities. Washbrook and Baker describe the appeal of the non-Brahman movement as factional. With a combination of naivety and anxious caution the College encouraged it as an indigenous reforming impulse. One of its "spin-doctors," Kandaswamy Chetty, was a student and later a lecturer in English literature at the College. He was also Miller's first, adulatory biographer, fluent in the rhetoric of Christian providentialism and imperially sanctioned national evolution, though he personally drew the line at the final step of conversion for obvious and entirely sensible reasons — he had not learned to quote Browning in order to be disowned by kin and caste.

The dominant faction in the Presidency, which crowded the available ministerial positions in the 1920s, had its roots in one of two shifting factions of lawyers, both of which were driven by an unideological hunger for political control. The College alumni in general gave a contingent and expectant loyalty to the Raj. In the 1930s, a period when Gandhian nationalism appeared to be faltering, its outstanding figures were riding high and decked in imperial honors. When, in the late 1920s, Hogg recognized that the College was no longer what it had been academically, he probably realized that a later generation was less convinced than its predecessors had been by Miller's reiterated imperial distinction between "good" and "bad" nationalism, and had come to judge that perhaps it was time to think of moving over to Congress.

VII

The ministries of the Westcott brothers represent a significantly different compounding of the elements of authority and faith, constitutional procedure, and improvisational opportunity. Allahabad in 1889 confronted them

69. E. Sharpe, *Not to Destroy but to Fulfill* (Lund, 1965); Timothy Yates, *Christian Mission in the Twentieth Century* (Cambridge, 1994), p. 26; Studdert-Kennedy, *British Christians*, p. 69.

with narrowly constricting problems: the Society for the Propagation of the Gospel (SPG) famine orphans, an agricultural settlement, the expatriate community, and a school. Over the years, as they provided industrial training for the orphans, developed the school into a College, and took on larger responsibilities, the Westcotts evoked in their SPG correspondence another dimension of Church structure. One senses routines that had come to be maintained by their own momentum and an atmosphere seldom communicated by Palmer, but instantly familiar to students of missionary reports. It is oppressed by heat and exhaustion, interpersonal abrasions, and frustrated aspirations.

In the mid 1930s, in the middle of the White Paper debate on India, the Archbishop of Canterbury, Cosmo Lang, grew irritated with Foss Westcott for losing touch with his responsibilities. The Metropolitan had compounded the offense by taking up with Frank Buchman's Oxford Group movement in England. This clearly provided him with a supportive moral community and a refreshed sense of organic spiritual life, which, as he publicly acknowledged, his institutional position failed to satisfy.[70]

Foss Westcott believed, perhaps correctly, that his brother had been "far better qualified" than himself as a Diocesan. When he became Bishop of Chota Nagpur in 1905, however, George continued in Allahabad. Four years later, Bishop Clifford of Lucknow wrote to the SPG that "George Westcott without Foss is not quite the same person," commenting on the mission's loss of "tone . . . smoothness and vigour."[71] A year later, however, George Westcott took over his diocese. Circumstances clearly account for a good deal. Palmer and Miller, in various ways, represent encounters dynamically structured by metropolitan churches, in each case a distinct and coherently mounted encounter with politically reactive native communities, but the Westcotts had it all to do, and that included raising funds at the margin.

Perspectives and personalities account for something. The Westcott brothers' sense of what constituted an organic Christian community was rather different from Palmer's. It entailed a less distanced response to the protagonist faiths of India. They shared Palmer's belief in bishops but for broad church rather than high church reasons. As dependable government servants, they believed in the imperial mission and shared Palmer's hostility to "Indian nationalism." Foss, however, unlike Palmer, did not hesitate to take Gandhi on at his own public game, but he did so with embarrassing results. Very briefly, Foss,

70. *The Times*, 21 September, 17 October, and 1 November 1933.

71. Oxford, Rhodes House, USPG Papers, F. Westcott to Bishop H. H. Montgomery, 23, III, 1905; A. Clifford to Bishop Montgomery, 15, VII, 1909.

who had an undistinguished degree in natural science from Cambridge, publicly advanced the argument that since "natural law" is absolutely fixed and reliable, and since Christ explicitly rejected the temptation to lead a nationalist movement against Rome, "the powers that be are ordained by God" and "they that resist shall receive to themselves damnation." J. C. Kumarappa, the Indian Christian who edited Gandhi's *Young India* at the time, had a field day and printed the entire correspondence. To be fair, Kumarappa had provoked the Metropolitan by challenging him to come out against violence inflicted by police on civil disobedience volunteers.[72] Foss's relations with nationalist-inclined Indian clergy seemed to them authoritarian and provocative. His sense of the reciprocity defining relations between political and ecclesiastical authority was undoubtedly confused.

Foss's confusions seem to reflect the larger significance of the Westcotts in that they represented the churchmanship of their saintly father, Foss Westcott, Bishop of Durham, and the interdenominational Maurician perspective he passionately but foggily expounded. It is useful to identify some essential ingredients in the broad church development of "F. D. Maurice and Company" before turning to a specific expression of this theological development in an attempted improvisation of George Westcott's.[73]

Samuel Taylor Coleridge is a point of departure with his vision of the "spiritual, Platonic old England,"[74] an organic, hierarchical, frankly elitist Christian society, by a "blessed accident" of history balancing church and state through the disinterested activity of its educating and progressive "clerisy." Schoolmasters following Thomas Arnold and George Ridding trained the clerisy, and their institutions sent them to serve across the Empire. What they had learned was industry, integrity, loyalty, and gentlemanly Christianity, for the most part on the simplest and most inclusive of theological foundations. Their historian was Sir John Seeley, Regius Professor of Modern History at Cambridge in the 1880s, who saw his scholarly function as that of identifying and exposing the impulses of a providential dispensation within history itself. The vehicle of providential

72. For more detail see Studdert-Kennedy, *British Christians,* pp. 157-62.

73. Alex Vidler, *F. D. Maurice and Company* (London, 1966); Studdert-Kennedy, "Broad Church," pp. 17-39; B. F. Westcott, *Social Aspects of Christianity* (London, 1908); A. C. Benson, "Bishop Westcott," in his *Leaves of the Tree: Studies in Biography* (London, 1911), pp. 21-48; David Newsome, *Bishop Westcott and the Platonic Tradition* (Oxford, 1969).

74. Coleridge's phrase is used as an epigraph for the series of thirteen pertinent sonnets by Geoffrey Hill entitled "An Apology for the Revival of Christian Architecture in England" of which 4, 5, and 6 constitute "A Short History of British India" (*Collected Poems* [London, 1985]).

intention is the organic nation and its imperial realization; its agents are politicians, clergy, administrators, and experts of all kinds — a socially integrated "clerisy." The broad church tendency was irenic, inclusivist, but in a nebulous sort of way. Its most influential intellectual at Balliol was T. H. Green, who had developed a Christian reading of Hegel in the 1860s and 1870s. Melvin Richter has delicately characterized this general irenic mentality in the thought of Green as a "disregard for clarity when it divided men."[75] Green's influence lived on with Palmer's friend and adviser A. L. Smith and with A. D. Lindsay, successively Masters of Balliol between 1916 and 1949. Both men were active for the Industrial Christian Fellowship (ICF) in the 1920s,[76] and Lindsay chaired the Commission on Christian Higher Education in India, whose 1931 report celebrated the achievements of the Madras Christian College. As an institution the interdenominational ICF movement was in lineal descent from Westcott of Durham's Christian Social Union, whose "liberal" theology Roundell Palmer suspected of dangerously socialistic tendencies.

This broadly based and conservative tendency in late Victorian thought, with its sacramental orientation, was one basis for reunion initiatives north and south of the Scottish border. In India it licensed the "fulfillment theology" of Farquhar and the Indian YMCA, which Palmer suspected and of which A. G. Hogg at the Christian College was an isolated critic. The Metropolitan's own "fulfillment" thinking was pedestrian, but a readiness in principle to recognize authentic religious insight in any quarter goes right back to the electrifying teaching of F. D. Maurice. Maurice had preached five agonized sermons as Chaplain of Lincoln's Inn, after the "Indian Crisis," as he called it, of 1857. The following quotations pick up their main thread:

> We cannot teach them of His true nature if we do not show them that He is a God Who maketh inquisition for blood; Who must have a land purged which has been defiled with it. . . .
>
> But so long as we think of Christianity chiefly as a Western or English religion, which is to drive out different Asiatic religions, so long I think it is good for us to find lions in our path of proselytism. . . . we think of every Hindoo feeling respecting Incarnation and Sacrifices as a feeling after Him Who truly became one with men.[77]

75. Melvin Richter, *The Politics of Conscience: T. G. Green and His Age* (London, 1964), pp. 192-94.

76. Gerald Studdert-Kennedy, *Dog Collar Democracy: The Industrial Christian Fellowship, 1919-1929* (London, 1982).

77. F. D. Maurice, *The Indian Crisis: Five Sermons* (Cambridge, 1857), from Sermons 1 and 2.

Implicit in the Duffian concentration on literature, at Miller's College, inclusivist and fulfillment thinking was a political necessity for Indian Christian communities, as Palmer was forced to recognize. It was also a convenience for imperial politicians since it tacitly abandoned ambitious evangelization as a prerequisite in an accelerating drift toward independence, though Tory diehards "stuck to their guns" well into the 1930s.[78] It can also be seen, however, as an invitation to dialogue. This brings us back to Bishop Clifford and George Westcott's "improvisation."

In his complaint about Westcott's loss of grip, Clifford chose not to recall that George had already reacted with alarm to the establishment by Muslims, Hindus, and Arya Samaj in north India of religious teaching centers. These centers were obviously part of the processes of communal self-identification and of varieties of nationalism. Clifford recognized their hostile potential and from 1908 had enthusiastically promoted the creation of a College of Study, with accommodation for both Christians and non-Christians. It would explore, in constructive confrontation, the correspondence of Christian and fundamentally valid non-Christian insights.

The project got nowhere and never had a chance of doing so. Westcott was defeated by what a sympathetic London Missionary Society man referred to as "chronic hardupness," and he had to stifle his resentment toward the London SPG, which would also shortly have the war to contend with. He had already indicated this new direction, in 1907, in his book *Kabir and the Kabir Panth,* which was well before Clifford's critical assessment.[79] Kabir, in the fifteenth century, had drawn on Hindu and Muslim devotional traditions. The Kabir *Panth* retained a substantial following in north India, and Westcott would have known of the community of *panthis* converted in Chanda, in Nagpur Diocese, by Alex Wood, subsequently Bishop of Chota Nagpur and, finally, of Nagpur.[80] Kabir became almost fashionable in England after 1915, with the translation of a hundred poems by Tagore assisted Evelyn Underhill.[81] Perhaps predictably, the Tagore-Underhill partnership stressed the ecstatic imagery of oneness with the Supreme, the aspect of the

78. Gerald Studdert-Kennedy, "The Christian Imperialism of the Die-Hard Defenders of the Raj," *Journal of Imperial and Commonwealth History* (October 1990): 342-62; reprinted as ch. 10 in *Providence.*

79. G. H. Westcott, *Kabir and the Kabir Panth* (Calcutta, 1907; reprinted Calcutta, 1953).

80. Eyre Chatterton, *Alex Wood, Bishop of Nagpur: Missionary, Sportsman, Philosopher* (London, 1939).

81. *One Hundred Poems of Kabir,* translated by Rabindranath Tagore, assisted by Evelyn Underhill (London, 1915). The 12th reprint was in 1961.

devotional *bhakti* tradition, that appealed particularly to members of Bishop Gore's Oxford Mission to Calcutta, as an Indian spiritual resource that they might tap. George Westcott, however, seems to make more of the proverbial gnomic wisdom in the Kabir canon, its rejection of sacerdotalism, of pointless austerity, ritualism, caste hierarchy, and the pretensions of religious authority, and its invitation to a life of dignity and integrity for the ordinary man. For example:

> In pride there is adversity, in sin there is suffering; in kindness there is stability, and in forgiveness there is God. . . .
>
> O Moulvie, what books are you explaining? Although day and night you remain babbling and jabbering you have not found out the one religion. . . .
>
> The Pundits are in error by reading the Vedas. They have no common sense. They daily go through their morning and evening rites and other ceremonies with great punctuality and regularity. . . . They consider themselves polluted by the touch of others: ask them who is lower than they are. . . .[82]

Westcott was not a professional scholar, but his book is an informed and interesting attempt to lay out common ground with a heterodox religious community of low caste. A brief acknowledgment in the preface makes it clear what this project represented for Westcott himself: "For help in this undertaking I am principally indebted to my Mali, Badlu Das, who is himself a member of the Panth. He has visited all places of interest in connexion with the Panth, has introduced me to many Mahants and conducted inquiries with great intelligence." Westcott was celebrated later for his success in cultivating roses in Allahabad, in the Bishop's garden. It is pleasant to think of him relaxing there and perhaps, despite the defeat of his generous and daring project, discussing common interests with his gardener Badlu Das.

VIII

Palmer, Miller, and the Westcotts have been taken to illustrate different configurations of "Church structure" when these differences were at the same time reflecting the highly complex, conditioning structures of the colonial situation and an evolving nationalist politics. Given the institutional forms of

82. Westcott, *Kabir.*

the imperial relationship and the fragmented diversity of metropolitan theologies already associated in a variety of ways with metropolitan political and social structures, it is difficult to see how the churches' engagement with South Asia's religious traditions could have been less limited and sporadic than it was.

There were, of course, radical critics at the time, but the careers of the four serve to emphasize the obstructed boundaries between the Church structures and the host societies these attempted to penetrate. The SPG north China missionary Roland Allen, a monotonic and relentlessly critical voice, argued that institutionalized Christianity, with the organized "uplift" of its schools, industrial training, agricultural settlements, hospitals, and, most dangerous of all, paid professional clergy, whether foreign or native, hindered the transmission of the gospel and the working of the Holy Spirit.[83] From the perspective developed here, however, this reads like an attempt to escape the inescapable conditions of existence for competing, communally centered beliefs.

When Allen visited India in 1927-28, in addition to making friends with Bishop Azariah he engaged the attention of Bishop Hubback of Assam, who tried hard with his tribal groups to take account of Allen's vision of gospel transmission. Hubback inevitably lost patience with Allen and eventually exploded *ex cathedra:* "*You* may hear the voice of our Lord speaking direct to you; others like myself are less highly honoured and have to depend for guidance on those in authority over us."[84] Some of this irritation, one suspects, may have been covertly directed at those superordinate figures themselves. The late Bishop Newbigin, among others, however, has acknowledged Allen's vision of a coherent universal Church that is yet free from what he called the "heavy structures" that have dominated it for centuries.[85] Such retrospective retrievals seem to bear out the present argument, for they are addressed to the contemporary environment of a postcolonial world of unstable secular or confessional states, presiding over competing communal identities of potentially threatening "religious" diversity. In many contemporary circumstances Allen's insights may have a compelling relevance to isolated communities of believers. In the structural context inhabited by those who have been introduced here, they were simply unintelligible.

Allen, much closer theologically to Palmer than to the Westcotts, had little interest in indigenous faiths. There was, finally, E. J. Palmer's notable impro-

83. For example, R. Allen, *Missionary Methods: St. Paul's or Ours?* (London, 1912).

84. D. M. Paton, *Reform of the Ministry* (London, 1968), p. 155.

85. Lesslie Newbigin, Foreword to Hubert J. B. Allen, *Roland Allen: Pioneer, Priest and Prophet* (Cincinnati, 1995).

visation, the foundation of the Christa Seva Sangh (CSS) *ashram* under Jack Winslow, formerly his pupil at Balliol. In an unpublished reminiscence, Palmer records that he had "recognized that God had given my son Jack Winslow a good idea."[86] Following C. F. Andrews, and disgusted by the separation of British and Indian Christians, Winslow was open to Gandhi's movement of national renewal, and to the richness of Hinduism's spiritual and cultural heritage.[87] He hoped to introduce Christ to working-class localities, first in Ahmednagar in 1920 and then in Poona, through Hindu forms of popular devotion *(bhajan* and *kirtan)* and in apostolic poverty. In the late 1920s, however, and more specifically following Gandhi's arrest after the 1930 Salt March, Winslow and the CSS faced a critical choice between commitment to Gandhian politics and a vague "nonpolitical" posture of reconciliation. Winslow responded initially by taking flight to England, and in the words of Ramachandra Guha it was Winslow's new associate, Verrier Elwin, who decided "to throw the *ashram* into the rebel camp."[88] That was a decision that projected Elwin himself through the institutional and conceptual boundaries of "Church structure," initially into the obscurity of his personal and sexual liberation among the Gond tribals, and later, as Deputy Director of the Anthropological Survey of India, into a friendship with Nehru, who saw him as the Englishman who had uniquely understood the social energies of the country with which he had come, by irregular stages but so completely, to identify. The English church in India had spoken finally to Elwin in the voice of Palmer's stubbornly impenetrable successor, Bishop Dyke Acland:

> You are very young, you are inexperienced, you are very foolish. You have greatly annoyed Government with your report on Gujerat. Personally I don't believe a word of it. I do not know of a single example where the authorities exceeded their duties. Even if they were brutal, they had to be. . . . Where would we be if we did not rule by force?[89]

86. Lambeth Palmer, "My Twenty Years As Bishop of Bombay," MS 3010, f. 177.

87. See, e.g., issues of *Christa Seva Sangha Review* (from March 1931). Copies survive at the United Theological College, Bangalore, and at St. Xavier's College, Calcutta.

88. Ramachandra Guha, *Savaging the Civilized: Verrier Elwin, His Tribals, and India* (Chicago, 1999), esp. ch. 3.

89. Guha, *Savaging the Civilized,* p. 52.

CHAPTER NINE

The Dornakal Church on the Cultural Frontier

SUSAN BILLINGTON HARPER

Christianity in India: Cultural Catalyst

The role of Christianity in India has been a sensitive political topic for much of this century, but never more so than in the last few years when critical rhetoric and violence against Christians have escalated dramatically. Christianity's alleged role in denationalizing its converts has been a central issue in many heated political exchanges. When sixty thousand members of the Rashtriya Swayamsevak Sangh (RSS) gathered in Agra for a Seventy-Fifth Anniversary celebration on 13-15 October 2000, their leader, or *sarsanghchalak*, K. S. Sudarshan, used the occasion to warn RSS volunteers about threats to the Hindu nation from Indian Christians. He argued that Christian conversions were undermining Hindu dominance and encouraging secessionist movements, that Christian churches were funded from abroad and dominated by foreigners, and that they encouraged an exclusivist rejection of Hindu culture. "How can we allow such people to work here?" Sudarshan asked. The *sarsanghchalak* particularly criticized Indian Christians for refusing to embrace their Hindu heritage and "called upon Christians to sever links with 'foreign' churches and set up a Church of India." Unless Christians and Muslims were willing to Indianize themselves, Indian national security would be threatened, Sudarshan warned.[1]

The *sarsanghchalak* was apparently unaware that India already has many indigenous churches, some of which have existed on the subcontinent since

1. Celia W. Dugger, "A Camp Meeting Celebrates the Vision of a Hindu India," *New York Times*, 16 October 2000, p. A3.

the earliest centuries of the Common Era. Moreover, the establishment of a fully indigenous church has been the primary goal of Western and Indian missionaries alike since at least the mid-nineteenth century. In calling for the creation of an Indian church, Sudarshan unwittingly joined great apostles of the Church, from Henry Venn onward, who have similarly advocated independence and self-support for the so-called younger churches in mission lands. Although Venn and his followers thought that indigenization would help the Church to grow, the contemporary RSS is not likely to have such outcomes in mind. If in the year 2000 the RSS leader exaggerated the continuing dependence of Indian Christians on foreign sponsors, he also seemed unaware that historically the Church has succeeded best when fully inculturated and not overly dependent on distant foreign mission boards. For example, indigenization of the Church in Africa has led to the dramatic flourishing of unique and vibrant forms of Christian faith across the continent in the last century.

Hindu nationalist attacks against the small Indian Christian community play upon India's most deep-seated cultural anxieties to galvanize the Hindu nationalist faithful without inflaming sizable non-Hindu communal groups, notably the Muslims. The political rhetoric, however, seriously misrepresents the reality of Christianity's historical role in India. Christianity has not entered Indian culture like a thief, robbing South Asia of its glories. Rather, it has entered like a catalyst, provoking an immensely varied and subtle history of cultural interactions that have neither denationalized the Indian Christian community nor diminished communities of other faiths. These catalytic reactions have changed all involved, usually in ways that can only be described as culturally complex and positive. The encounters between the many Christianities that have arrived on the subcontinental shores over the last two millennia and India's many religious traditions have not resulted in the improvement of one at the expense of the other, but rather in a fluid and dynamic mix that has enriched each tradition and community.

Cultural Interactions in the Dornakal Diocese

The cultural interactions that occurred in the Anglican diocese of Dornakal during the early twentieth century provide an excellent illustration of this fluid and dynamic process of cultural change. The Dornakal diocese was a vast, bifurcated province, one section of which was located in the Madras Presidency, the other in the Nizam of Hyderbad's Dominions, and all of whose inhabitants shared a common Telugu linguistic and cultural heritage.[2] Under the leadership of Bishop Vedanayagam Samuel Azariah (1874-1945), Dornakal became the fastest growing Anglican diocese in South Asia.[3] The total Anglican Christian population in the Dornakal diocese increased from 56,681 in 1912 to 225,080 in 1941, a number that exceeded the total number of Anglican converts for all of Japan, Korea, and China combined.[4] In 1936 the Dornakal Church baptized over 200 converts each week, and a total of 11,400 converts that year, and sustained this general level of accession throughout the decade.[5]

This growing Indian Christian community in Andhra was composed almost entirely of former "Untouchables" who lived on meager daily wages from agricultural and leather work. The Malas were traditionally weavers, al-

2. The classical name, Andhra, is generally preferred by Telugu speakers. The name of today's state, Andhra Pradesh, translates as "country of the Andhras." "Andhra" was commonly used alone to refer to Telugu-speaking regions as they existed before incorporation into the modern state. The diocese included both fertile coastal areas watered by the Kistna (Krishna) and Godavari Rivers and hilly inland regions of the Eastern Ghats and the great plains of the Deccan. The diocesan center, Dornakal, was in a forested area used by the Nizam for game hunting.

3. During this period in South Asia, the Indian Christian population grew at a faster rate than other major communal groups. In the 1920s, e.g., the Indian Christian population of India and Burma increased at a rate of 32.5%, with Protestant Christians increasing at a rate of 41% (compared with 13% for Muslims and 10.4% for Hindus) (*Directory of Christian Missions and Churches in India, Burma and Ceylon, 1940-1941* [Nagpur, 1940], pp. 34, 36, 38). The growth rate in Azariah's Telugu-speaking areas was among the fastest on the subcontinent. The number of Protestant Christians increased at a rate of 183.8% in Hyderabad State and 54.8% in the Madras Presidency, the greater part of this increase taking place in the Telugu regions (*Directory of Christian Missions,* p. 42; "Statistics of Telugu Christianity," *Dornakal Diocesan Magazine (DDM),* 11.8 [August 1934]: 6-7). Increases in the Telugu districts for Protestant and Roman Catholic Christians were 52% for the Madras Presidency and 152% for the Hyderabad State (V. S. Azariah, "Evangelization and Its Challenge," *National Christian Council Review (NCCR),* 54.1 [January 1934]: 9).

4. Statistics of Anglican Church growth in the Dornakal diocese may be found in *DDM* 5.1 (January 1928): 1-2; 5.4 (April 1928): 11; 5.11 (November 1928): 6; 5.12 (December 1928): 1; 6.6 (June 1929): 3; 8.11 (November 1931): 1; 10.1 (January 1933): "Statistics for the Year 1931"; 10.5 (May 1933): "Statistics for the Year 1932"; 10.11 (November 1933): 4; 11.6 (June 1934): 19; 11.8 (August 1934): 6-9; 11.11 (November 1934): 6; 12.4 (April 1935): 19; 13.5 (May 1936): 2; 14.3 (March 1937): 2; 15.3 (March 1938): 1; 18.4 (April 1941): 1. See also V. S. Azariah, *A Charge Delivered at Bezwada on Wednesday, October 29th, 1941* (Dornakal, 1941), p. 4.

5. *DDM* 10.11 (November 1933): 4. V. S. Azariah, "India: A Present Urgent Opportunity," in *The Spirit of Missions* (U.S., Autumn 1937), p. 543; Azariah, *Charge Delivered at Bezwada,* p. 4.

though competition from industrial mills had forced most of them to become agricultural workers by Azariah's time. The Madigas were traditionally leather workers engaged in the tanning of skins and the making of leather articles. Certain other social functions were exclusively performed, but never shared, by these two castes. They dug graves and monopolized two key roles in festivals for village goddesses: cutting the neck of the sacrificial animal and sprinkling blood-soaked grain in the fields. They provided village officers with manual assistance, beat drums, and provided trumpets and fanfares on festive occasions. Both castes also had the license to eat the carrion of village cattle, and they performed other specialized communal tasks in certain villages such as *neerukattu* (watering the fields). The Malas and Madigas were both prohibited from drawing water from common wells and from living in the main village. Their touch was considered to be polluting, and washermen and barbers would not serve them. In addition, these two untouchable groups had a long-standing rivalry over which occupied the higher position in the social hierarchy, causing them to observe strict segregation even among themselves, living in separate hamlets and refusing to share the same food or the same wells.[6]

Some segments of the Telugu non-Brahmin castes also converted to Christianity at this time, including the Telagas, Kammas, Kappus and Reddis (landowners and farmers), and Yadowas (shepherds, or Gollas),[7] as well as the borderline and tribal groups, such as the Waddars (stonecutters and diggers, also known as Vadderas or Oddars), Yerukalas (pig traders, basket mak-

6. For more on these groups and on the age-old animosity between them, see Sydney Nicholson, "Social Organization of the Malas — An Outcaste Indian People," *Journal of the Royal Anthropological Institute of Great Britain and Ireland* 56 (January-June 1926): 91-103; T. R. Singh, *The Madiga: A Study in Social Structure and Change* (Lucknow, 1969); N. Subha Reddi, "Community-Conflict among the Depressed Castes of Andhra," *Man in India* 30.4 (October-December 1950), pp. 1-12; Edgar Thurston, *Castes and Tribes of Southern India* (Madras, 1909), 4:292-325, 329-87; J. Abraham, *Fifty Years' History of the Indian Missionary Society of Tirunelveli, 1903-1953* (Palayamkottai, 1955), pp. 76-77; Knud Heiberg, *V. S. Azariah af Dornakal* (Copenhagen, 1950), p. 79; and C. Graham, *Azariah of Dornakal* (London, 1946), p. 53.

7. V. S. Azariah, "The Bishop's Letter," *DDM* 9.6 (June 1932): 1-4; G. A. Oddie, "Christian Conversion among Non-Brahmans in Andhra Pradesh, with Special Reference to Anglican Missions and the Dornakal Diocese, 1900-1936," in *Religion in South Asia: Religious Conversion and Revival Movements in South Asia in Medieval and Modern Times,* edited by G. A. Oddie (New Delhi, 1977), pp. 67-99; James G. Manor, "Testing the Barrier between Caste and Outcaste: The Andhra Evangelical Lutheran Church in Guntur District," *Indian Church History Review* 5.1 (1971): 27-41; Abraham, *Fifty Years' History,* pp. 71-79; J. W. Pickett, *Christ's Way to India's Heart* (Lucknow, 1937), pp. 2, 40-45, 48-50, 100-107.

ers, and soothsayers, also known as Erukalas and Erkalas), Lombadies (nomadic gypsies or "carriers," also known as Banjaras, found throughout western and southern India),[8] and Mandulas (another nomadic tribe of snake charmers and swine traders, many of whom apparently converted to Christianity to obtain protection from their ruthless headman Kunda Puchiah of Masulipatam).[9] By 1935, there were about eight hundred thousand Christians from all church missions in the Telugu country, including roughly two hundred thousand Anglicans in the Dornakal diocese.[10]

Indo-Anglican Christianity in Andhra had little direct cultural impact beyond the Untouchables and low castes except in the area of education. Here Christian schools served many upper-caste non-Brahmin and Brahmin students, resulting in significant indirect cultural influence of Christianity on elite groups. Within the lower strata of society, the church played an increasingly important role as the bearer not only of the Christian religion but also of social uplift.[11] By 1935, the Dornakal diocese, with 250 ordained Indian clergy and more than two thousand village teachers,[12] was sponsoring an extensive network of schools that offered elementary education for children and teachers and literacy and vocational classes for adults. Medical dispensaries, temperance campaigns, cooperative societies and banks, printing presses, agricultural settlements, and industrial projects all supplemented the diocese's central task of leading the worship and providing pastoral services for over 218,879 Anglicans.[13] The church also instituted a pioneering program for women's leadership in the villages through elections as church elders. By 1944 there were almost two thousand women elders serving on *panchayats* in eight hundred Dornakal villages, perhaps only twenty of whom could read or write but each of whom was perceived to be the leader of her community.

The church mobilized a powerfully challenging social movement in Andhra against what Azariah called the "four Demons — Dirt, Disease, Debt, and Drink," which plagued the rural villages.[14] Tobacco smoking was discour-

8. Thurston, *Castes and Tribes,* 4:207-32; Abraham, *Fifty Years' History,* pp. 68-70; Manor, "Testing the Barrier," pp. 29-30; Pickett, *Christ's Way,* pp. 106-7.

9. Abraham, *Fifty Years' History,* pp. 73-76.

10. V. S. Azariah, "The Bishop's Letter," *DDM* 12.12 (December 1935): 4.

11. *DDM* 13.4 (April 1936): 3-4. See also V. S. Azariah, "The Church in Rural India," *DDM* 5.10 (October 1928): 1-12. ("Where Christianity goes education, civilization and habits of cleanliness in body, dress and food, in speech and conduct, are the concomitant results" [Azariah, "The Church in Rural India," p. 3].)

12. Elva Jackson, *Indian Saga* (Devonport, New Zealand, 1980), p. 7.

13. *Directory of Christian Missions.*

14. V. S. Azariah, "The Bishop's Letter," *DDM* 11.12 (December 1934): 4.

aged.[15] Lying, quarreling, cheating, and taking bribes were condemned and reduced,[16] and crimes such as theft, poisoning cattle, and murder were regularly denounced.[17] The church also encouraged thrift,[18] discouraged costly weddings and dowries,[19] established programs of direct assistance as well as cooperative credit societies to free converts from debt,[20] and arbitrated land disputes.[21]

In an effort to help new congregations become self-supporting, the diocese adapted, in 1912, the indigenous system of *inam* or endowment lands where a small piece of arable, tax-free, church land (3-4 acres) was purchased and provided with a house, a plow, and a pair of bullocks. Christian teachers cultivated this land on the condition that they led village worship and conducted evening classes for children and adults.[22] The church also bought land

15. *DDM* 5.11 (November 1928): 4; 6.9 (September 1929): 3.

16. *DDM* 13.4 (April 1936): 1-4; K. Luke, *Ḍārnakal Tiranalvēli Inḍiyan Miṣanarī Sanghamu* (Vijayawada, 1956), p. 101; Pickett, *Christ's Way,* pp. 42-43.

17. *DDM* 5.4 (April 1928): 3; 8.10 (October 1931): 15; 9.5 (May 1932): 13-14; 10.1 (January 1933): 9-11; 13.3 (March 1936): 2-3; 13.4 (April 1936): 1-4; Luke, *Darnakal Tiranalveli,* pp. 97-101; Pickett, *Christ's Way,* p. 42; Henry Whitehead, "The Bishop's Diary," *Madras Diocesan Magazine (MDM)* 16.3 (March 1921): 51-59; David Packiamuthu, *Vaḻikāṭṭi* (Tirunelveli, 1963), act 2, scene 1; Thamil Selvan, "Research on Bishop Azariah and His Theology," B.D. thesis, Tamil Theological Seminary, Madurai, 1985, p. 32; Graham, *Azariah of Dornakal,* p. 58. Cattle poisoning was considered a more serious crime to Indian Hindus who venerated the cow than it was to Westerners. It was a crime to both nevertheless.

18. Converts claim they often gave up "spending lots of money" after baptism. Interview with Padamuthyam Joseph, 4 April 1986, Thirumapalayem, A.P.

19. Azariah was opposed to expensive marriages (his own cost RS 40) and to the dowry system (he took no dowry from his son's wives, nor did he ask his wife to provide one). Interview with Grace Aaron, 24-26 September 1985, Ottawa, Canada.

20. *DDM* 11.3 (March 1934): 18; V. S. Azariah, "Sermon Preached by the Bishop of Dornakal on Sunday, 28 November 1920, at St. George's Cathedral, Madras, on behalf of the CMS Centenary Celebrations," *MDM* 16.10 (January 1921): 13-22; Heiberg, *Azariah,* pp. 94-95; J. Z. Hodge, *Bishop Azariah of Dornakal* (Madras, 1946), pp. 32-33. The IMS liberated one of its first converts, Kodama Gundula Luka, from debt slavery for RS 7 (Packiamuthu, *Vaḻikāṭṭi,* act, scene 3). Mrs. Whitehead initiated one of the diocese's early efforts to establish cooperative societies by founding the Khammamett Workers Society (*MDM* 11.1 [January 1916]: 8). On cooperatives, see also *Proceedings of the Indian Missionary Society (PIMS),* 14 July 1915, Indian Missionary Society of Tirunelveli Archives (IMSA), Palayamkottai.

21. One case led indirectly to conversion. A Christian priest helped a "rich Sudra" to win a land dispute, but then the priest refused to accept three acres of land worth RS 900 offered to him by the grateful victor. "This aroused the Sudra's interest and he eventually became a Christian" (*DDM* 9.8 [August 1932]: 12).

22. *Madras and Tinnevelly Diocesan Magazine (MTDM)* 7.5 (May 1912): 139.

to establish several special Christian "Villages of Refuge," Vedanayagapuram, for persecuted converts,[23] and Kiritipuram for famine relief victims who converted to Christianity.[24]

Medical and health assistance was an integral part of the church's work. Vaccinations were distributed with gospel tracts, inoculations with magic lantern talks about Jesus. The church sponsored an annual "medical evangelistic tour," which it viewed as part of its broader commission to further "health propaganda and preventative work."[25] It dispensed Christian prayer with Western medicines, such as quinine, eyedrops, and dysentery remedies,[26] through several hospitals and clinics.[27] A Tamil missionary, Dr. J. S. William, traveled frequently throughout the diocese giving talks on disease (leprosy, yaws, and cholera were particularly prevalent) and sanitation while providing medicines and vaccinations.[28] He established the Rural Medical Relief Association, which sent trained workers into the villages with medicines, and hosted an annual Health Week for all diocesan workers.[29] During a cholera epidemic in 1928, the church distributed chlorogen (a water sterilizer) and assisted officials in disinfecting water reservoirs and wells.[30] Village

23. The land for Vedanayagapuram was purchased, with the help of Bishop Whitehead, to provide for a group of Banjara converts who were barred from burying their dead in their own village. The settlers built their own homes, worked the land, and paid a rent/tax to the church. Interview with Rev. M. Daniel, 29 March 1986, Dornakal.

24. This practice, based on Old Testament patterns, had been revived during the Tinnevelly mass movements, and so it was one with which Azariah was personally familiar. In Andhra, Kiritipuram was settled by Mala workers who constructed the Dornakal Cathedral. Construction jobs and rice from Burma were provided as relief during the *thella jonnala karuvu,* or "white corn famine" of 1920. Interview with Rev. M. Daniel, 8 April 1986, Dornakal.

25. *DDM* 9.7 (July 1932): 10-11.

26. Interestingly, Christians often accepted Western remedies but still continued to go to village medicine men for native cures for ailments such as jaundice or when it was believed that *diams* (possessing evil spirits) were responsible. Christians in Dornakal today apparently continue to visit a Hindu woman for treatments. Interview with Rev. M. Daniel, 31 March 1986, Dornakal.

27. The 1932 annual report for the Bishop Whitehead Hospital recorded 11,686 outpatients and 131 inpatients (*DDM* 9.7 [July 1932]: 10-11).

28. *DDM* 5.1 (January 1928): 8-9; 5.12 (December 1928): 1-2; 6.5 (May 1929): 1; 6.7 (July 1929): 16.

29. *DDM* 8.1 (January 1931): 12-15.

30. While the epidemic strengthened the faith in some villages, it caused others to renounce the faith by joining non-Christians in making vows to "Maramma [sic], the cholera goddess." Azariah observed: "An epidemic of this kind is a searching test to many a religious profession . . . it confirms one village in the faith, and drives back another to Hinduism. It tests the teachers: one runs away and another suffers with his people" (*DDM* 5.9

dais (midwives) were trained and equipped, bore-hole latrines were introduced,[31] and Christian villages developed the tradition of having an annual "house whitewash."[32] Although the persistent problem of impure water was not solved, diocesan records suggest a marked improvement of general sanitation in Christian villages.[33] Before conversion in one village

> the Zamindars . . . would consider it pollution to walk through the village: they stood on the road and called for the men. Now they do not hesitate to walk through the street; they even go into the court-yard and knock at the door of the teacher. [Azariah] asked for the reason for this change. Cleanliness was the answer.[34]

Christianity's arrival set in motion a thorough reevaluation of the most important issues defining and regulating local village life: caste *(jati,* Telugu: *kulam)* relations, the prescribed ritual rights and responsibilities for village subgroups, the composition and authority of village *panchayats,* local codes governing marriage and sexual morals, and the ingestion of defiling substances (alcohol, certain meats, and carrion).

Insofar as conversion permitted previously outcast or marginal groups to turn away from the stigma of their previously degrading beliefs, practices, and social customs, the Dornakal conversion movements are correctly understood as protests against those indigenous systems. However, the conversion movements were themselves also indigenous movements fully embedded in wider processes of socioeconomic and cultural change at the local and regional levels. The cultural changes that accompanied conversion in Dornakal proved to be both unpredictable and surprising to both Western and Indian missionaries because many of them were generated "from below" according

---

[September 1928]: 2-3). Rev. Daniel, of Dornakal, described how Hindu Malas and Madigas of his native village worshipped the same gods, but each had a different *Muthyalamma gudi* (shrine) at which they sacrificed animals. If Muthyalamma got angry, he said, she would send cholera and other serious diseases. The Malas offered goats and sheep as sacrifices; the Madigas offered chickens. When the Sudras sacrificed a buffalo, they would give all but the leg to the Madigas to eat. (The Malas would not eat the buffalo.) "People were afraid of Muthyalamma, but not the Christian God" (interview with Rev. Daniel, 8 April 1986, Dornakal).

31. "Thirty Years' Report of the Dornakal Mission," *DDM* 11.12 (December 1934): 7-8.

32. *DDM* 5.2 (February 1928): 6.

33. *DDM* 8.10 (October 1931): 13. Some wells were provided by a "Well Fund" established for villages otherwise reliant on surface water (see *DDM* 5.4 [April 1928]: 1-2).

34. *DDM* 13.4 (April 1936): 2.

to values and standards of social rank and precedence indigenous to Andhra and quite foreign to both Western and Christian values, practices, and traditions. The fast-growing institutional church in Dornakal mediated and influenced some of the profound cultural adjustments that accompanied conversion, but it was often unable either to foresee or to control the results because of the movements' deeper indigenous relevance. The arrival of Christianity may have set a process of catalytic cultural change into motion, but, once begun, even the church could not control the outcome of this accelerating process of cultural change and interaction.

Christianity's Interaction with the Caste System

Bishop Azariah believed that the growing Christian community in Dornakal should resist the pressure experienced by the other "introduced" religions in India (Islam, Zoroastrianism, and Judaism) to adopt the prevailing social order by participating in India's established system of *jati* or *kulam* relations. He argued that most beliefs, rituals, practices, and cultural manifestations of the caste system were incompatible with Christianity and should be renounced at baptism, particularly its dehumanizing conceptualization and rationalization of "pollution" and "untouchability" that relegated up to one-fifth of society to perpetual thralldom.

The church required new converts to give up animosities that formerly divided them from different *jati* groups. "The moment a person is baptized, he is no longer a Mala, a Madiga or a Sudra, but all are one in Christ Jesus," Azariah asserted.[35] Converts of different caste backgrounds were required to attend the same chapels, to drink from the same communion cup, to send children to the same schools (where they could receive training in occupations reserved traditionally for their own, or for rival, castes), and to eat together at public celebrations such as marriages, harvest festivals, and other community *jatras*. Azariah frequently enjoined his diocese to pray against the "the spirit of faction" caused by "caste."[36] Caste appellations were abandoned for new Christian names taken either from the Bible (Rachel, Job, and Abraham) or from Telugu and Sanskrit words for important virtues (*Dina* for hu-

35. *DDM* 13.1 (January 1936): 10-11.

36. For example, *DDM* 5.5 (May 1928): 2.

37. *DDM* 9.9 (September 1932): 16; 10.5 (May 1933): 7, 10; 12.8 (August 1935): 8-9; interview with Rev. Daniel, 31 March 1986, Dornakal. This was also the practice in the neighboring diocese of Medak (P. Y. Luke and J. B. Carman, *Village Christians and Hindu Culture* [London, 1968], pp. 190-92).

mility),[37] converts were required to shave the *juttu* (the tonsure, or tuft of hair, that signified their Hindu identity), and women were required to remove the caste mark (traditionally removed at the death of a husband).[38] Christianity aimed, it seemed, to create a new type of community in which old caste symbols and inter-*jati* animosities would play no role.

The church required converts to abandon the performance of *jati*-based duties previously required of them in Hindu sacrifices, rituals, and festivals. As a result, new Christians were often threatened with physical harm or loss of income. To lessen social and economic disruption, the church drew some distinctions between "harmless" duties performed by the depressed classes for *ryots* at village festivals (cleaning up houses, preparing grain, etc.), "debatable" duties (leading animals for slaughter as offerings to Hindu gods), and those "definitely forbidden to Christians" (sprinkling the blood of the sacrifice, i.e., taking part in Hindu *puja*).[39] Nevertheless, diocesan records are filled with stories of conflict arising from new conversions. One Madiga convert recorded the loss of customary gifts and income (*mamool* or "custom") earned previously from *zamindars* (landholders) for performance of certain sacrifices. Another convert named Yesuratnam narrowly missed a beating and loss of wages when he refused to perform the traditional boundary sacrifice in which the blood of a sacrificed chicken was poured on boiled rice and sprinkled on the land's boundaries to invoke the blessing of a local goddess on the crop.[40] One Hindu *pujari* (or priest, described as a devout "worshipper of Ganganamma") gave up his regular sacrifices after his conversion; another *asadi* who used to tell the story of Peddamma (the village goddess) in a drunken state for the amusement of caste onlookers at Hindu festivals also gave up this practice.[41]

This rejection of hereditarily ascribed roles represented not just the repudiation of old idols by new converts, but also a challenge to the social order and to local authorities by long-suppressed lower classes. The higher castes were quick to disparage efforts by members of the depressed classes to assume "new airs."[42] Sometimes the persecution became so intense that converts migrated to the new Christian "Villages of Refuge."

There is much we cannot glean from diocesan and missionary archives regarding the full sociological and cultural ramifications of conversion to

38. *DDM* 13.4 (April 1936): 1; 9.8 (August 1932): 12.

39. *DDM* 15.8 (August 1938): 10.

40. *DDM* 7.9 (September 1930): 8-9; 5.4 (April 1928): 3-4.

41. *DDM* 6.5 (May 1929): 3; 12.3 (March 1935): 16.

42. S. Manickam, *The Social Setting of Christian Conversion in South India* (Wiesbaden, 1977), pp. 105, 249.

Christianity. Most contemporary written accounts were devoid of the sort of subtle ethnographic distinctions found in modern scholarly studies.[43] Primary records combined with interviews with elderly church leaders in Dornakal suggest that, although some progress was made, the church did not succeed in changing many of the caste or *jati*-based practices it condemned.[44] Although in one sense this means that the Christianization of Azariah's diocese always remained incomplete, in another it suggests that something entirely new was being created in Dornakal through the cultural interaction between Christianity and local traditions.

Indeed, evidence of significant lapses in the church's anti-caste policy suggests that, despite the church's efforts to repudiate caste and its many stigmas, the new church in Dornakal became the institutional focus for a broad effort on the part of the depressed and marginal classes to improve their status in society via changes that were sometimes surprisingly consistent with caste-based values. In attempting to build a new community with a new identity that replaced and transcended old caste identities, the church almost inadvertently created new social organizations, rituals, and customs that bore remarkable similarities to the old ones they replaced.

Azariah recognized that caste could serve a positive function as an integrative system that helped to preserve the community life of its members. In particular, caste structures provided natural and effective instruments for publicizing the gospel and vehicles for encouraging group conversions along caste lines, which were much less socially disruptive than individual accessions.

Membership in the new Christian community in Dornakal entailed many

43. Whether Mala converts belonged to the "land-holding," right-handed, Saiva section *(Reddi-Bhumalu)* or to the "service-giving," left-handed, Vaishna sections *(Murikinai* or *Pokanati)* was clearly less important to the church than the numbers of Malas converting. Neither diocesan journals nor missionary accounts provide much sense of whether certain subgroups of Malas or Madigas tended to be more receptive to conversion, of whether conversion was linked to particular social changes (such as the breaking of rules related to group endogamy), or even of the precise *jati* identity of most converts. Nor do the *Church Censures* that recorded all infractions of diocesan rules contain much detail about the nature of the "heathen practices" and the "Hindu rites" for which its members were so frequently excommunicated. See Singh, *The Madiga;* Nicholson, "Social Organization of the Malas," pp. 91-103. Henry Whitehead's ethnographic writings provide relatively detailed observations of depressed class practices. See, e.g., his description of Mala priests *(Pambalas)* in *MDM* 1.7 (July 1906): 320; *Village Gods of South India* (London, 1916); and "A Lecture on Some Religious Customs of the Hindus in South India . . . Delivered in the Regimental Theatre at Wellington," *MDM* 1.5 (May 1906): 207-17.

44. Luke and Carman, *Village Christians.* This was also the conclusion drawn by M. V. Rajagopal in *Andhra Pradesh District Gazetteers: Khamman* (Hyderabad, 1977), p. 40.

social rights and responsibilities similar to those imposed formerly by caste. Ideally, the Christian community, like the former *kulam*, was an endogamous group not marrying outsiders. Azariah condemned "mixed marriages" between Christians and non-Christians, although on the biblical grounds that Christians ought not to be "yoked with unbelievers"[45] rather than on the basis of the indigenous practice of marrying within the *kulam*. He prescribed excommunication, like "outcasting," as the proper punishment for the offense.[46] Such disciplinary actions were executed in a manner similar to that of the former *kulam*. Bodies of church elders were constituted as informal village *panchayats* in every village and entrusted with limited disciplinary powers.

In most cases the same people who served as village elders *(peddagarus)* before conversion continued to serve as church elders after baptism.[47] "The congregation elders are for the most part none other than the old community elders, for in the mass movement as a rule the whole community has come over to Christianity together," wrote one observer in 1933.[48] Like their non-Christian counterparts, the informal *panchayats* of Christian elders settled quarrels, inquired into misdemeanors, and had the power to inflict small fines. The church elders were associated with the local lay Christian teacher and area pastor in a manner similar to the association between non-Christian elders and village headmen. Both the Christian pastor and the village headman officiated as priests in marriages and arbitrated difficult matters affecting the village by calling formal *panchayats* composed of the village elders (and, occasionally, elders from other villages). The Christian *panchayat*'s findings in matters of discipline were reported to the Bishop's Local Council (of clergy and laymen) and, if necessary, to the bishop, who held the final power of excommunication or restoration of church privileges. Non-Christian *panchayats* possessed more serious sanctions (heavy fines and excommunication) and usually functioned as the final court of appeals in caste affairs, unlike their Christian counterparts who deferred to the bishop's decision on heavier penalties. Some non-Christian castes had regional *panchayats* ruling over specific territories; others had caste gurus judging on caste affairs in a manner somewhat comparable to Christian bishops.

Excommunication from the church, by now an historical relic in the Western Church, was revived in Dornakal as a punishment not all that different from outcasting from the *kulam*. Azariah forbade Christians to "keep on

45. 1 Cor. 7:39; 2 Cor. 6:14-16.

46. V. S. Azariah, "Mixed Marriages," *NCCR* 61.11 (November 1941): 528-34.

47. Although with one major exception as Azariah made an effort to include women elders on the *panchayats*.

48. "Lay Work in Dornakal Diocese," *DDM* 10.4 (April 1933): 8.

friendly terms with the excommunicated" and insisted that they "hold no intercourse with such and not even to eat with them."[49] He based his policy of prohibiting dining and social intercourse with Christian outcasts on "apostolic command" rather than on Indian social traditions, but he clearly saw the advantage of preserving traditional or "natural" social mechanisms that could be helpful in establishing an independent Indian Christian community and need not be incompatible with its ideals. The church's disciplinary system closely resembled the system it replaced, even if many of the rules by which crimes and misdemeanors were judged had been adjusted to be consistent with Christian social ethics.[50]

Christianity's Interaction with Local Ritual and Customs

Azariah believed that some dimensions of local Hindu culture and institutions ought to be incorporated into indigenous expressions of Indian Christianity, particularly in order to attract more caste people to a faith they were initially inclined to dismiss as an exclusively "outcast's religion." By incorporating certain spiritually neutral, culturally familiar elements from Hindu ritual and custom into Christian life and worship, Dornakal Christians developed creative and theologically acceptable ways to insert their new religion into traditional rituals, such as using prayers to Jesus as a substitute for previous sacrificial incantations during the traditional boundary sacrifice.[51]

Azariah himself drew from Hindu and, occasionally, Muslim traditions in devising indigenous new forms of liturgy, music, drama, architecture, festivals, and Christian expression in his diocese. He devised a new Christian marriage service that adapted Hindu symbols (rather than circling a fire, the bride and groom walked around a cross), and advocated use of the Christian *tali* (a small gold cross, anchor, or heart fastened by a string round the neck of a married woman) as a substitute for the Western wedding ring.[52] This service was intended especially to satisfy caste converts who objected to the brev-

49. *DDM* 5.5 (May 1928): 2.

50. *DDM* 10.4 (April 1933): 8-9; *PIMS*, 14 July 1915, IMSA.

51. *DDM* 5.4 (April 1928): 3-4.

52. Azariah did not invent the idea of a Christian *tali*, but he abandoned the practice of placing it on a plate that was passed around to receive blessings of the elderly. Rather, he suggested that the *tali* be put around the bride's neck and the groom touch it while saying his vows (Selvan, "Research on Bishop Azariah"). Azariah designed a *tali* for his family decorated with a cross, anchor, and heart representing faith, hope, and charity, respectively (interview with Grace Aaron, 24-26 September 1985, Ottawa, Canada).

ity of the Christian marriage service. As one missionary recalled, "A Brahmin wedding goes on for five days. What is twenty minutes in a church?" Bishop Azariah's new wedding service accommodated these traditional sensibilities "by having plenty of singing and processions round the church [which] made the service last for two hours."[53]

Hoping to provide a substitute for the Hindu festival of Divawli, Azariah instituted a Festival of Lights in which families lit oil lamps in church and then distributed the light throughout the village, symbolizing the idea that Christ was the light of their homes, of their hearts, and of their families.[54] Although the bishop required the cutting of the *juttu*, he permitted use of a vermilion cross on the forehead as a substitute for traditional caste markings.[55]

Azariah's most visible contribution to indigenization was his Dornakal Cathedral, which mixed architectural elements and symbolism from Hindu, Muslim, and Christian traditions into a wholly unique synthesis. Taking twenty-five years to build, the Cathedral Church of the Epiphany combined the domes of Muslim mosques with the pillars of South Indian Hindu temples, and was suffused with Christian symbolism. Thus, twelve pillars bearing up the church nave symbolized the twelve apostles and were decorated by each apostle's symbolic shield and by carvings of the lotus flower, symbolizing India, of the datura flower, symbolizing death, and of the shoot from the banana tree, which brings new life. All of these symbols were placed under the cross, which symbolized their ultimate reconciliation in Christ. This cathedral, entirely hand-carved and hand-built by local people, was the bishop's most dramatic statement of Christianity's potential as the fulfillment of Indian faith and culture.[56]

The Problem of Marriage

In the area of marriage and sexual morals the church faced the difficult task of trying to impose its standards upon a great variety of local practices. Bishop Azariah had to adapt the Christian law of marriage, as defined by the

53. Jackson, *Indian Saga*, p. 226. See also in *DDM* 9.6 (June 1932): 2; 12.10 (October 1935): 8.

54. In this idea, Azariah borrowed from Easter (and probably also Epiphany) traditions of the Greek Orthodox Church (see Selvan, "Research on Bishop Azariah").

55. Selvan, "Research on Bishop Azariah."

56. For examples of relatively positive assessments of Hinduism in Azariah's writings, see V. S. Azariah, *India and the Christian Movement* (Madras, 1935), pp. 55-58 and *The Church and Evangelism* (Madras, 1936), pp. 36-37.

Table of Kindred and Affinity included in the *Book of Common Prayer*, to Indian conditions and to sometimes divergent civil and ecclesiastical regulations. The handbook on marriage he published for Anglican clergy and religious workers in India[57] traced the origins of Christian laws of marriage to universally applicable natural laws ("the need to secure the preservation of the human race"), to Jewish laws, and, finally, to Christological and apostolic injunctions. He argued that peoples in India had "trespassed" on these laws with child marriage, which violated both the natural law of mutual consent and the Christian tradition of free consent between marriage partners. He saw divorce and remarriage as violations not only of a natural law demanding lifelong partnership but also of declarations by Christ and the apostles concerning the permanence of marriage. Several widely practiced unions in India (those of a sister's daughter and of a deceased wife's sister) also violated the unions declared permissible under Anglican guidelines.[58]

Azariah argued that the Anglican Church in India forbade marriages of Christians with non-Christians even though such "mixed" marriages were deemed legal under the Indian Christian Marriage Act of 1872 (which made the children of such marriages legitimate and qualified them for property inheritance). This was one of several areas in which the Dornakal church decreed excommunication for the violation of a marriage that was, strictly speaking, legal. As Azariah wrote in 1941:

> Christian standards and ideals stand firm and unaltered, whatever the State legislation may say. Mixed marriages are wrong according to Christian ideals, and it is the duty of the Churches by ecclesiastical action to give clear guidance to their ministers and to uphold the Christian standards by Church discipline.[59]

Regarding child marriage, the church adhered to standards set by the 1872 Act that required parental consent in cases where either party was under twenty-one years of age and the Child Marriage Restraint Act of 1929 (the Sarda Act) that prohibited marriages of men under eighteen years of age and

57. V. S. Azariah, *Holy Matrimony: Being Chapters on the Christian Law of Marriage* (Madras, 1941; revised and enlarged, 1942). Published also in Tamil, Telugu, Hindi, Urdu, and Marathi.

58. An "Archbishop's Commission on Kindred and Affinity as Impediments to Marriage" recommended in the 1940s greater lenience regarding marriages of a deceased wife's sister but still prohibited marriages of a sister's daughter (Azariah, *Holy Matrimony*, pp. 84-85).

59. Azariah, "Mixed Marriages," p. 533.

of women under fourteen years of age in British India.[60] Azariah also called for the abolition of the dowry system and its bargain marriages in order to foster harmonious Christian family life.[61]

Azariah and fellow church leaders in Andhra had more difficulty changing local marriage practices than any others. When the Indian Missionary Society (IMS) of Tirunelveli, whose Tamil missionaries had first introduced Anglicanism to Dornakal, conducted its first Christian marriage ceremony in the Manukota pastorate in 1917, it ran up against three local customs that were particularly deeply rooted. By insisting on the English tradition of reading the banns of marriage on three consecutive Sundays before the wedding, it went directly against the village custom of holding a marriage as soon as possible after the completion of marriage negotiations (and in accordance with an auspicious date set by a Brahmin priest usually less than a week in advance).[62] By requiring marriages to be held in the village place of prayer, it took the ceremony out of the family home. By insisting that marriages be held during the day, it defied the custom of night marriages. These last changes proved so hard to accomplish that Azariah sometimes sent Christian teachers to wedding houses with musical instruments to provide evening "entertainment" and thereby insure that no ceremony could be held until the following morning.

Elsewhere in Andhra, Telugu Baptists found that child marriage could be regulated only with strict discipline.[63] A study of Christianity in formerly Methodist areas of Andhra concluded that, despite all legislation, child marriages still persisted among Christians and that mixed marriages were more common than unmixed ones. Indeed, Christians were more inclined to marry non-Christians of their own *jati* than Christians of different *jatis,* demonstrating the relative importance of traditional caste allegiances in comparison with introduced religious affiliations.[64]

Although the *Dornakal Diocesan Magazine* claimed that the church had successfully introduced Christian marriage rites and celebrations free of alcohol consumption in a community free of "early marriage,"[65] church disciplin-

60. Azariah, *Holy Matrimony,* p. 46; *DDM* 6.10 (October 1929): 4-5.

61. Azariah, *Holy Matrimony,* pp. 63-65.

62. IMS, *The Missionary Intelligencer (TMI)* 14.5 (May 1917): 45; Luke and Carman, *Village Christians,* pp. 195-96.

63. A. T. Fishman, *For This Purpose* (Madras, 1958), p. 83.

64. Luke and Carman, *Village Christians,* pp. 5-6, 192-98.

65. For example, *DDM* 6.9 (September 1929): 2. It is interesting to note that the first girl to attend the IMS Boarding School, established in 1906, had taken refuge with the missionaries from child marriage (*DDM* 11.12 [December 1934]: 6). Also, a census commissioner whom Azariah described as "an impartial student of racial progress," praised the

ary records reveal significant violations. The *Church Censures* for the years 1914 to 1945 contain more excommunications for improprieties connected with marriage and sexual relations than for any other type of sin. Among the volumes' 6,347 entries (giving name, offense, and punishment), the most frequently mentioned transgressions were "heathen marriages," "arranging, contracting, conducting or abetting heathen marriages," and "adultery." Other offenses mentioned were "marrying wife's sister," "living in sin with a heathen," "living in sin with a married non-Christian woman," "living with a man without any legal marriage," and "fornication."

It is difficult to derive anything but general conclusions from diocesan disciplinary records because the exact nature of each offense was not usually specified. For instance, it is unclear if the frequently used term "irregular marriage" meant child marriage, mixed marriage, or something else entirely. In 1920, a couple was excommunicated for "giving their junior daughter in heathen and irregular marriage in Kurnool/Nandyal." However, such detail was rare for these records, the usefulness of which thus lies in their testimony to the general fact that the church encountered much more resistance to its regulations, particularly in the area of marriage and sexual morals, than is indicated by published records.[66]

On average, there were about 200 excommunications in Dornakal diocese each year. Of 972 excommunications that occurred during one four-year period, 425 were for "non-Christian practices," 281 were for "living in adultery," and 255 were for "apostasy."[67] "Non-Christian practices" usually referred to "non-Christian connections" associated with sexual immorality, Bishop Azariah explained:

> A large proportion of these cases arise out of bad social customs. Parents very often arrange the marriages; free consent is not obtained of the young people; ignorance and incompatibility soon drive them apart, resulting in one or both of them seeking other connections after their own hearts.[68]

Azariah reported in 1941 that a seemingly large total number of excommunications for "immorality" (i.e., 281 for adultery and 425 for non-Christian

---

church in 1921 for abolishing child marriage and permitting widow remarriage (*DDM* 5.10 [October 1928]: 3).

66. *Church Censures: Diocese of Dornakal,* I (1914-32); II (1933-45), Dornakal Diocesan Archives (DDA).

67. Azariah, *Charge Delivered at Bezwada,* p. 5.

68. Azariah, *Charge Delivered at Bezwada,* p. 20.

connections) represented a great improvement over previous years: "These figures are about half of what they were ten years ago, which shows that the younger generation on the whole are setting before themselves higher standards of Christian family life."[69]

Surviving marriage registers also suggest continued child marriage among Christians in Azariah's diocese. The register for the IMS Telugu mission reveals a large number of marriages involving partners of age fourteen and fifteen, just over the legal limit of fourteen for girls. One entry in 1924 involved a wife eleven years of age; another in 1925 involved a wife of age ten and a husband of age fourteen.[70] Individuals still living in Dornakal confirm the continuance of this practice. One elderly Christian woman, a sweet seller in Dornakal, described how she became a Christian at the age of five (changing her name from Venkamma to Nama Ruth) and was married at the age of ten to a Hindu (who subsequently became a Christian and changed his name from Narsaiah to Jeremiah).[71] Another pastor who worked under Azariah confirmed that Christians and non-Christians continued to intermarry despite church prohibitions, prompting the bishop to compromise by allowing such marriages if non-Christians were first baptized.[72] It is evident that the number of both child marriages and mixed marriages were reduced but were by no means eradicated in the diocese.

The Problem of Alcohol

Dornakal's converts accepted other areas of reform more readily, chiefly because they satisfied the moral scruples of Christian missionaries without offending higher-caste Indian notions of defilement via certain forms of ingestion. Azariah scored one of his biggest successes by opposing alcohol consumption in the villages. On this issue, Indo-Anglican bishops were influenced by both Western and Indian temperance movements.[73] They joined critics of the government's liquor laws and condemned the exploitation of in-

69. Azariah, *Charge Delivered at Bezwada,* p. 20.

70. Indian Missionary Society of Tinnevelly, Telugu Mission, Marriage Register, DDA.

71. Interview with Nama Ruth, 9 April 1986, Kiritapuram.

72. Interview with Rev. Daniel, 31 March 1986, Dornakal.

73. By the late nineteenth century, there were already several Anglican temperance societies at work in England: the Church of England Temperance Society, the Army White Cross, and the Church of England Purity Society. Report of the Episcopal Conference, 1897 (handwritten), Bishop's House Archives (BHA), Calcutta.

digenous demand for liquor to increase revenues via taxes *(abkari)*, a practice inherited from pre-Raj times. The problem of liquor consumption in India was not an indigenous problem, according to a report from *The Christian Science Monitor* republished in the *Madras Diocesan Magazine* in 1918, but was created by British self-interest.[74] The Indo-Anglican leadership adopted a moral position of opposition to alcohol consumption and supported (although not unanimously) new prohibition decrees instituted by Congress ministries elected to provincial legislatures in 1937.[75]

Through the Dornakal diocese's enthusiastic support for prohibition[76] and its establishment of a popular temperance society, the Andhra Christo Purushula Samajam (ACPS), the church achieved notable successes in lowering the rate of alcohol consumption among its adherents in Andhra.[77] Founded in 1914, the ACPS boasted 1,142 branches by 1941 with a total of 10,486 adult members and 1,673 junior members.[78] Upon admission, ACPS members promised to abstain from drink and to witness to the power of Jesus Christ through both their improved moral lives and their conversations with friends and family. Each member received a cross and a prayer card, which recorded their date of admission.[79]

74. "Prohibition Issue in India," n.a., *MDM* 13.11 (November 1918): 263-64.

75. Herbert Anderson, *Prohibition Progresses in India* (London, 1938).

76. *Proceedings of the Eighth Session of the Dornakal Diocesan Council Held at Bezwada on 6-7 January 1938,* 5: 2/2, Dornakal, Metropolitan Archives of the Church of India, Pakistan, Burma and Ceylon (MACIPBC), Bishop's College, Calcutta. This session applauded the Prohibition Act of 1937 and pledged to continue to aid the now-supportive government in the cause of temperance. The Anglican Church was much more in harmony with Indian public opinion on this issue than the British government. See "Prohibition Issue in India," pp. 263-64.

77. For evidence of reduced alcohol consumption, see *DDM* 5.4 (April 1928): 4; 5.11 (November 1928): 4; 6.5 (May 1929): 1; 6.6 (June 1929): 14; 6.9 (September 1929): 3; 7.5 (May 1930): 6-7; 7.9 (September 1930): 8; 9.5 (May 1932): 13; 10.10 (October 1933): 9; 13.4 (April 1936): 2-3. See also Pickett, *Christ's Way,* p. 42; "The Bishop's Diary," *MDM* 16.3 (March 1921): 51-59; Rajaiah D. Paul, *"V. S. Dornakal": Birth Centenary of Bishop Azariah, 1974* (Madras, 1974), p. 59; Luke, *Ḍārnakal Tiranalvēli,* p. 101. There is relatively little published evidence that drinking alcohol remained a severe problem in Christian congregations, but for some indication of intemperance in the church, see *DDM* 5.5 (May 1928): 2; 12.4 (April 1935): 4; also "The Bishop's Diary," *MDM* 9.2 (February 1914): 26.

78. 1,293 of its adult members and 400 of its junior members were on "probation" in 1941 ("ACPS Report," *Proceedings of the Twentieth Meeting of the Standing Committee of the Diocesan Council, 29 October 1941,* Bezwada, 5: 2/2, Dornakal, MACIPBC; *MDM* 9.6 (June 1914): 167; G. B. Redman, "Telugu Church Temperance Society," *MDM* 11.4 (April 1916): 121-22. See also IMS, *TMI* 27.6-7 (June-July 1928): 49-52.

79. Interviews with Alfred Bunyan, 29 and 30 March 1986, Dornakal.

The ACPS became the diocese's most important social improvement agency, sponsoring about sixty-three conferences per year in which the virtues of temperance were presented alongside the claims of the gospel. Its members engaged in activities such as cleaning streets and houses, visiting the sick, tutoring in reading and writing, discouraging the use of indecent language, and assisting the village teacher by promoting regular attendance at morning prayers and participation in evangelistic activities such as the "week of witness."

Where drinking remained a problem among Christians, it was treated at first as a relatively minor offense punishable by suspension from holy communion.[80] With the introduction of prohibition in 1938, however, Azariah made drinking and illicit distilling a cause for excommunication:

> The time when drinking among Church workers was treated as a minor fault and given a slight punishment has passed. . . . Our Christian congregations must be made to pledge themselves not to allow any toddy at marriage feasts, funerals or festivals. Any village that does these things must be severely dealt with.[81]

By 1941 Azariah reported that "about half the Pastorates say that there is still some drinking among the older people, and that too on festival and marriage occasions" but added that much progress had been made: "There are many Pastorates in which public drinking has entirely gone out of fashion. 'The second generation [of Christians] has entirely given up drink,' says one Deanery Chairman."[82]

Azariah's campaign against alcohol consumption would clearly not have been so successful without the aid of indigenous abhorrence for the "doubly-defiling" substance of alcohol. The drinking of strong liquor was considered especially polluting to higher *jatis,* not so much because it was defiling in itself but because it was distilled by *jatis* of lower rank and had thus been touched by polluting people. The abandonment of distillation and of drinking alcohol was a well-recognized means of *jati* mobility throughout Indian society, for non-Christians as well as Christians.[83] The Dornakal converts' enthusiastic support for temperance was therefore motivated by an indigenous desire for elevated ritual rank in the Hindu social order as much as, or per-

80. *Church Censures: Diocese of Dornakal,* I (1914-32), II (1933-45), DDA.

81. *DDM* 15.7 (July 1938): 11.

82. Azariah, *Charge Delivered at Bezwada,* p. 20.

83. David G. Mandelbaum, *Society in India* (Berkeley, 1970), pp. 201, 217, 479-81, 569.

haps more than, being simply an effort to conform to the church's ethical standards for sobriety.

The Problem of Eating Meat

Perhaps no area more clearly illustrates the degree to which Christian conversion movements provided the depressed classes with the opportunity for social mobility than the area of carrion and meat ingestion. Here, many of Dornakal's converts voluntarily adopted certain indigenous eating prohibitions that were not advocated by the church at all but were regarded as highly desirable within India's broad criteria of ritual purity and impurity.

Although the eating of meat, any meat, was one of the main factors associated with pollution and untouchability, there was in practice a hierarchy of meat pollution, with chicken, fish, and mutton ranking as relatively less polluting, and bats, cats, rats, dogs, crows, and snakes ranking as relatively more polluting and even unmentionable.[84] Beef and pork were considered by the higher castes to be defiling because the former came from the most sacred of all animals, the cow, and the latter came from swine, which ate excrement. Indeed, one of the myths commonly used to explain the low position of Malas and Madigas in the caste hierarchy involved the killing and eating of a divine cow belonging to Parvati and Siva.[85] Dornakal diocesan records contain numerous examples of converts forsaking carrion, beef, and pork in an obvious bid to improve their social rank, as defined more by India's ritual criteria than by Western or "Christian" standards.

Both Western missionaries and caste neighbors disapproved of carrion eating but for different reasons. The depressed class practice of eating carrion *(tsachina mamsamu)* was condemned by missionaries on the grounds that the meat of animals that had died of themselves from disease, old age, or starvation was dangerously insanitary. In contrast, the higher castes disapproved of eating *tsachina mamsamu* because, as in the case of the Madigas, this almost always meant eating relatively cheap but ritually defiling beef (cattle or buffalo).[86] Caste people felt that pollution was contracted not through the ingestion of dead animals *per se* (some people of higher castes ate the carrion of other animals) but through the ingestion of ritually impure meats.

84. R. E. Frykenberg to author, 20 October 1990.

85. P. Wiebe, *Christians in Andhra Pradesh* (Madras, 1988), pp. 53-54.

86. Fishman, *For This Purpose,* p. 80. Other types of highly polluting meats (bats, etc.) were not specified in the literature, only beef and pork.

Unlike prohibitions regarding Sunday work, participation in Hindu rituals, and child marriage, which interfered with village traditions and provoked resistance from higher-caste Hindus, the prohibition against eating *tsachina mamsamu* was welcomed by dominant Hindu groups and was accepted eagerly, at least by those Christian converts with adequate dietary alternatives.[87] A pastor reported in 1931 that "the Madiga Christians of L——— who used to eat dead flesh have now entirely left off eating it. This is a marvellous thing."[88] Baptist Christians of Ongole became known for sitting apart when carrion was boiling in the pot.[89]

The movement against eating carrion was also part of a seemingly spontaneous wider movement among Dornakal's depressed classes to abandon eating beef, pork, and presumably other defiling but unmentionable meats. Diocesan records reported that many Christian congregations (and particularly Madigas and Yerukulas) decided to abstain from eating beef and pork voluntarily, without pressure from the church, in order to remove any hindrance to caste people who wanted to become Christian. In 1928, the church reported that Christians in a pastorate headquarters had given up pork "so that the use of it may not be an offence to others," and that Christians in another area had "three years ago bound themselves to give up drink, beef, pork and tobacco; and are keeping faithful."[90] In 1930 church representatives from an area in which Telagas and other Sudras were pressing for baptism reported:

> For the last two or three years we have been making a vehement campaign against beef-eating since it is a hindrance in the way of caste people coming in. They deem it as abominable and the eaters thereof wicked and sinful. As a result of this campaign six families in this congregation have given it up, and the drink habit as well.[91]

These decisions were often made by whole villages (sometimes including numerous non-Christians) and enforced by village elders as a matter of policy. So, for example, a Deanery chairman reported in 1930 that a big hamlet of 800 Madigas, about 350 of whom were Christians, had decided to give up

87. A. T. Fishman, *Culture Change and the Underprivileged* (Madras, 1941), pp. 5, 13-15; Fishman, *For This Purpose*, pp. 14-15, 80.

88. *DDM* 8.10 (October 1931): 15. It was standard practice in such journals to omit village names.

89. Emma Rauschenbusch-Clough, *While Sewing Sandals: Or Tales of a Telugu Pariah Tribe* (London, 1899).

90. *DDM* 5.11 (November 1928): 4.

91. *DDM* 7.9 (September 1930): 8-9.

drink and eating beef four months before. All had been faithful to their pledge except a few transgressors who were summoned by the village elders and implored "not to be unfaithful to the solemn oath they had taken." There were apparently immediate economic benefits to this action. The Christians estimated that they had already saved RS 200 previously spent on drink and had also been saved the expense of killing four to five cows per week for meat. Though they continued as shoemakers to use the ritually defiling skins of the dead cattle for tanning, the chairman reported that they now "bury the flesh so that no one may eat it. Almost all of them were eating the flesh of dead cattle before." The Madiga's pledge quickly gained the attention of the higher castes. "The Hindus are wondering at the sudden and remarkable change which has come over them. The surrounding villages also are trying to follow suit."[92]

Azariah sympathized to some extent with neighboring Baptist missionaries who continued to eat beef in order to demonstrate their freedom from Hindu reverence for the cow.[93] The bishop was not a vegetarian and ate meats according to his personal tastes. (As it happened, inevitably poor quality beef was not a favorite.) But unlike the Baptists who regarded beef eating as something of a test for converts, Azariah encouraged the anti-beef (pork, etc.) campaigns in his diocese. He attested to the long-term benefits of an anti-beef campaign in 1936 when he visited a village whose Christians had been baptized eleven years before. Their voluntary commitment to giving up "drink, beef, theft and lies" had so improved their "cleanliness" in the eyes of village *zamindars* that distance requirements had been abandoned.[94] Abstention from defiling meats was one of several means by which Christians attempted with some apparent success to raise their status in the eyes of higher castes. Although not initiating these efforts, Azariah welcomed them to demonstrate to higher castes the ability of Christianity "to drive away degrading habits"[95] and to increase caste conversions.

The church therefore actively encouraged this unexpected outcome of Christianity's interaction with the local Telugu culture. In 1929 Bishop Azariah visited a village in which outcast Christians had given up beef eating in order to remove an alleged obstacle to caste conversions to Christianity. This had apparently helped to remove some of the stigma associated with the local Christian congregation. As Azariah recounted: "A Komati [village

92. *DDM* 7.5 (May 1930): 6-7.
93. Fishman, *For This Purpose*, p. 80.
94. *DDM* 13.4 (April 1936): 2.
95. *DDM* 13.4 (April 1936): 2.

banker or merchant] recently remarked of Christians of a certain village that he had no objection to their coming to his shop or his touching them since now they had altogether given up beef." The bishop added:

> I was very much amused at this anti-beef campaign by our Christians. That it should have started from them entirely and that, too, solely for the sake of removing the prejudice of the caste people against the Christian faith are most encouraging facts. If the whole of India took a similar attitude on such questions there will be no communal conflicts. The Christian spirit is certainly the best solution for all communal troubles.[96]

Far from condemning the anti-beef resolutions as symptomatic of the continuing hold of caste prejudice or of heathen cow veneration among Christians, the Dornakal church welcomed these movements as generous expressions of a new, gospel-motivated desire to reconcile communal differences. The fact that converts had spontaneously opted to give up eating beef and pork without a mandate or recommendations from the church was not viewed as insubordination but rather as an encouraging sign that outcast Christians desired to improve their reputation among higher-caste groups and, ultimately, to help the Christian (not to mention the outcast) cause. The issue of eating beef had been discussed at the 1910 Edinburgh World Missionary Conference, where it was concluded that "to refrain from eating beef would remove a serious obstacle to the acceptance of the Christian faith by Hindus."[97] Yet abstaining from beef had not become a policy in Dornakal, nor even a practice followed by Azariah and most other Indian church leaders.

Consistent with Azariah's generally optimistic attitude about the gospel's power to transform aspects of Indian culture, he viewed the grassroots anti-beef campaign as an expression of Christian power to heal communal differences rather than as the self-serving attempt by one *jati* to improve its ritual status by adopting a higher-caste practice. That the latter motivation may often have been the more compelling is suggested by the fact that the anti-beef campaign was not confined to Christian groups, although Christians often took the lead in initiating broad resolutions on the subject. In the mainly non-Christian Madiga hamlet cited above, whose eight hundred inhabitants had agreed to stop drinking alcohol and eating beef, the minority Christians

96. *DDM* 6.5 (May 1929): 2-3.
97. Quoted in Fishman, *For This Purpose*, p. 80.

held all but one of the positions on the village *panchayat* responsible for the initiatives. Since Indian national independence, a sizable part of the non-Christian Madiga community has continued this effort to stop eating carrion and dealing with dead cattle.[98] The rise in economic position and political power, which Madigas have experienced in urban areas to which they have been migrating, has been accompanied by an attempt to claim better status in the eyes of higher-caste groups. The abstention from beef eating and from handling cattle has been the Madigas' main concession to values derived from the Sanskritic tradition. Madiga elites attempting to raise their *jati*'s status have not engaged, except sporadically, in the process of Sanskritization, have avoided incorporating Brahmin priests into their socio-religious life, and have worshipped local territorial and caste deities rather than "the all-India gods of classical Hinduism."[99] Their models for emulation have been derived only occasionally and partially from the Sanskritic tradition and more often from a variety of cultural heritages that include local, regional, modern Western, and secular national traditions. For example, modern Madiga interfamily relationships have been modeled increasingly on patterns established by upper-caste Andhra agriculturalists rather than by Brahmins.[100] Refraining from eating beef appears to have been the only Brahmanical practice widely adopted.

Conclusion

Christianization in the Dornakal diocese with its variety of socioeconomic and cultural repercussions is, thus, perhaps best understood as one of many facets of change that occurred in the wider context of *jati* upward mobilization. Unlike some Western missionaries, Azariah accepted his converts' accommodation to certain values defined by India's broad ritual criteria whereby different meats were accorded different degrees of ritual pollution. This was a realistic recognition that, although his formerly outcast converts resented their ostracism from Hindu society, they were still inclined to assimilate some of that wider culture's values in order to gain greater respect. Insofar as those indigenous values did not offend Christian values, Azariah chose to focus instead on their potential for improving the lives of both his converts and of Indian society as a whole.

98. Singh, *The Madiga,* p. 76.
99. Singh, *The Madiga,* p. 76.
100. Singh, *The Madiga,* pp. 73-74.

The church hoped to bring about dramatic changes in the values and practices of the depressed classes while also adapting and invigorating certain positive elements of their culture. By requesting baptism, the mass movement converts apparently welcomed many of these changes. There is little doubt that conversion to Christianity in Dornakal and in other mass movement areas entailed, in addition to spiritual experiences, the quest for a better life both economically and socially and for greater individual and group dignity.[101] The question of which motivations took priority was one of the more vexing issues Azariah had to face during his episcopal career and, indeed, became the focus of Mahatma Gandhi's criticisms of Indian Christians in Dornakal.[102]

A more recent scholarly debate over motives for depressed class conversions has refocused upon the somewhat different question of whether Indian Christian converts regarded their baptism as a means of protest and escape from the hierarchical values of the Indian caste system (as the missionaries, many Indian Christians, and some scholars have claimed), or whether they were merely trying to improve their positions within the traditional Indian social order. Studies of Indian Christian communities suggest that converts

101. Whether these goals were really met remains a complex subject whose results vary according to locality and time. For useful assessments see Henry Whitehead, "Mass Movement Appeal," *MDM* 13.6 (June 1918): 131-34; Manickam, *Social Setting of Christian Conversion,* pp. 101-3, 108-11, 257-58; J. C. B. Webster, *The Christian Community and Change in Nineteenth Century North India* (Delhi, 1976), pp. 61-72, and his *A History of the Dalit Christians in India* (San Francisco, 1992). The Indian Christian community became better known for its educational than its economic attainments. Literacy gave converts the opportunity to enter new professions (in railways, the postal system, government, and missions). Although this mobility contributed to a significant long-term rise in social status, persecution was often the only short-term result of such conversions; see S. Manickam, *Social Setting of Christian Conversion,* pp. 108-11; Wiebe, *Christians in Andhra Pradesh,* pp. 128-31. In a report on the research of Methodist Bishop J. W. Pickett, the *Dornakal Diocesan Magazine* claimed that church-sponsored activity led to general economic improvement for the "Untouchables": education and the breakdown of occupational restrictions led to increased earnings; improved medical care prevented loss of working days; and reduced drinking meant less wasteful expenditure and greater productivity. Pickett pointed out, however, that conversion worsened the economic condition in some respects. Educated converts often migrated to urban areas so that villages did not benefit from their education; converts adopted new standards of expenditure on clothes; and "false ideas of dignity" prevented them from doing ordinary work, caused them to boycott certain occupations, and created "the occasional development of a spirit of dependence upon the Mission" (see "Mass Movements and Economic Reconstruction," n.a., *DDM* 11.3 [March 1934]: 16-19).

102. See my *In the Shadow of the Mahatma: Bishop V. S. Azariah and the Travails of Christianity in British India* (Grand Rapids, Mich., and Cambridge, U.K., 2000) for further treatment of the issues.

often continued to adhere to Hindu standards of social rank and precedence and that conversion movements in India cannot be properly understood in isolation from these values.[103] This seems to have been the case in Dornakal, where conversion served, among other functions, as a means by which depressed groups tried to improve their social and economic status, to gain new self-respect, and to win the respect of higher castes.[104] Although optimistic Western missionaries of this period tended to regard mass movements as a

103. S. B. Kaufmann, "Popular Christianity, Caste and Hindu Society in South India, 1800-1915: A Study of Travancore and Tirunelveli," Ph.D. thesis, University of Cambridge, 1980, pp. 15-26, 382-490, and his "A Christian Caste in Hindu Society: Religious Leadership and Social Conflict among the Paravas of Southern Tamilnadu," *Modern Asian Studies* 15.2 (April 1981): 203-34. Kaufmann's argument that Christian conversion is best understood as a sectarian movement operating according to Hindu concepts of rank and social advancement (similar to *bhakti* movements such as *Virasaivas*) challenges the notion that Christian converts were seeking liberation from those values. For representative Christian missionary views, see S. C. Neill, *Out of Bondage* (London, 1930), pp. 48-50, 127; W. Paton, *Christianity in the Eastern Conflicts* (Westminster, 1937), p. 93; J. W. Pickett, "The Untouchable," in *Moving Millions,* United Study of Foreign Missions (Boston, 1938), pp. 42-74; and J. W. Pickett, *Bombay Representative Christian Council: Report on the Survey of Evangelistic Opportunities in Maharashtra, 1938-39* (Mysore City, 1940), p. 10. For other modern scholarly assessments of this question, see the works by R. E. Frykenberg, R. Hardgrave, G. A. Oddie, J. Manor, and D. Washbrook cited by Kaufmann, and Mark Juergensmeyer, *Religion as Social Vision: The Movement against Untouchability in 20th-Century Punjab* (Berkeley, 1982), pp. 181-92; R. Frykenberg, "On the Study of Conversion Movements: A Review Article and a Theoretical Note," *Indian Economic and Social History Review* 17.1 (1980): 121-38; D. Forrester, "The Depressed Classes and Conversion to Christianity, 1860-1960," in *Religion in South Asia: Religious Conversion and Revival Movements in South Asia in Medieval and Modern Times,* edited by G. A. Oddie (New Delhi, 1977), pp. 35-66; J. W. Gladstone, *Protestant Christianity and People's Movements in Kerala, 1850-1936* (Kannamoola, Trivandrum, 1984), pp. 9-10, 76-81, 151-60, 201-4, 421-28; Walter Fernandes, *Caste and Conversion Movements in India* (Delhi, 1981), and "Caste, Religion and Social Change in India: Christianity and Conversion Movements," in *Scheduled Castes and the Struggle against Inequality,* edited by Jose Kananaikil (Delhi, 1983); Manickam, *Social Setting of Christian Conversion,* pp. 101-12, 245-49; L. L. and S. H. Rudolph, *The Modernity of Tradition: Political Development in India* (Chicago, 1967), pp. 136-37; and Dick Kooiman, *Conversion and Social Equality in India* (New Delhi, n.d.), pp. 168-208. Although this literature has not been subjected to systematic analysis, as Frykenberg notes in his "Review Article and Theoretical Note," it suggests generally that conversion provided a means of challenging caste disabilities and of bidding for elevation within Indian society, rather than of eradicating caste *per se.*

104. *DDM* 13.6 (June 1936): 6. See also Pickett, *Christ's Way,* pp. 42-43; Fishman, *Culture Change and the Underprivileged,* p. 26 (Fishman notes that the prestige of association with missionaries was not unimportant); Juergensmeyer, *Religion as Social Vision,* p. 187.

means by which outcasts and low castes were rejecting not only their particular position in the caste hierarchy but also the entire hierarchical value system upon which it was based,[105] conversion to Christianity seems primarily to have provided an effective instrument for improving the status of depressed class groups within that same caste hierarchy.

Most of the cultural changes advocated by the Dornakal church, and at least partly achieved in the villages, were considered "improvements" universally according to both Indian/Hindu and Western/Judeo-Christian values. Converts to Christianity were expected to give up a range of habits that were regarded by everyone (although often for entirely different reasons) as contributing to their state of "degradation." Unexpected developments, however, such as the grassroots Christian anti–beef-eating campaign, suggest that Christianization in Dornakal cannot be properly understood in isolation from prevailing Hindu values that determine local standards of social rank and precedence. Many of Dornakal's converts voluntarily adopted eating prohibitions not advocated by the church but regarded as highly desirable within India's broad criteria of ritual purity and impurity. Many converts also enthusiastically embraced the church's anti-alcohol campaign. The popularity of the temperance movement, led by the ACPS, stands in marked contrast to the relative unpopularity of new Christian standards for marriage, sexual, or inter-*jati* relations. The differential rate of success between these different areas of church work is surely at least partly accounted for, not just by a negative "lack of discipline" on the part of new converts but also by a more positive interplay between the new Christian standards of morality and the old indigenous notions of ritual defilement and obligation.

Evidence from the Dornakal diocese therefore supports the view that the conversion movements to Christianity were less a means of rejecting Hinduism and the prevailing caste system than a means by which subordinate groups tried to elevate their rank in the social hierarchy by accommodating and, sometimes, transforming the values of dominant, non-Christian groups.

105. This sort of perspective is reflected indirectly in Forrester's "Depressed Classes and Conversion," pp. 35-66. He concludes that these classes were attracted to the Protestant emphasis on equality, among other factors. This difference in perceptions of missionaries and converts has been noted in other contexts. Juergensmeyer *(Religion as Social Vision)* claims that, for the missionaries, "Christianity in the Punjab was something that rose above caste, hardly an instrument of caste identity and mobility" (p. 184); and that "even in the cheeriest piety of church fellowship there were tensions between the global perspective of the missionaries and the parochial concerns of village Christians, and in the end the illusion of Christendom as a new society remained mostly that, an illusion" (p. 192).

Azariah's contribution was to allow his church the short-term freedom to order its affairs according to a creative mixture of principles important to local culture and principles important to external cultures, in the expectation that the gospel would transform and benefit local culture over the longer term. This produced a new kind of Indo-Anglicanism specific to Andhra and different from anything that has emerged before or since: an inculturated hybrid tradition that neither denationalized its converts nor diminished their nation.

CHAPTER TEN

The "Pure Tamil Movement" and Bible Translation: The Ecumenical Thiruviviliam of 1995

MICHAEL BERGUNDER

Bible Translation and "Church Tamil"

Over several centuries Christianity has had a profound impact on the development of the Tamil language. Western missionaries are highly respected by Tamil pandits for producing modern linguistic tools for the Tamil language. At least three names, C. J. Beschi (Italian Jesuit, 1680-1747), Robert Caldwell (British Church of England missionary, 1814-91), and G. U. Pope (British Church of England missionary and scholar, 1820-1908), are mentioned even in the most concise histories of Tamil literature.[1]

The Tamil research of the missionaries was motivated by their efforts to communicate the Christian message in the local language, and one of their main projects was, of course, the translation of the Bible. The search for a meaningful biblical terminology was particularly difficult because religious language in Tamil was greatly shaped by Hindu religious traditions.[2] Tamil

1. V. M. Gnanaprakasam and M. Mathialagan, "Contribution of Foreign Scholars to Tamil," in *Encyclopaedia of Tamil Literature,* vol. 1: *Introductory Articles,* edited by J. Samuel (Madras, 1990), pp. 367-79; S. Ramaswamy, *Passions of the Tongue: Language Devotion in Tamil India, 1891-1970* (Berkeley, 1997), pp. 189-94.

2. See B. Tiliander, *Christian and Hindu Terminology: A Study in Their Mutual Relations with Special Reference to the Tamil Area* (Uppsala, 1974), for an excellent discussion of

I am especially grateful to Daniel Jeyaraj for valuable insights and criticisms on an earlier version of this paper.

terms that could render key Christian concepts, such as God, sin, and grace, were already highly loaded with specific connotations deriving mainly from Hindu philosophy and *bhakti* traditions.

The serious challenges that any translation of Christian ideas into Tamil has to face might be best illustrated by the fact that, in some cases, the early missionaries were unable to find any adequate equivalent. Early Catholic missionaries, for example, translated Holy Spirit as *ispirīttu cāntu* (Latin *Spiritus Sanctus*) in the Lord's Prayer, and this usage was even continued by the early Lutheran Tranquebar missionaries in the eighteenth century until they introduced a Tamil phrase *(paricutta āvi)*.[3]

It was a long process before a consistent and mature Christian vocabulary in Tamil was established, and, at least among Protestants, the Bible translations had an extraordinary impact on that development. The history of the Tamil Bible is quite complicated in detail, but three major, and closely interwoven, threads may be distinguished: a Lutheran, a non-Lutheran Protestant, and a Catholic tradition.[4]

From the very beginning, the Tranquebar missionaries had planned to translate the whole Bible into Tamil, but it was only Johann Philip Fabricius (1711-91) who brought together all earlier efforts and prepared a complete Bible translation that was posthumously published in 1796.[5] This so-called "Fabricius Version" became the standard Bible translation within the Tamil Lutheran Church, and, apart from very minor revisions, it was regularly reprinted until 1951.[6] Its terminology and phrases have shaped the liturgical and religious language of the Tamil Lutherans right up to the present.

In the first half of the nineteenth century many Protestant missionary so-

---

this issue. Some helpful word lists are found in U. Sandgren, *The Tamil New Testament and Bartholomäus Ziegenbalg: A Short Study of Some Tamil Translations of the New Testament* (Uppsala, 1991).

3. S. Rajamanickam, *The First Oriental Scholar* (Tirunelveli, 1972), pp. 186-87, 196; Tiliander, *Christian and Hindu Terminology*, p. 252.

4. Sabapathy Kulandran, *Kiṟistava tamiḻ vētākamattiṉ varalāṟu* (Bangalore, 1967); B. Tiliander, "Tamulische Bibelübersetzungen von Anfang an bis heute," in *Fides pro mundi vita*, edited by T. Sundermeier (Gütersloh, 1980), pp. 268-83; I. H. Victor, "A Brief History of the Tamil Bible," *Indian Church History Review (ICHR)* 18 (1984): 106-18; S. Packiamuthu, *Viviliyamum tamiḻum* (Madras, 1990); Sandgren, *Tamil New Testament.*

5. Quoted (abbreviated as "Fabricius") according to the following editions: J. P. Fabricius, *Paḻaiya ēṟpāṭu* [Old Testament] (Madras, 1841); J. P. Fabricius, *Putiya ēṟpāṭu* (Tranquebar, 1878).

6. I. H. Victor, "Tamil Translations of the Bible by the Danish-Halle Mission during the Eighteenth Century," *ICHR* 16 (1982): 82; Victor, "Brief History of the Tamil Bible," p. 110.

cieties began their work among the Tamil-speaking population of southern India and Ceylon. Initially, they adopted the Fabricius Version, but in the course of time they started their own translation projects, and, finally, a joint Protestant effort for a new Tamil Bible translation was planned. A thorough revision of the Fabricius Version was undertaken under the leadership of the Anglo-Indian, H. Bower, and it was published as the Union Version (nowadays known as Old Version — OV) by the British and Foreign Bible Society in 1871.[7] For all non-Lutheran Protestants this remains the authoritative Bible translation. The Lutherans did not join this revision project, and their Fabricius Version remained the only officially acknowledged translation because long usage had made that text almost sacred for them.

In the twentieth century several efforts were made to revise the Union Version, but it was only in 1956 that a moderately changed version (Revised Version — RV) gained wider approval.[8] In contrast to the Old Version, this translation had the firm support of the Lutherans, and C. G. Diehl, later bishop of the Tamil Evangelical Lutheran Church, played a very important role in the project.[9] Although the Revised Version was (irregularly) reprinted, it did not gain approval within the Protestant congregations where the Old Version is still in use today. Ironically, the publication of the Revised Version helped indirectly to popularize the Old Version among the Lutherans too. The Lutheran Church authorities stopped printing the Fabricius Version and thought to replace it with the Revised Version. Lutheran congregations, however, did not adopt the Revised Version and began to use the Old Version, even though passages from the Fabricius Version are still read in some Lutheran churches and some old terminology of Fabricius has survived in the Lutheran liturgy and hymns.

The Catholics, who traditionally have given more weight to catechetical books, did not print a complete Bible before the end of the nineteenth century. The Jesuit J. B. Trincal translated the complete New Testament, which was printed in 1890, and Bishop Bottero from Kumbakonam brought out another translation that was printed as a complete Bible in 1912 (the so-called Pondicherry Bible). Both translations were independent of the Protestant versions.[10]

7. Quoted (abbreviated as "OV") according to the following edition: Bible Society of India, ed., *The Holy Bible Tamil — O.V.* (Bangalore, n.d.).

8. Quoted (abbreviated as "RV") according to the following edition: Bible Society of India, ed., *Holy Bible Tamil R.V.* (Bangalore, 1980).

9. H. Grafe, *The History of Christianity in Tamilnadu from 1800 to 1975* (Erlangen, 1990), p. 251; Sandgren, *Tamil New Testament,* p. 9.

10. Grafe, *History,* p. 250.

The publication of widely recognized complete Bible translations indicates that denominational "church Tamil" had been well established by the beginning of the twentieth century. Spiritual and liturgical life was shaped by the biblical language that constituted the basis for a special "church Tamil." The younger generations were socialized in a fixed technical Tamil terminology that gradually became the only way to speak about Christian doctrines within the congregations. As a result, this specific religious language also began to serve as a socio-religious marker that helped to reaffirm the identity of denominational Tamil Christian communities through their own dialect or "branch language" *(kiḷaimoḻi),* which clearly distinguished them from other religious groups.

At the turn to the twentieth century, G. U. Pope thought that church Tamil, based on Bower's Union Version, would become the starting point for the development of a genuine Christian contribution to Tamil literature:

> There exists now much of what is called Christian Tamil, a dialect created by the Danish missionaries of Tranquebar; enriched by generations of Tanjore, German, and other missionaries; modified, purified, and *refrigerated* [*sic*] by the Swiss Rhenius and the very composite Tinnevelly school; expanded and harmonized by Englishmen, amongst whom Bower (a Eurasian) was foremost in his day; and, finally, waiting now for the touch of some heaven-born genius among the Tamil community to make it as sweet and effective as any language on earth, living or dead.[11]

Nevertheless, Pope did not foresee that, during the twentieth century, Tamil-speaking South India would undergo such a radical political and linguistic revolution that nineteenth-century church Tamil would become outdated and would have to be thoroughly renewed to cope with the rapid language changes.

The "Pure Tamil Movement" and Its Impact on Tamil Theology

The multi-faceted, so-called Dravidian movement that started at the beginning of the twentieth century, though its roots go back further, caused very considerable ethnic mobilization and generated a vigorous nationalism that

11. G. U. Pope, *The Tiruvacagam or "Sacred Utterances" of the Tamil Poet, Saint and Sage Manikka-Vacagar* (Oxford, 1900), p. xii.

has now become a recognized part of the Tamil identity.[12] One striking feature of the emerging Tamil nationalism was strong and powerful initiatives toward language purism.[13] From the very beginning this language purism was especially connected with Maraimalai Adigal (1876-1950).[14] In 1916, it is said, he consciously decided that he would no longer use words of supposedly foreign origin when speaking or writing in Tamil. This decision is popularly seen as the official beginning of the "Pure Tamil movement" *(taṉittamiḻ iyakkam)* that tried fervently to eradicate all words that were thought to be of Sanskrit origin.

In some aspects, this movement must be seen as a backlash against a new wave of "Sanskritization" that had flowed into the Tamil language in the second half of the nineteenth century. At that time, the Brahmanical Tamil, which was always heavily mixed with Sanskrit words, enjoyed great social prestige because of the high status ascribed to Brahmans in the colonial society. Consequently the new non-Brahman middle classes also imitated Sanskritized Tamil. It is very characteristic of that period to find a Tamil grammar of 1878 observing that "at the present time a stream of pure, unaltered Sanskrit words is continually flowing into Tamil prose literature."[15]

Like all branches of the Dravidian movement, the Pure Tamil movement was anti-Brahmanical, and, as "Aryan" Brahmanism became one of the main targets of the Tamil nationalists, Sanskrit terminology was considered to be a vehicle of Brahman domination. In the view of Maraimalai Adigal it was clear, as he declared in 1927, that "liberation from Aryanism and its language, Sanskrit, constituted the first *cuyarājyam* (independence) for Tamilians."[16]

The purists achieved their greatest popularity in the 1940s and 1950s when they were in the forefront of the anti-Hindi agitation in the Tamil-speaking south.[17] Moreover, since 1967, when the Dravida Munnetra Kazhagam (DMK) swept the state polls and Madras State was renamed Tamilnadu (*tamiḻnāṭu* = land of the Tamils), Tamil purism became an official

12. See especially M. R. Barnett, *The Politics of Cultural Nationalism in South India* (Princeton, 1976); K. Nambi Arooran, *Tamil Renaissance and Dravidian Nationalism* (Madurai, 1980); D. Hellmann-Rajanayagam, *Tamil: Sprache als politisches Symbol* (Wiesbaden, 1984); E. F. Irschick, *Tamil Revivalism in the 1930s* (Madras, 1986); N. Subramanian, *Ethnicity and Populist Mobilization: Political Parties, Citizens and Democracy in South India* (Delhi, 1999).

13. Ramaswamy, *Passions*, pp. 144-61.

14. See, for example, I. Ilangumaran, *Maṟaimalaiyaṭikaḷ* (New Delhi, 1995).

15. J. Lazarus, *A Tamil Grammar* (Madras, 1878), p. 163.

16. Ramaswamy, *Passions*, p. 150.

17. A. R. Venkatachalapathy, "Dravidian Movement and Saivites, 1927-1944," *Economic and Political Weekly*, 8 April 1995, pp. 765-66; Ramaswamy, *Passions*, pp. 168-78.

government policy. Looking back at nearly a hundred years of puristic enterprise, one has to admit that this movement has effectively changed the Tamil language and that the usage of words of a supposedly Sanskrit origin has declined dramatically.

From a linguistic perspective, however, many shortcomings of the Pure Tamil movement are obvious. First of all, the movement concentrated only on the elimination of Sanskrit words and never considered foreign grammatical influences on Tamil. It was also hardly interested in reflecting upon proper grammatical rules for a good modern Tamil prose style. On the contrary, looking back to the classical literature as their preferred model, proponents of the movement often introduced strange archaisms into their speeches and writings, although political leaders in the Dravidian movement, such as E. V. Ramasami Naicker (Periyar), or C. N. Annadurai, consciously tried to speak a pure Tamil that could be well understood by the people. Moreover, leaders of the movement never reflected on the problem of diglossia and different levels of language but simply propagated the idea that "pure Tamil" is "good Tamil" and thus the grammatical norm that should be taught at schools.

Western missionaries and Tamil Christians were not prominently involved in the Dravidian movement, but they were certainly sympathetic with many of its aims. After all, it was Caldwell's *Comparative Grammar of the Dravidian or South Indian Family of Languages* and the Tamil-English dictionaries of Winslow and Fabricius that had already asterisked every word with a Sanskrit origin.[18]

As all higher education was to be in English, however, the small Christian middle class was more English-oriented and less interested in questions of Tamil literature and grammar. That might be the reason why "church Tamil" was not affected by the new developments initiated by the Tamil purists. Christian congregations were quite comfortable with a sectarian language that was a kind of identity marker. This fact was made explicit by L. Newbigin, Bishop in Church of South India, 1947-74, in his autobiography:

> Meanwhile a colossal revival of Tamil culture was going on under the stimulus of C. N. Annadurai and his colleagues. New novels, poetry and

18. M. Winslow, *A Comprehensive Tamil and English Dictionary of High and Low Tamil* (Madras, 1862); H. Beisenherz, ed., *A Dictionary Tamil and English Based on Johann Fabricius's "Malabar-English Dictionary," Second Edition, Revised and Enlarged* (Tranquebar, 1910); D. Bexell, ed., *A Dictionary Tamil and English, Based on Johann Fabricius's "Malabar-English Dictionary," Third Edition, Revised and Enlarged* (Tranquebar, 1933); C. G. Diehl, ed., *J. P. Fabricius's Tamil and English Dictionary* (Tranquebar, 1972).

drama, and new films were flooding the whole state with new ideas. But the church was out of effective contact because its theological leadership was oriented towards the English-speaking world.[19]

This situation changed somewhat in 1969 when the Tamilnadu Theological Seminary (TTS) at Madurai came into being. It was a merger of a Church of South India seminary and one from the Lutheran Church, and it was planned for Tamil-medium education. Its Tamil name, *iṟaiyiyal kallūri* instead of *vētacāttirak kalācālai,* showed at the outset a clear move toward pure Tamil, and it tried to make this new Tamil style part of the whole theological teaching program; a deep reform of traditional church Tamil was high on the agenda.[20] Moreover, a Tamil Theological Book Club was founded in order to produce theological and spiritual literature in pure Tamil, a small quarterly theological magazine *(iṟaiyiyal malar)* was launched in 1970, and a theological book series (*tirumaṟaikkut tirumpuvōm* = Back to the Bible), in 1981.[21] In the course of time, TTS developed a major theological thrust on questions of social justice and later became one of the centers for Dalit liberation theology. As a result of that, the idea of a contextualized Tamil theology was pushed somewhat into the background. Nevertheless, as Dalit theology is highly critical of Brahmanical Hinduism and its caste system, and also very receptive of anti-Brahmanical ideas in the Dravidian movement, teaching pure Christian Tamil is still an important part of the TTS curriculum.

As mentioned above, Roman Catholics were not as concerned with a codified church Tamil, and only after the Second Vatican Council was a conscious Tamilization process started. Thereafter this had a considerable impact. At the regional college for Catholic priests, St. Paul's Seminary *(tūya ciṉṉappar iṟaiyiyal kallūri)* at Tiruchchirappalli, pure Tamil was actively promoted and a Tamil theological magazine (*maṟai aruvi* = the fountain of scripture) was started in 1977. Yet it was the Tamilnadu Biblical Catechetical and Liturgical Centre (TNBCLC, Tamil *tamiḻnāṭu viviviliya maṟaikkalvi tiruvaḻipāṭṭu naṭunilaiyam*), founded in 1974 at Tindivanam, that became the focal point for the introduction of pure Tamil into the liturgical and spiritual

19. L. Newbigin, *Unfinished Agenda: An Autobiography* (Geneva, 1985), p. 145.

20. V. P. K. Sundaram, *"Kallūri vaḷartta tamiḻum tamiḻ paṇpāṭum,"* in *Venturing into Life: The Story of the First Twenty Years of the Tamilnadu Theological Seminary,* edited by S. Amirtham and C. R. W. David (Madurai, 1990), pp. 190-202.

21. Dayanandan Francis, *"Irupatu āṇṭukaḷil iṟaiyiyal ilakkiyap paṇi,"* in *Venturing into Life; The Story of the First Twenty Years of the Tamilnadu Theological Seminary,* pp. 204-18. For a general survey on Tamil theological literature in the 1960s and 1970s see S. Arulsamy, "Theology in Indian Languages," *Indian Theological Studies* 14 (1977): 390-402.

life of the congregations.[22] All liturgical publications of TNBCLC show a preference for pure Tamil and traces of the former Catholic Church Tamil can only be found in some traditional prayers and songs.[23] Moreover, it seems that the Catholic congregations are quite open to the changes of their church Tamil.

Towards an Ecumenical Translation

Soon after the DMK came to power in 1967 and pure Tamil became an official state language policy, new Bible translations were published. It seems as if some church leaders had felt a pressing need to bring out new versions of the Tamil Bible that adequately addressed the new situation.

Responding to this pressure but also encouraged by changes through the Second Vatican Council, the Catholics published a New Testament in 1970, and in 1973 the Old Testament followed.[24] These were radical new translations that freely adopted modern purist Tamil. Perhaps inspired by the Catholic endeavor, the Lutheran theologian D. Rajarigam also produced a completely new translation of the New Testament in a similar pure Tamil style that was published in 1975; he followed it with the Psalms one year later.[25]

In this situation, and because ecumenical Bible translation projects were taken up all over the world, the time was ripe to consider a joint translation project by Catholics and Protestants.[26] In 1972, representatives from the different churches agreed to undertake a common translation of the Old Testament. This work progressed steadily though not without long delays, and between 1975 and 1992 thirty-nine books of the Old Testament were published

22. See http://www.tnbclc.org (20 August 2000).

23. During 1981-82, the Tamilnadu Bishops' Council decided that the language of five traditional prayers should not be changed (Sign of the Cross, Glory Be to the Father, Our Father, Hail Mary, and the Apostles' Creed); see www.tnbclc.org/litcom.html (20 August 2000).

24. Quoted (abbreviated as "RC") according to the following edition: TNBCLC, ed., *Paricutta vētākamam: tiruttiya patippu* (Tindivanam, 1986).

25. Quoted (abbreviated as "Rajar") according to the following edition: Bible Society of India, ed., *Putiya ēṟpāṭum caṅkītaṅkaḷum, putu moḻipeyarppu kirēkka mūla nūliliruntu ceyyappaṭṭatu* (Bangalore, 1979). Rajarigam's manuscript with unpublished translations from the Old Testament are in the Lutheran Heritage Archives at Gurukul Lutheran Theological College, Chennai.

26. V. Mariadasan, "A Brief History of the Interconfessional Tamil Bible Project," in *Niṉaivu malar. tiruviviliyam potu moḻipeyarppu*, edited by TNBCLC (Tindivanam, 1995), pp. 48-49.

as trial editions. Meanwhile, in 1980, the project was extended to the whole Bible, and in 1992 trial editions of the four Gospels were published. By December 1993, the complete translation of the Bible was ready for print. As leading Catholic and Protestant Tamil theologians and bishops had been very supportive of this new translation, a powerful committee had been formed in the 1980s to push forward the project,[27] and in 1995 Thiruviviliam was printed.[28]

Language and Terminology in Thiruviviliam

Pure Tamil as Common Language

In a souvenir *(niṉaivu malar)* printed on the occasion of the release of the voluminous book, some of the translators commented on the linguistic principles of the translation.[29] The new Tamil Bible was thought to be a "common language" translation. In the terminology of the international Bible Societies this meant a special kind of Bible translation that differs from the so-called "standard versions." This classification originated in Western countries. Despite the fact that traditional Bibles were regularly revised (like the Revised Standard Version and the New Revised Standard Version in English), it was felt that new translations should also be undertaken that were not so dependent on traditional language and terminology and that were written in a simple modern prose style.

As seen above, the Tamil context was quite unique. Of course, the translation of Thiruviviliam was based on the critical editions of the original Bible text in Hebrew and Greek (*Biblia Hebraica Stuttgartensia* and Nestle-Aland's *Novum Testamentum Graece*), but the idea about "common language" in Tamil was unique since it was decisively influenced by the Pure Tamil movement. When the translation committee of Indian theologians and Church leaders met for the first time to discuss the translation principles, they were surprised to find that Catholics and Protestants alike were all fervent supporters of the Pure Tamil movement. A Catholic participant remembers this situation vividly:

> We were wondering whether our [Protestant] Christian brethren would

27. For a complete list of the members see TNBCLC, *Niṉaivu malar*, pp. 118-20.

28. Quoted (abbreviated as "Thiruviviliam") according to the following edition: TNBCLC, ed., *Holy Bible Thiruviviliam* (Tindivanam, 1995).

29. TNBCLC, *Niṉaivu malar.*

> accept these new readings, since they almost know their Tamil Bible by heart and the Pastors, Evangelists and common people were all using the old Tamil. . . . But we were pleasantly surprised, that our BSI [Bible Society of India] brethren at the very start accepted our suggestion for the use of Modern Tamil.[30]

The few theologians in the Tamil churches who were thought to be Tamil experts were deeply influenced by the language environment of the Dravidian movement. Moreover, it seems that no Protestant church leader or theologian openly opposed this translation strategy that radically broke with the language tradition of the Old Version. So, the commitment to pure Tamil became a strong unifying ecumenical factor during the period of the translation project.

As a consequence, one of the foremost principles in the translation work was the replacement of Sanskrit words. This was done with great energy, as one of the translators remembers: "The whole day we were preoccupied with searching for pure Tamil terms."[31] In accordance with the common usage in modern Tamil prose, especially in the journalistic field, the honorific plural *(mariyātaip paṉmai)* was transformed into an inclusive form for the third person singular denoting all rational persons irrespective of their gender. Making use of this grammatical potential, all social hierarchies, which are usually consciously marked in Tamil, are evened out in the text, and women, servants, and beggars receive the same reverence as anyone else. However, there are interesting exceptions. For people "who work against the will of God" (such as Herod, Judas), for those who use "abusive speech" (e.g., Mark 3:22), and for those in a "close friendship" (e.g., John 11:11 for Lazarus), the third person singular *is* used.[32] These are very significant changes, but, because in modern secular prose there is a similar trend, it is not at all unreasonable.

The translators were convinced that they closely followed the principles of a common-language translation and therefore believed that they wrote in a "natural, high standard and easy Tamil language style."[33] This kind of

30. Fr. P. P. Xavier, in an English comment in TNBCLC, *Niṉaivu malar,* p. 41.

31. TNBCLC, *Niṉaivu malar,* p. 68.

32. *iṟaittiṭṭattiṟku etirāṉavaraik kuṟippiṭumpōtum, paḻitturaikkum cūḻalilum, neruṅkiya naṭpuṟavai veḷippaṭuttumpōtum mariyātaippaṉmai tavirkkappaṭukiṟatu* (Thiruviviliam, preface); see also C. M. Hieronimus, "*Mariyātaip paṉmaiyum irupālārukkum poruntap pēcalum,*" in TNBCLC, *Niṉaivu malar,* pp. 76-80; V. M. Gnanapragasam, "*Putiya potu moḻipeyarppil mariyātap paṉmai,*" in TNBCLC, *Niṉaivu malar,* pp. 84-86.

33. *iyalpāṉa, taramāṉa, eḷiya tamiḻmoḻinaṭai* (Thiruviviliam, preface). A. Antony Crun speaks of "easy, sweet, straight good Tamil" *(eḷiya iṉiya nēraṭiyāṉa nalla tamiḻ),* cf. "*Tiruviviliyap potu moḻipeyarppiṉ tamiḻmaṇam,*" in TNBCLC, *Niṉaivu malar,* p. 60.

rather unreflective understanding can only be understood from the assumption of the Pure Tamil movement that pure Tamil is always good Tamil. As a consequence, the language of Thiruviviliam shares the above-mentioned linguistic shortcomings of the Pure Tamil movement. Admittedly, the translators made the grammatical constructions very simple, especially in contrast to Tamil conventions that always tend to construct long and complicated compound sentences, even in ordinary speech.[34] Even with regard to the original text the grammatical constructions are often simplified,[35] but, in contrast to the simple grammar, there are many words that belong to a very high literary level and that are only familiar to people acquainted with classical Tamil. Such difficult words are, for instance, used to denote, "epistle,"[36] "wrath,"[37] "flesh,"[38] "heaven,"[39] "descendant (of Abraham),"[40] and "glory."[41] Nevertheless, from the perspective of the translators the language style is that of the future because they were convinced that high literary Tamil would become increasingly popular, and that their translation would be very appropriate for the demands of the twenty-first century.[42] As one translator wrote: "we adopted a specific language and style keeping in mind the people of 2100 A.D."[43]

Theological Terminology

It is obvious that, by eliminating all words with supposed Sanskrit origin, the new translation deliberately changes the theological key words too. Unfortu-

34. Crun, "*Tiruviviliyap potu mol̲ipeyarppin̲ tamil̲maṇam,*" p. 63.

35. See Mark 1:13a where Thiruviviliam, unlike all other Tamil Bible translations before, splits even one simple Greek sentence into two: "*pālai nilattil avar nar̲patu nāḷ iruntār; appōtu cāttāṉāl cōtikkappaṭṭār.*"

36. *tirumukam;* OV: *nirupam;* RC: *tirumukam;* Rajar: *kaṭitam.*

37. *cin̲am* (Rom. 1:18, Greek *orgḗ*); OV: *tēvakōpam* (Sanskrit *deva-kopa*); RC: *cin̲am;* Rajar: *cin̲am.*

38. *ūn̲iyalpu* (Rom. 7:5, Greek *sárx*); OV: *māmcam* (Sanskrit *māṃsa*); RC: *ūn̲iyalpu;* Rajar: *pāva iyalpu.*

39. *viṇṇakam* (Rom. 10:6, Greek *ouranós*); OV: *paralōkam* (Sanskrit *paraloka*); RC: *vān̲akam;* Rajar: *vān̲am.*

40. *(āpirakāmin̲) val̲imarapin̲an̲* (Rom. 11:1, Greek *spérma* = semen); OV: *(āpirakāmin̲) cantati* (Sanskrit *saṃtati*); RC: *(āpirakāmin̲) val̲ivantavan̲;* Rajar: *(āpirakām) marapil vantavan̲.*

41. *māṭci* (Luke 2:9, Greek *dóxa*); OV: *makimai* (Sanskrit *mahimā,* nominative of *mahiman*); RC: *viṇṇoḷi,* Rajar: *māṭcimai.*

42. Crun, "*Tiruviviliyap potu mol̲ipeyarppin̲ tamil̲maṇam,*" p. 64.

43. TNBCLC, *Nin̲aivu malar,* p. 68.

nately, there is, as yet, no published source that explains the theological guidelines that lay behind that change of terminology.[44] From the text, however, it can be inferred that the translators tried to find pure Tamil equivalents that were used mainly in a secular context and were not so imbued with religious meaning. The translations for "salvation," "faith," and "trance" stand as examples for this translatory method.

Salvation

At least among Protestants the technical term for salvation (Greek *sōtēría*) has been *iraṭcippu* for centuries. *Iraṭcippu* means protection, help, and, in a wider sense, "rescue from peril."[45] It is derived from the verb *iraṭci* (Sanskrit *rakṣ*) and is rarely found in Hindu theistic devotional literature; it is rather used in a "profane" sense.[46] In modern Tamil, a religious connotation of *iraṭcippu* is rather confined to the Christian translation for salvation. For a long time, however, Christian poetry has used *mīṭpu* as a pure Tamil equivalent for *iraṭcippu*. Although initially a range of other Tamil words was considered, such as *īṭēṟṟam, kaṭaittēṟṟam, viṭutalai,*[47] the Tamilnadu Theological Seminary in particular promoted the exclusive use of *mīṭpu.*[48] It is no wonder therefore that the translators of Thiruviviliam chose to replace *iraṭcippu* with *mīṭpu*. This was a good choice; *mīṭpu,* like *iraṭcippu,* is mainly used in the profane sense and means "to release a debt or a mortgage or to redeem a slave by paying the price for him."[49] That makes this term very suitable to express the "salvation through Christ, who paid the ransom for the sins of mankind by

44. The only thing that is extensively discussed is the problem of rendering biblical names under strict observance of their phonological value according to their original form (cf. Jones Muthunayagam, "*Tiruviviviliyattil ciṟappup peyarkaḷ,*" in TNBCLC, *Niṉaivu malar,* pp. 65-67). This meant a radical change for the Catholics, who, in a peculiar method of contextualization, used Tamilized forms for some important saints, e.g., *aruḷappar* (father of grace) for John, *irāyappar* (father of the king) for Peter, and *ciṉṉappar* (little father) for Paul. Even here, one finds some remarkable inconsistencies. For "Michael" (Hebrew *mīkā'ēl,* Greek *michaēl*) the Catholic form *mikkēl* is used throughout Thiruviviliam, though the traditional Protestant usage *mikāvēl* (= OV/RV/Rajar; cf. Fabricius: *mīkavēl*) would probably be the best rendering of the original pronunciation.

45. Tiliander, *Terminology,* pp. 173-74.

46. Tiliander, *Terminology,* p. 174.

47. G. Robinson, *Iṟaiyiyaṟ payiṟcit tōḻaṉ* (Madurai 1982), p. 77.

48. Samuel Amirtham and Israel Selvanayagam, *mīṭpu* (Madurai, 1981); I. Selvanayagam, ed., *Viviliya, iṟaiyiyal ceñcol kaṭṭuraik kōvai* (Madurai, 1993), pp. 267-72 (art. *mīṭpu*).

49. Tiliander, *Terminology,* p. 175. Nevertheless, the verb *mīḷ* (to save) is sometimes used in devotional Saiva literature (see *Tiruvācakam,* 5, 94).

the sacrifice of himself on the cross, thereby releasing mankind from the captivity and slavery under the evil powers."[50]

Faith

Faith (Greek *pístis*) is one of key words of Christian self-understanding, and in Tamil the word *vicuvācam* (Sanskrit *viśvāsa*) was used for it.[51] *Vicuvācam* was never a prominent term in Tamil Hindu devotional literature, and in the course of the centuries, in its religious meaning, it became a purely Christian Tamil word. In Thiruviviliam *vicuvācam* was replaced by the pure Tamil word *nampikkai*. Like *vicuvācam*, *nampikkai* (hope, trust, confidence) is a secular word widely used in contemporary Tamil.

Trance

The Tamil translation for "trance" (Greek *ékstasis;* cf. Acts 10:10) was traditionally *ñāṉatiruṣṭi* (Sanskrit *jñāna-dṛṣṭi*), which means, in the Hindu context, spiritual illumination and the ability to know the past, the present, and the future. Thiruviviliam speaks instead of a state in which one forgets oneself and loses consciousness *(meymmaṟanta nilai)* and uses a pure Tamil word that has fewer religious connotations. This is remarkable since all other new translations (RV, RC, Rajar) replace that misleading term *ñāṉatiruṣṭi*, which goes back to the Fabricius Version, by *paravacam* (Sanskrit *paravaśa*), which is the common term for ecstatic phenomena in contemporary popular Tamil Hinduism, though this word does have a Sanskrit background.[52]

It is clear that it was sometimes unavoidable for the translators of Thiruviviliam to use Tamil words with an explicit Hindu connotation. Nevertheless, it seems that in these cases the translators tried to appropriate only those terms that have a very broad meaning and are not confined to any specific system of Hinduism. This complex field of translatory contextualization can

50. Tiliander, *Terminology*, pp. 175-76.

51. Tiliander, *Terminology*, pp. 227-32.

52. Nevertheless, in a rather strange way *paravacam* also finds its entry into Thiruviviliam. The phenomenon of "speaking in tongues" (Greek *glṓssais laleín* or *génē glṓssōn*, etc.) is translated as *paravacap pēccu* (ecstatic speech; cf., e.g., 1 Cor. 12:28, 30). Thiruviviliam is not the first in that kind of interpretative translation (Fabricius: *palavita pāṣaikaḷ/pāṣaikaḷ*, cf. Sanskrit *bhāṣā;* OV: *palavita pāṣaikaḷ/anniya pāṣaikaḷ;* RV: *palavita nāvu varaṅkaḷ/nāvukaḷāl pēcu;* RC: *palvakaip paravacap pēccu/paravacap pēccu;* Rajar: *paravacappaṭṭup palavakaiyākap pēcu/paravacap pēccu*).

be illustrated by the terms that are chosen to render "baptism," "God," and "grace" in Thiruviviliam.

Baptism

Since the times of De Nobili the term "baptism" was translated as *ñāṉasnāṉam* (Sanskrit *jñāna-snāna*), which means "bath of knowledge."[53] Sanskrit *snāna* refers explicitly to the many kinds of ritual baths and ablutions in Hinduism, but *ñāṉasnāṉam* is a neologism that became the standard term for baptism in all Christian denominations. Nevertheless, in his New Testament translation from 1975 Rajarigam replaced this word with *tirumuḻukku,* that is, "holy dip," because of the Sanskrit origin of *ñāṉasnāṉam.* Moreover, at Tamilnadu Theological College the usage of this new word was fervently supported.[54] *Muḻukku* (dip, bath) is the pure Tamil equivalent of *snāṉam* but has hardly any religious meaning. Because of that, *tiru* (holy) is added to the word. Though the Tamil lexicon knows *tirumuḻukku* as a synonym for *tirumañcaṉam* (ritual bathing of the deity of a temple) and as a "bath taken by women after fasting in honour of Pārvatī in the month of Mārkaḻi,"[55] the word is not used in contemporary Tamil and has no explicit meaning in modern Tamil Hinduism.

God

In the search for appropriate terms for God, Tamil Bible translations were always experimental. In the Old Version God (Hebrew *ʾælohīm,* Greek *theós*) is usually referred to as *tēvaṉ* (Sanskrit *deva*), and Lord (Hebrew *jhwh,* Greek *kýrios*) as *karttar* (Sanskrit *kartṛ* = creator) or *āṇṭavar* (ruler), though there were some inconsistencies.[56] This is now completely Tamilized into *kaṭavuḷ* and *āṇṭavar* only, and previous inconsistencies are deleted. From a theological point of view, *kaṭavuḷ* is a much better choice than *tēvaṉ* because, whereas *tēvaṉ* has strong polytheistic connotations, *kaṭavuḷ* means something like "transcendent

53. Rajamanickam, *Scholar,* p. 189.

54. Samuel Amirtham and Israel Selvanayagam, *Tirumuḻukku* (Madurai, 1982); Robinson, *Iṟaiyiyaṟ payiṟcit tōḻaṉ,* p. 10; Selvanayagam, ed., *Kōvai,* pp. 166-69 (art. *tirumuḻukku*).

55. University of Madras, ed., *Tamil Lexicon,* 3:1913.

56. Tiliander, *Terminology,* pp. 108-11. Both words *(karttar/āṇṭavar),* though rarely found in theistic literature, are synonyms of *īsvaraṉ* (Sanskrit *īśvara*) and can therefore be associated with *bhakti* traditions. In the Christian context both words are mainly used in the above given honorific plural forms. This is not the practice in Tamil Hinduism, where the third person singular *(karttaṉ* and *āṇṭavaṉ)* is normally used.

existence."[57] Furthermore, *kaṭavuḷ* is not confined to a particular religious system, and the word is in very widespread and popular. Previous terms, such as the philosophical *parāparaṉ* (Sanskrit *parāpara*) in the Fabricius Version, were not that suitable. Discarding the Sanskrit word *karttar* in favor of the sole usage of the pure Tamil *āṇṭavar* not only avoids the Sanskrit term but also in contemporary Tamil confines the word *karttar* to its Christian meaning. *Karttar* is no longer used by non-Christian Tamils,[58] whereas *āṇṭavar* (in the form of *āṇṭavaṉ*) is still widely used in the context of Tamil Hinduism.

Holy

Since the time of the first Protestant Tranquebar missionary, B. Ziegenbalg, the word *paricutta* was the standard term for designating "holy" (Hebrew *qādoš/qādōš*, Greek *hágios*) in Bible translations. It is derived from Sanskrit *śuddha*, but the combination with the prefix *pari-* is seldom used because *viśuddha* is the established Sanskrit form to express completeness.[59] Because of that, *paricutta* became a term that was easily understood by non-Christians but that had a certain Christian flavor. In the course of the centuries *paricutta* became the standard term used by Protestants and Catholics alike, and non-Christians started to consider it a genuine Christian term. In Thiruviviliam *paricutta* is now replaced by the pure Tamil word *tūya; tūya* is an adequate equivalent, and it is commonly used in the Tamil language. It no longer, however, bears the subtle Christian connotation that *paricutta* does. In modern Tamil *tūya* was also used to render the Hindu concepts of holiness. Nevertheless, in popular usage *tūya* had already been an established term within Christian circles for a long time. The Catholics used it (besides *puṉitam*) to denote the saints, like St. Francis Xavier, *tūya cavēriyār*,[60] and it is widely used in Protestant Christian hymns sung in the churches.[61]

It is very important to note that there are cases in which the translators of Thiruviviliam could not find pure Tamil words that were without specifically religious meaning in Tamil Hindu traditions. To cope with that problem, dif-

57. Tiliander, *Terminology*, pp. 132-36.

58. Nevertheless, the Sanskrit form *karttā* (= Sanskrit *kartā*, nominative of *kartṛ*) is still used for "doer, author, etc." P. R. Subramanian, ed., *Kriyāviṉ taṟkālat tamiḻ akarāti* [Dictionary of Contemporary Tamil, Tamil-Tamil-English] (Madras, 1992), p. 257 (s.v. *karttar/karttā*).

59. Tiliander, *Terminology*, p. 144.

60. Subramanian, *Akarāti*, p. 573 (s.v. *tūya*).

61. Tiliander, *Terminology*, p. 147.

ferent solutions were tried. The extreme case is the name "Thiruviviliam" that was chosen for the new translation itself. Here, the translators rejected any kind of Tamilization and preferred to introduce a Greek loanword to render the word "Bible." In other places the translators even retained the old Sanskrit words because they were apparently not convinced that new pure Tamil equivalents would give an adequate meaning. There are also cases, however, where pure Tamil words were adopted, despite their very strong Hindu connotations, as the translation of "grace" will illustrate.

Holy Bible

The new Bible translation bears the artificial name *tiruviviliyam.* It is a combination of the Tamil word for "holy" *(tiru)* with a corrupted form of the Greek word *biblía (viviliyam).* At least in written Tamil it is quite a new word.[62] For a long time, within Protestant circles "True Veda" *(cattiya vētam,* Sanskrit *satya veda)* was the common name for Holy Bible.[63] In 1956, this was changed to "Holy Veda-Āgama" *(paricutta vētākamam),* a name also adopted by the new Catholic Bible translation (RC) from 1970. This name had the advantage of being less polemic and more neutral than "True Veda," and by the addition of *āgama* an interesting reference to the strong Tamil Agamic traditions was made.

With the growing desire to use pure Tamil, however, the newly introduced Sanskrit name Veda-Agama also became unacceptable within theological circles that were influenced by Dravidian ideas. Particularly at the Tamilnadu Theological Seminary it was felt that the anti-Brahmanism of the Dravidian movement had much in common with liberationist and contextual approaches to a Tamil Christian theology. At TTS Christian theology was taught in pure Tamil, and it was those scholars who replaced the usage of "Holy Veda-Āgama" with two new words: *viviliyam* and the Tamil term *tirumaṟai.*[64] *Maṟai* is a Tamil equivalent for Veda and means literally "concealment, secret." This meaning made it very difficult for many people to accept this new term. Out of that, the artificial loanword *viviliyam* became popular among the adherents of pure Tamil, as this was at least not a Sanskrit word.

One should also note that in the New Testament the word for Scripture

62. As *viviliyanūl* it is listed in University of Madras, ed., *Tamil Lexicon,* but not found in Winslow, *Dictionary;* Beisenherz, *Dictionary;* Bexell, *Dictionary;* Diehl, *Dictionary.* It seems that it was first used as the official name of the Bible in the form *viviliyanūl* as a subtitle to the Revised Version (RV) from 1956.

63. Tiliander, *Terminology,* pp. 67-69.

64. Robinson, *Iṟaiyiyaṟ payiṟcit tōḻaṉ,* p. 11.

(Greek *graphḗ*) is rendered as *maṟainūl,* not *vētavākkiyam* (Sanskrit *veda-vākya*) (as in the Old Version). *Vētam* (Sanskrit *veda*) and *piramāṇam* (Sanskrit *pramāṇa*), which stood for "law" (Hebrew *tōrāh,* Greek *nómos*) in the Old Version, is now rendered by the pure Tamil word *caṭṭam* (or sometimes *tiruccaṭṭam*). In modern Tamil *caṭṭam* is a purely secular legal term that means "law" or "rule."

Retaining of Traditional Sanskrit Terminology

In some cases the traditional terminology is retained. For instance, the word for sin, *pāvam* (Sanskrit *pāpa*), remains the only translation for Greek *hamartía,* although the Tamilnadu Theological College experimented with the pure Tamil word *tīviṉai* (bad action) as a possible alternative.[65]

Furthermore, the word *ñāṉam* (Sanskrit *jñāna*), which was traditionally used to translate wisdom (Hebrew *ḥåkmāh;* Greek *sophía*), is also retained, and a wise person is still called *ñāṉi.* However, compounds containing *ñāṉam* were abolished, as we already discussed in the cases of *ñāṉasnāṉam* (baptism) and *ñāṉatiruṣṭi* (trance). Another rather strange example is the use of the word *tarmam* (Sanskrit *dharma!*) in Matthew 6:2-4 in the sense of "alms" (Greek *eleēmosýnē*). It is not clear why this word was not replaced by a better one.[66]

Grace

For a long time the established Tamil word for grace (Greek *cháris*) was *kirupai* (Sanskrit *kṛpā*). This term was a good equivalent, especially because in the terminology of the Alvars we find a kind of *kirupai* that is said to be "without cause or reason" *(nirhētukam,* Sanskrit *nirhetuka)* and renders very well the biblical concept of unconditional grace.[67] Nevertheless, since *kirupai* is of Sanskrit origin, it had to be replaced by the translators, and this was done with the pure Tamil word *aruḷ,* which had sporadically been in Christian use before. The word *aruḷ* is highly loaded with meaning in the context of devotional Saivism, and its meaning differs significantly from *kirupai. Aruḷ* is very much connected with *cakti* (Sanskrit *śakti*), as Tiliander points out:

> In its spiritualized sense, Aruḷśakti means a divine power working within the human soul. . . . This dynamic aspect of "grace" is not foreign to the

65. Robinson, *Iṟaiyiyaṟ payiṟcit tōḻaṉ,* p. 80.
66. Like RC: *nī piccaiyiṭumpoḻutu;* or Rajar: *nī ēḻaikku utavi ceyyumpōtu.*
67. Tiliander, *Terminology,* p. 185.

> biblical concept of Cháris. The N[ew]. T[estament]. meaning of "grace" is not only an attitude of benevolence and forgiveness on the side of the divine subject, it is a power that aims at transforming the selfish nature and will of man in order to make it subject to the divine will.[68]

In some way, one could say that the biblical *cháris* has two aspects: *kirupai*, that is, the spontaneous aspect of divine grace; and *aruḷ*, that is, the dynamic, transforming power of God. Replacing *kirupai* with *aruḷ* brings a neglected aspect of a biblical word to new light but also tends to be one-sided. Moreover, because the Pure Tamil movement is very much connected with efforts to revive Saivism as the true "religion of the Tamils" *(tamiḻar matam)*,[69] much of the religious vocabulary that was popularized as replacement for Sanskrit words have a Saivite background. In that way, in contemporary Tamil, *aruḷ* is very much associated with the neo-Saivite *bhakti* traditions.

Thiruviviliam and Cultural Interactions

Thiruviviliam shows that Indian Christian theologians had no problems in adopting the radical language approaches of the Pure Tamil movement for their new Bible translation. This could not be taken for granted because the Christian minority participated only very marginally in the development of modern Tamil literature, despite the existence of a few very famous Christian devotional poets who are regarded as Tamil classics.[70] As a consequence, a kind of sectarian church Tamil developed that is particularly strong within non-Lutheran Protestant circles that have been familiar with the Old Version for nearly 130 years. In the Old Version, common secular Sanskrit words were infused with a Christian meaning. Because of the changes caused by the Pure

68. Tiliander, *Terminology*, pp. 195-96. See also J. J. Raj (*Grace in the Saiva Siddhantham and in St. Paul: A Contribution in Inter-faith Cross-cultural Understanding* [Madras, 1989]), who explores differences and similarities between the understanding of *cháris* in the Pauline letters and *aruḷ* in Tamil Saiva Siddhanta.

69. Maraimalai Adigal, *Tamiḻar matam* (Chennai, 1999; first ed. 1941).

70. The history of Christian Tamil literature is still a much neglected field of scholarly research, but see D. Rajarigam, *The History of Tamil Christian Literature* (Madras, 1958); T. Dayanandan Francis, *Christian Poets and Tamil Culture* (Madras, 1978); R. Arokiasamy, *Ikkālak kiṟistava tamiḻ ilakkiyam* (Madras, 1983); S. Innasi, *Kavitaic celvam* (Madras, 1989); J. Samuel and L. R. John, "Christianity and Tamil Culture," in *Encyclopaedia of Tamil Literature*, vol. 1: *Introductory Articles*, edited by J. Samuel (Madras, 1990), pp. 391-409; P. S. Jesudasan, *Tamiḻk kiṟittava ilakkiyattil caiva vaiṇava ilakkiyattākkam* (Trichy, 1991); S. Innasi, *Dimensions of Tamil Christian Literature* (Madras, 1994).

Tamil movement, many of these Sanskrit words are no longer used in modern Tamil and survived primarily in church Tamil. This kind of Sanskritized Christian language became an explicit socio-religious marker that is often considered to be part of the Tamil Christian identity.[71] As a result, congregations received the new Bible translation with a mixed response.

Among Catholics there seems to be a broad consensus that Thiruviviliam is now the standard Bible.[72] This is probably due to the fact that the first Catholic standard Bible translation was quite late and was very similar to that of Thiruviviliam. Moreover, on 19 November 1995, the Tamilnadu Bishops' Council wrote a pastoral letter to all congregations, introducing Thiruviviliam officially.[73]

Much more complex is the situation within the Protestant mainline churches.[74] The Tamilnadu Theological Seminary is actively engaged in promoting a pure Christian Tamil. Consequently, Thiruviviliam it is now widely used in the classes at this seminary, and most of the Protestant bishops are also promoting the use of the new Bible wholeheartedly. Yet the Christian minority in Tamilnadu, especially in the south, is rather conservative concerning any change in church life and liturgy, and it feels comfortable in a certain state of isolation. Moreover, as these circles are focused on English-medium education, they are often not very interested in modern Tamil literature and do not feel a pressing need for a modern-language translation.

Criticism comes also from the Pentecostals and charismatics whose worldview and spiritual life is shaped by the terminology and style of the Old Version and who know many Bible passages by heart. They have struggled hard to understand the difficult language of the Old Version, and since the translators of Thiruviviliam are known in these circles as "liberal" theologians, they are viewed with suspicion, and there is concern about whether their new translation is "right" or "wrong." There is even a chance that some Tamil counterpart to the "King James only" controversy might develop.[75] Yet some Pente-

71. Nevertheless, in certain aspects Thiruviviliam has some affinity to neo-Saivite *bhakti* traditions (e.g., *āṉṭavar, aruḷ*), but this would need further investigation.

72. At the beginning of 2000, the TNBCLC had already brought 170,000 copies of the full Bible and 160,000 copies of the NT with Psalms; see www.tnbclc.org/bibcom.html (20 August 2000).

73. Tamilnadu Bishops' Council: *Viviliya potu moḻipeyarppup paṟṟiya tamiḻaka āyarkaḷiṉ cuṟṟumaṭal*, in TNBCLC, *Niṉaivu malar*, pp. 121-25.

74. Up to 2000, the Bible Society of India had only published 31,500 full Bibles and 22,000 NT with Psalms (see e-mail from G. D. V. Prasad, Bible Society of India, 15 September 2000). Moreover, the Bible Society of India still publishes mainly the Old Version.

75. P. J. Thuesen, *In Discordance with the Scriptures: American Protestant Battles over Translating the Bible* (New York, 1999).

costal churches take a positive view of the new translation: the Assemblies of God, one of the largest Pentecostal churches in Tamilnadu and a member of the Bible Society of India, for example, officially supports Thiruviviliam.

From the perspective of religious interactions it is important to note that the translators of Thiruviviliam tried to avoid any adoption of strong vocabulary from Hindu traditions. They were well aware of the problem that, as a small minority, it is nearly impossible to "Christianize" religious key words of Hinduism and to make that new usage known to all Tamil speakers. Thiruviviliam shuns any direct reference to religious concepts of Hinduism and has apparently no explicit agenda of religious contextualization, though most of the translators are presumably fervent supporters of a radical contextualized Indian theology. It is important to note that the translators of Thiruviviliam exercised the same restraint as the translators of all major Tamil Bible translations before them.[76] As Thiruviviliam continues the translatory strategies of previous Bible translations, there are no theological reasons why that new translation, though some further revisions are certainly necessary,[77] should not gain acceptance throughout the Tamil Christian community in the course of time. However, only the future will tell the fate of this ambitious Bible translation within the Tamil Christian community.

In the theological debates, Bible translations are usually considered to be powerful vehicles for the inculturation of the Christian message.[78] This is certainly also true for Thiruviviliam when it tries to translate the biblical terminology within a cultural context that is greatly shaped by Hinduism, and when it defies sectarian church Tamil by embracing the doctrines of Tamil-language purism.

76. In the rare cases where the OV had strong Hindu terms, these were deleted in all later translations: e.g., Titus 3:5, where the Old Version translated Greek *palingenesía* with *maṟujeṉmam* (rebirth), which stands mainly for the Hindu concept of reincarnation (Sanskrit *punarjanman*) and is itself not a bad translation because *palingenesía* literally means "rebirth." Nevertheless, later translations changed the teminology — RC: *putuppiṟappu* (new birth); Rajar: *piṟappu* (birth); Thiruviviliam: *putup piṟappu.* See also Matt. 19:28 where *palingenesía* is translated with *maṟujeṉmakālam* (time of rebirth); later translations: RV: *putitākkappaṭum kālam;* RC: *ulakam puttuyir peṟum nāḷ;* Rajar: *putitākkappaṭum kālam;* Thiruviviliam: *putuppaṭaippiṉ nāḷ.*

77. The senior committee, noted earlier, met again December 1997 and approved the revision of some words and phrases that were suggested by the Old and New Testament coordinators and by other members of the translation team. In addition to that, the "Committee" suggested a periodical revision of Thiruviviliam at least once every five years. email from G. D. V. Prasad, Bible Society of India, 15 September 2000.

78. L. Sanneh, *Translating the Message: The Missionary Impact on Culture* (New York, 1989).

Index